Approaches to Teaching the Plays of August Wilson

Approaches to Teaching the Plays of August Wilson

Edited by

Sandra G. Shannon

and

Sandra L. Richards

The Modern Language Association of America
New York 2016

85 Broad Street, New York, New York 10004
www.mla.org

To order MLA publications, visit www.mla.org/books. For wholesale and international orders, see www.mla.org/bookstore-orders.

The MLA office is located on the island known as Mannahatta (Manhattan) in Lenapehoking, the homeland of the Lenape people. The MLA pays respect to the original stewards of this land and to the diverse and vibrant Native communities that continue to thrive in New York City.

Cover illustration of the paperback and electronic editions:
photograph of the Signature Theater's production of *The Piano Lesson*. © Joan Marcus

Approaches to Teaching World Literature 140
ISSN 1059-1133

POD 2022 (first printing)

Library of Congress Cataloging-in-Publication Data

Names: Shannon, Sandra Garrett, 1952– editor. | Richards, Sandra L., 1946– editor.
Title: Approaches to teaching the plays of August Wilson / edited by Sandra G. Shannon and Sandra L. Richards.
Description: New York : The Modern Language Association of America, 2016. | Series: Approaches to teaching world literature | Includes bibliographical references and index.
Identifiers: LCCN 2016006381 (print) | LCCN 2016010750 (ebook) | ISBN 9781603292580 (cloth : alk. paper) | ISBN 9781603292597 (pbk. : alk. paper) | ISBN 9781603292603 (EPUB) | ISBN 9781603292610 (Kindle)
Subjects: LCSH: Wilson, August—Study and teaching. | Wilson, August—Criticism and interpretation.
Classification: LCC PS3573.I45677 Z54 2015 (print) | LCC PS3573.I45677 (ebook) | DDC 812/.54—dc23
LC record available at http://lccn.loc.gov/2016006381

CONTENTS

ACKNOWLEDGMENTS

A theater truism asserts that behind every great production there is an even greater production. While we leave it to readers to assess the quality of this production, we do want to acknowledge some of the behind-the-scenes folks who have been critical to this enterprise. Sandra G. Shannon is grateful for the expert technical assistance offered by Wallace C. Baxter III and Candice A. Pitts, two Howard University English Department graduate students and brilliant millennials who, together, were able to edit the hefty manuscript meticulously and to master several pesky formatting issues. Sandra L. Richards wishes to acknowledge the subvention generously offered by Everette E. Dennis, the dean and CEO of Northwestern University in Qatar. The independent copy editor Keith Monley and the Northwestern librarians Iman Khamis, Beth Clausen, and Kathleen Bethel were also instrumental in helping to bring this project to fruition. We are indebted to the MLA editors Sonia Kane, James C. Hatch, and Michael Kandel, who shepherded this project through its various stages with a rigor that was always supportive.

Though this volume's contributors certainly were not behind-the-scenes, we both want to thank them for the incredible patience they exercised through the long twists and turns that this manuscript has taken. Finally, we are wonderfully indebted to the playwright himself. August Wilson has given us powerful portraits of humanity in much of its resilience, contradiction, and hope. We trust that on this last point, you, the reader, will agree.

Sandra G. Shannon
Sandra L. Richards

PREFACE

The award-winning playwright August Wilson was an avowed "race man" committed to justice through an exploration of the richness and resilience of twentieth-century black American life through the medium of drama. His plays pose particular interpretive and pedagogical challenges in the second decade of the twenty-first century, a period that many have proclaimed either postrace or postblack. How does one talk about racialized privilege and dispossession in the public arena of the classroom when Americans in general lack a robust, nuanced language and civil protocols to discuss issues of difference and when voters in several states, backed by the Supreme Court, have declared affirmative action considerations unacceptable for admission to college? An engaging narrative can offer a starting point, and, happily, Wilson's plays provide such a jumping-off point for venturing into what may feel like uncharted, challenging terrain. Wilson stages basic desires that drive almost all dramatic narratives—the quest for work and dignity, love, self-worth, and security—through the prism of African American experiences. Thus attention to history, documented in official sources as well as in blues music, vernacular speech, creative literature, gesture, and popular culture, provides the compass by which one can navigate. That examination of cultural histories and their contemporary resonances, along with pedagogical strategies for prompting student analysis, is what our essays offer. The classroom challenge that we seek to address is thus one of cultural literacy, whereby students are affirmed in what they know and supported in identifying the sociohistorical contexts in which that knowledge is embedded while being encouraged to critically explore what is different, probe the history of that difference, and engage the current legacy of a shared yet differentiated national past.

Sandra L. Richards

Part One

MATERIALS

Introduction

Because several fine books document Wilson's life and explore connections between his biography and his creative work (Shannon, *Dramatic Vision*; Snodgrass; and Bryer and Hartig), this brief introduction rehearses only the bare biographical basics in order to focus attention upon resources for teaching the plays. Although Wilson overtly argues for what appears to be a black essentialism, his aesthetic is always already hybrid, emerging from a dynamic synthesis of cultures that the nation has invested energy and law in keeping oppositional. In fact, it is that hybrid quality that both attracts and puzzles some spectators. A play like *Fences*, for example, seems to offer a realistic representation of the father-son dynamic that theatergoers have experienced in Eugene O'Neill's *Long Day's Journey into Night* or Arthur Miller's *Death of a Salesman*, but its anthropomorphization of death and its presentation of the transformative capacities of storytelling and music signal that the teleological assumptions of realism will not suffice as an appropriate critical lens. As is elaborated in the critical introduction in part 2 of this volume, Wilson creolizes the familiar or norms of the West by suffusing them with values rooted in African and African American cultures and thereby produces powerful, astonishing theater that offers new, restorative possibilities.

Born Frederick August Kittel in Pittsburgh in 1945, August Wilson first came to national attention in 1984 when *Ma Rainey's Black Bottom* was produced on Broadway and subsequently nominated for a Tony Award for Best Play. It won the New York Drama Circle Critics Award for Best American play. Since then, nine other Wilson plays have followed to constitute a cycle dramatizing twentieth-century African American history and culture. Four other plays have also won the New York Drama Circle Critics Award—*Joe Turner's Come and Gone* in 1988, *The Piano Lesson* in 1990, *Seven Guitars* in 1996, and *Jitney* in 2000—while *Fences* and *The Piano Lesson* garnered the prestigious Pulitzer Prize for Drama in 1987 and 1990, respectively. Wilson himself won many awards, the most prestigious of which may be the National Humanities Medal (1999), and a Broadway theater and Pittsburgh cultural center were posthumously named after him.

Access to the Plays

While some of the earliest Wilson scholars had difficulties accessing play scripts, happily all ten plays are now available in paperback. Paul Carter Harrison's pioneering anthology, *Three Plays by August Wilson,* brings together the earliest and most popular plays—namely, *Ma Rainey's Black Bottom, Fences,* and *Joe*

Turner's Come and Gone. Further, Harrison offers one of the best analyses of what he terms Wilson's "blues poetics." More recently, Theatre Communications Group has published the August Wilson Century Cycle as a handsome, ten-volume hardback set. Introduced by John Lahr, a *New Yorker* drama critic, it offers forewords and commentaries by some of the most illustrious of Wilson's peers and by distinguished actors who performed his works.

Full-Length Critical Resources

Since the mid-1990s, scholarly activity on Wilson has escalated steadily, paralleling the playwright's growing reputation as a major American dramatist. If one wishes to adopt a biographical-contextual approach, then there is no better starting point than Sandra G. Shannon's *Dramatic Vision of August Wilson* (1995), which tracks his evolution and provides insightful commentaries on the seven plays produced at the time of the book's publication. Mary Ellen Snodgrass has authored *August Wilson: A Literary Companion* (2004), which contains an annotated chronology of the playwright's life and work; a time line that correlates events in Wilson's life with those of his characters; and more than one hundred fifty citations of primary and secondary sources on topics as varied as the blues, Malcolm X, the gothic mode, and the cultural significance of roosters. Though her book was published before Wilson's last play, *Radio Golf* (2005), Snodgrass generously offers some forty topics for further study and classroom discussion. Jackson R. Bryer and Mary C. Hartig offer access to Wilson's nontheatrical pronouncements in their compilation of published interviews titled *Conversations with August Wilson* (2006). Here readers will find his reflections on such issues as his writing process, his relationship with the director Lloyd Richards, literary and musical influences on Wilson, and his conviction that black Americans must be in control of their cultural production.

Moving more toward the arena of literary criticism, readers will discover that Mary Bogumil's revised *Understanding August Wilson* (2011) provides accessible, thoughtful commentaries on each Wilson play as well as an opening chapter rich in information about his unpublished work. For this information, she relies upon the observations of Todd Kreidler, whom Wilson designated as his dramaturge and who directed the playwright in his one-man show *How I Learned What I Learned,* produced by the Seattle Repertory Theatre in 2003. Kim Pereira's *August Wilson and the African-American Odyssey* (1995) serves as another foundational reference, having a wealth of contextual information and providing an analysis of recurring themes. As its title indicates, Shannon's *August Wilson's* Fences*: A Reference Guide* (2003) focuses on a single text. It may have particular comparative appeal to those seeking to insert Wilson into an American drama survey or to those using sports—in this instance, baseball—as a lens into wider issues in American culture.

For instructors more interested in the craft of playwriting, Joan Herrington's *"I Ain't Sorry for Nothin' I Done": August Wilson's Process of Playwriting* (1998) compares successive drafts of his first three plays. *The Past as Present in the Drama of August Wilson* (2004), written by Harry J. Elam, Jr., will prove particularly helpful to those who wish to understand and possibly teach the cycle as a single epic, for Elam weaves together multiple themes at work in individual plays and draws connections between overarching ideas that appear throughout the cycle. Elam's study also offers a substantial bibliography that reflects the explosive, upward trajectory of Wilson scholarship.

Key Essays and Critical Anthologies

In 1991, Paul Carter Harrison published "August Wilson's Blues Poetics" as an afterword to the first collection of Wilson plays. In this seminal essay, Harrison explicates Wilson's insistence that an African sensibility constitutes the foundation of African American culture by arguing that a blues poetics recognizes no distinction between the sacred and the secular. Rather, it understands performance as potentially a moment of intensive challenge that opens a space for spiritual apprehension on the part of the blues singer or character and the audience of the singer or character. Harrison's analysis in this essay, as well as his introductions to anthologies like *Kuntu Drama: Plays of the African Continuum* (1974), paved the way for subsequent scholarship on an African sensibility in Wilson's work.

Instructors may want to pursue this line of inquiry in Alan Nadel's anthology *May All Your Fences Have Gates: Essays on the Dramas of August Wilson* (1994), for several articles elaborate on the theme of African sensibility in plays like *Ma Rainey* and *The Piano Lesson,* while others explore Wilson's deployment of history and relation to neoclassical jazz. For specific links between Wilson and Yoruba cosmology, readers may consult Amadou Bissiri's "Aspects of Africanness in August Wilson's Drama: Reading *The Piano Lesson* through Wole Soyinka's Drama" (1996), Sandra L. Richards's "Yoruba Gods on the American Stage: August Wilson's *Joe Turner's Come and Gone*" (1999), and Sandra Shannon's "Audience and Africanisms in August Wilson's Dramaturgy" (2001).[1]

Though eclectic in subject matter and approach, Marilyn Elkins's *August Wilson: A Casebook* (1994) also offers at least four essays that emphasize Africanity in Wilson's work. Because critics often make casual reference to the four Bs in Wilson, readers will appreciate Mark William Rocha's exploration of the influence of Romare Bearden, Amiri Baraka, Jorge Luis Borges, and blues music ("American History"). The 2004 anthology *August Wilson and Black Aesthetics,* edited by Sandra Shannon and Dana Williams, documents a range of critical responses to Wilson's 1996 speech "The Ground on Which I Stand": some recognize continuity between his position and earlier African American performance history, while others propose an Afrocentric aesthetic that also links to hip hop. Noteworthy are a previously unpublished interview in which Wilson muses about projects that he plans to undertake after completing the ten-play cycle and about a play that demonstrates how his spirituality and activism have inspired a generation of younger African American women playwrights (Shannon and Williams, "Conversation"). Also edited by Shannon, the twentieth volume of the *Zora Neale Hurston Forum* (2006–08) offers new directions in Wilson studies, containing essays that probe the playwright's construction of Caribbean identity, politics of food, and relation to Frederic Franklin's 1988 choreography of *Creole Giselle* for the Dance Theatre of Harlem (*August Wilson*).

Christopher Bigsby's 2007 *Cambridge Companion to August Wilson* offers perceptive essays on such popular Wilson plays as *Ma Rainey's Black Bottom* and *Fences* along with analyses of the later plays, arranged chronologically so that readers can ascertain the playwright's conception of historical development. Of particular note is Brenda Murphy's essay on *Seven Guitars*, a play for which the editors of this MLA volume were unable to attract substantive critical attention. Not only does Murphy explore Wilson's acknowledgment that the play is rooted in Aristotelian tragedy (127) but she also extends earlier analysis of the ways in which this later play rewrites Wilson's first award-winning drama, *Ma Rainey* (see Elam, *Past*). A special issue of the *New England Theatre Journal* (2008), edited by Heather Nathans, offers essays on Wilson as an activist and his dramatization of tensions between memory and history but also spotlights the artistry of Jefferson Pinder and Chandra Dieppa Ortiz, who translate Wilson's "abstract verbal imagery" into arresting quilts and collages (Nathans, "Infinite Variety" 5). In contrast to some of the essayists in this journal, the editors of a 2009 special issue of *College Literature* emphasize Wilson's universality as framing device in order to introduce the playwright's oeuvre to new audiences, who seem to be more familiar with the high canon of Western literature (Caywood, Elkins, and Floyd). But readers will find that many of the essays of this issue offer penetrating insights into the cultural particularities of Wilson's dramaturgy that contradict and productively complicate the dominant, American national narrative. Surprisingly, given the "dubious" quality and "tendentiousness" that Harold Bloom finds in Wilson's plays (*August Wilson* 1, vii), he has also edited a collection simply titled *August Wilson*. Despite the editor's admitted befuddlement, readers will find strong essays by some of the most respected Wilson critics.

In 2010, Nadel edited a second anthology, entitled *August Wilson: Completing the Twentieth-Century Cycle*, which features essays on *Seven Guitars*, *Jitney*, *King Hedley II*, *Gem of the Ocean*, and *Radio Golf*. Steven C. Tracy's essay ("Holyistic Blues") and accompanying discography ("Appendix") focus attention on *Seven Guitars*, a play that arguably best demonstrates Wilson's extensive knowledge of the corpus of blues music. Building upon the assertion of Wilson that he constructed characters in this play as though they were guitars, Tracy explicates how their notions of identity and love are both determined by and clash with dominant narratives ("Holyistic Blues" 51). Certainly, this is an insight that can be applied to the entire Wilsonian corpus. Indeed, essays by Donald Pease, by Soyica Diggs Colbert, and by Herman Beavers in this volume by Nadel resonate with yet extend Tracy's perspective to include the sequel play, *King Hedley II.*

Student Resources

Because today's young people are particularly attuned to visual media, the instructor may want to direct students to some of the materials discussed below as a way of introducing Wilson's biography, African American history in Pittsburgh, or the influence of his drama on American drama and culture. The *South Bank Show,* produced first in 1999 by Films for the Humanities and Sciences, and then retitled simply *August Wilson* and reissued in 2004, follows the playwright as he travels to Pittsburgh locations like the Crawford Grill—once a well-known jazz club—and reminisces about the musicians, playwrights, and ordinary people who frequented these spaces and served as inspiration for his plays. Given Wilson's references to people like Charley Burley, a black boxer who was denied entry into the profession and subsequently became a garbage collector and whose biography seemingly anticipates Troy Maxson's narrative in *Fences,* students begin to appreciate how Wilson uses history to serve his own artistic purposes. Bill Moyers's 1988 interview of Wilson, entitled *A World of Ideas,* offers insight into the playwright's identification of the blues as a source of his art. In addition, the program includes scenes from *Joe Turner's Come and Gone* and *Fences.* It is available either as a part of the DVD collection *Bill Moyers: A World of Ideas* (http://billmoyers.com/series/a-world-of-ideas/) or directly at the Web site www.pbs.org/moyers/journal/archives/wilsonwoi_flash.html.

Students enrolled in an American drama course may find the comparative approach of *The Drama of Creation: Writers on Writing* (2006) particularly illuminating because the film asks a variety of well-known writers to reflect upon the process by which a few scribbled words, the sudden appearance of a character or idea, and rewrites become treasured texts that the public takes to heart. It is available either as a video recording or an electronic resource.

Numerous Internet sites are also readily available. Instructors may want to direct students to sites like www.augustwilson.net, by Michael Downing, a Kutztown University English professor, which offers a slide show of Wilson's life and work, bibliographies of critical as well as production reviews, a posting of a news article concerning the infamous 1997 Town Hall debate between Wilson and Robert Brustein, and seven analytic papers that Downing has somewhat idiosyncratically chosen to feature. The Kennedy Center, which produced many Wilson plays, offers a "Watch and Listen" section that contains a lengthy interview with the playwright and performers' reflections on acting in his plays (www.kennedy-center.org/programs/festivals/07-08/wilson/#watch). Indeed, students will discover that almost every regional theater that has produced a Wilson play now includes actor commentary and video performance on its Web site. But they would be well advised to read the play before going to the Web site in order to observe how words on a page can accrue added or different meanings once they emerge out of actors' mouths into a particular spatial context.

Though students are likely to find this next resource visually static and thus perhaps less appealing, instructors will want to utilize the Greene Space Audio project, because it houses audio recordings of the full Wilson cycle. A project produced by New York City's Public Radio station in 2013, the site offers, along with professional readings, reflections by directors, actors, designers, other theater practitioners, and academics who have devoted substantial portions of their careers to the playwright (www.thegreenespace.org/story/258319-august-wilson-american-century/).

Additional Resources

Undoubtedly instructors and more advanced students will want to avail themselves of more specialized resources, concerning, for example, African American history in Pittsburgh or the Negro Baseball League. To that end, one can pursue a comparative then-and-now history of Wilson's Hill District at http://multimedia.post-gazette.com/ThenNow/Hill/Devillers/default.asp or through the Carnegie Library of Pittsburgh's site (www.clpgh.org/exhibit/neighborhoods/hill/hill_n102.html).

Digitized photographs of ordinary African Americans as well as visiting celebrities, taken by Charles "Teenie" Harris, a *Pittsburgh Courier* photojournalist from the 1920s through the 1970s, can be accessed through the Carnegie Museum of Arts' *Teenie Harris Archives* (www.clpgh.org/exhibit/neighborhoods/hill/hill_n102.html) or through the smaller (541 images) Teenie Harris Collection within the University of Pittsburgh's *Historic Pittsburgh* site (http://digital.library.pitt.edu/images/pittsburgh/teenieharris.html). Cheryl Finley, Laurence Glasco, and Joe W. Trotter have also published a book of Harris's photographs entitled *Teenie Harris, Photographer: Image, Memory, History*.

Instructors preparing to teach *Fences* should include a virtual visit to the Negro Baseball League Web site (www.negroleaguebaseball.com). As Shannon reports in her essay in this volume, Howard University has developed a robust site that links resources specific to Wilson to the large universe of African American history and cultural production (see http://libguides.howard.edu/augustwilsoninterdisciplinarycourse). Because Wilson often located an originating black authenticity in the southern United States, instructors may want to use *Motion: the African American Migration Experience* (www.inmotionaame.org/home

.cfm). The *American Memory* Web site, produced by the Library of Congress, offers a treasure trove of photos, sound recordings, and written documents on topics like culture and folk life, performing arts (including music) and African American history (http://memory.loc.gov/ammem/index.html), but instructors will want to develop in-class exercises to guide young researchers in negotiating these collections.

As this review suggests, there is a wealth of print, audiovisual, and digitized materials that will enhance the teaching of Wilson's ten-play cycle. The essays in part 2 of this volume document some of the innovative methods instructors have used to inspire and support students in exploring the complex beauty and enduring relevance of his dramatic vision.

NOTES

"Key Essays and Critical Anthologies" and the sections that follow it have benefited significantly from the research assistance provided by Patricia A. Lott and Michael W. Young.

[1] Those wishing to explore more generally links between the Yoruba trickster god and African American literary and dramatic production would do well to consult Femi Euba, *Archetypes, Imprecators, and Victims of Fate: Origins and Developments of Satire in Black Drama* (1989), and Henry Louis Gates, Jr., *The Signifying Monkey: A Theory of African-American Literary Criticism* (1989).

Part Two

APPROACHES

A Critical Frame

In one sense, one can understand August Wilson as engaged in a decades-long dialogue with the preeminent scholar and activist W. E. B. Du Bois, who declared in 1897 that the problem of the twentieth century was the color line that elevated whites as culturally and politically superior to nonwhites. Du Bois went on to diagnose the consequences of this racialized paradigm for black Americans as "double consciousness" or

> this sense of always looking at one's self through the eyes of others, of measuring one's soul by the tape of a world that looks on in amused contempt and pity. One ever feels his twoness,—an American, a Negro. . . . He simply wishes to make it possible for a man to be both a Negro and an American, without being cursed and spit upon by his fellows, without having the doors of Opportunity closed roughly in his face. (9)

Undoubtedly, the young Frederick August Kittel experienced this existential war as the son of a German immigrant baker, August Kittel, Sr., and Daisy Wilson, an African American cleaning woman left to raise six children by herself in the Hill District of Pittsburgh. Subjected to racist abuse in school and in the white working class neighborhood of Hazelwood, where Daisy Wilson eventually moved her family, the tenth-grader dropped out of Gladstone High School in 1960, when an African American instructor—impressed with the substance of his report on Napoléon I of France—accused him of plagiarism, and no one took notice of the young man hanging around the school yard in the hope of being asked to return. The Carnegie Library became Wilson's new school, and he made such good use of its resources that many years later the library conferred an honorary degree upon the playwright, the only such one given to date.

Coming into adulthood in the tumultuous period of the 1960s, when youth were inspired by black liberation movements at home and decolonization struggles in Africa, Wilson rejected Du Bois's formulation of an alienated, double consciousness. He argued for the essential Africanness of black America. In numerous assertions outside the world of his plays, he consistently posited a unified, black consciousness in terms that tended toward the categorical. Thus I start with his overt pronouncements before analyzing ways in which his dramaturgy complicates predominant American constructions of race as an either-or black-white binary. For example, the same year that *Joe Turner* opened on Broadway (1988), the playwright asserted in an interview with Bill Moyers, "We are Africans who have been in America since the seventeenth century" ("August Wilson on Blackness"). When pressed by Moyers, who interpreted Wilson's insistence as a disavowal of his white father, Wilson explained that the cultural environment that shaped him was black. Racism had denigrated that world as dysfunctional, but he understood its nobility and resilience when he first listened to a record of Bessie Smith singing the blues. That experience shifted his thinking, prompting him to recognize that "the contents of my mother's life—her myths, her superstitions, her prayers, the contents of her pantry, the smell of her kitchen, the song that escaped her sometimes parched lips, her thoughtful repose and pregnant laughter—are all worthy of art" ("Note"). Since that pivotal encounter, Wilson understood his life mission as placing onstage the history and worldview of African Americans in the twentieth century as a powerful, affective medium for orienting African Americans—and, by implication, all Americans—toward a future built from the solid foundation of accurate self-knowledge.

Nearly a decade later, Wilson delivered a manifesto on this theme, entitled "The Ground on which I Stand" at a gathering of theater professionals.[1] Two motifs run throughout this provocative speech: the distinct, African-based culture that has developed in the United States and the economic as well as aesthetic implications of a national presumption of white superiority. Noting that in writing plays and addressing a theater audience, he stands on terrain that playwrights like Euripides, Shakespeare, and Eugene O'Neill have traversed, Wilson declares himself a race man and emphasizes instead the ground upon which Nat Turner, Marcus Garvey, Elijah Mohammed, and Daisy Wilson's father toiled:

> I stand myself and my art squarely on the self-defining ground of the slave quarters and find the ground to be hallowed and made fertile by the blood and bones of the men and women who can be described as warriors on the cultural battlefield that affirmed their self-worth. As there is no idea that cannot be contained by black life, these men and women found themselves to be sufficient and secure in their art and their instructions. (496)

Expanding upon his definition of culture as a combination of eating habits, religious beliefs, and gestures, as well as of concepts of beauty and justice or responses to pain and pleasure learned and transmitted intergenerationally, Wilson issues a challenge to American society as a whole:

> The term black or African American not only denotes race; it denotes condition and carries with it the vestige of slavery and the social segregation and abuse of opportunity so vivid in our memory. That this abuse of opportunity and truncation of possibility is continuing and is so pervasive in our society in 1996 says much about who we are and much about the work that is necessary to alter our perceptions of each other and to effect meaningful prosperity for all. (495)

To those critics like Robert Brustein, a prominent writer-director, who characterized the then-emerging support for nonwhite artists as the use of sociological criteria where artistic criteria alone should obtain,[2] Wilson vigorously argues that the systemic enforcement of white privilege masquerades as aesthetic worthiness. Were discrimination removed, artists of color would meet their white competitors and expand the horizons of American theater; black theaters would receive a level of financial support, staff professionalization, and critical acclaim commensurate to regional theaters that were and are predominantly white-oriented in their repertoires and staffing. They would do so not by producing colorblind versions of white culture but by delving into their historical, cultural distinctiveness from the mainstream. What would be shared across cultural differences? "The common values of the American Theater that we can share are plot . . . dialogue . . . characterization . . . design. How we both make use of them will be determined by who we are . . . what ground we are standing on and what our cultural values are" (497).

Not surprisingly, Wilson's manifesto sparked controversy from a number of quarters: people who thought Wilson was being racist in pointing to racism in American theater; people who were puzzled by the discrepancy between his championing black theater while having his own work produced in white, regional theaters; people who objected to his locating the origins of black authenticity solely in the rural South; and people who were troubled by his relentlessly masculinist frames of reference.

What is important for those reading and teaching Wilson is not only his self-perception but, equally important, nuances within this speech, amplified within the plays, that project a Wilsonian worldview that is *both* based in an Africanist aesthetic and creolized in its deployment of Euro-American cultural values and idioms. By creolized, I mean the tactical appropriation of dominant culture by a marginalized minority that redefines master codes in concert with its own subaltern or subjugated experiences (Mercer 255). The result is a syncretic dynamic that both looks like and departs from hegemonic culture. Thus, for example, the contentious father-son dynamic in Wilson's *Fences* will be familiar to most spectators (or readers) regardless of race because they too have had to struggle with parental authority, but Troy Maxson's absolute refusal to support his son's dream of playing professional baseball, based in a personal and collective history of racism, critiques the white, national convention of optimism about the future.

Returning to Wilson's "The Ground on which I Stand" essay, we can discern elements of a creolized practice. Acknowledging the actual terrain on which he is standing—namely, a New York theater and before a distinguished group of theater professionals—he chooses to locate himself instead on the oppositional ground of the slave quarters and the Nation of Islam, both of which actively resisted racial domination and vigorously challenged the disjuncture between the foundational premise of inalienable rights guaranteed by an omnipotent creator and the practice of oppression. Yet his essay title and sense of the writer's responsibility echo Paul Robeson's book *Here I Stand,* thereby suggesting a socialist paradigm that rejects the black-white binarism of American racial constructions and anticipates solidarity across boundaries. Further, Robeson's articulation of the battlefield against oppression as being everywhere (52) may explain the seeming contradiction in Wilson's own practice of premiering his plays at historically white, regional theaters. Introducing yet another contradiction—or complicating nuance—the closing paragraph of the speech reaffirms his belief in an American theater that has in fact been performatively reconstituted through an insistence upon artistic validity and the inclusion of "minority" perspectives. This paragraph echoes Shakespeare, that pinnacle of Western drama, in deploying imagery of holding a mirror up to nature, but it also repeats elements of the founding American discourse in celebrating the power of art to bring "the unencumbered pursuit of happiness to the ground on which *we* stand" (503; emphasis added). Wilson repeats but creolizes, having redirected master codes to produce a new theater and a new collectivity.

An examination of what Wilson termed the four Bs that influenced his art offers further elaboration on this creolizing practice and vision. In numerous interviews, Wilson pointed to blues music, the playwright Amiri Baraka, the painter Romare Bearden, and the short story writer Jorge Luis Borges as critical to his development.[3] Important to note at the outset is that the musical idiom of the blues is a product of modernity, and all three artists can be classified as modernists. All disavow the old verities and a teleology anchored by a divine entity or secular belief in human rationality and enlightenment. Ignoring cultural borders and aesthetic hierarchies, these four Bs borrow, reassemble, and juxtapose to produce dynamic, high-affect truths that often lead to confrontation, astonishment, and contradiction. Ralph Ellison's analysis of black history captures the qualities that Wilson shares with his four models, when Ellison writes of "sharp breaks, leaps in consciousness, distortions, paradoxes, reversals, telescoping of time and Surreal blending of styles, values, hopes and dreams which characterize much of Negro American history" (qtd. in Rocha, "August Wilson" 11). As Mark William Rocha argues, the blues constitute a language for narrating an America that is not, given the utter discrepancy between its founding ideals and its dehumanizing practices, particularly in relation to African Americans. Wilson, listening to singers like Bessie Smith and Ma Rainey (who figure in his first nationally successful play), began to hear the coded language in which ordinary black folk sought to surmount the near-devastating pain of broken promises and aspirations, indexed in phrases like "my man's gone now," "good morning heartache," and "boll weevils ate the crop."[4] For Wilson, the blues became the "sacred book" of Africans displaced in the United States. The blues were "an entire philosophical system at work," so the playwright argues (Rocha, "August Wilson" 9). Or, as he scripts for Ma Rainey, the blues are "life's way of talking. You don't sing to feel better. You sing because that's a way of understanding life" (82).

For Amiri Baraka (aka LeRoi Jones), blues music served as a matrix that advanced an African sensibility even as black people were migrating out of the rural South and becoming more deeply enmeshed in the values of industrial America. In *Dutchman,* Baraka crafts a character much like himself in the

1960s—and like the young August Wilson—namely, a young, fledgling poet, educated (self-educated in Wilson's case) in the modernist canon of Euro-American literature, desirous of integration into the white mainstream, but ultimately provoked to reveal a deeply buried, smoldering rage and resistance to racist hegemony. As Rocha notes, Baraka's protagonist proclaims in the climactic moment: "[The ofays, i.e., whites] say, 'I love Bessie Smith.' And don't even understand that Bessie Smith is saying, 'Kiss my ass, kiss my black unruly ass.' Before love, suffering, desire, anything you can explain, she's saying, and very plainly, 'Kiss my black ass'" (*Dutchman* 34–35). Art is conceptualized as a weapon at this moment, but interestingly for the character Clay, for the playwright Baraka, and for the younger Wilson, the generative, combative capacity of art would become even clearer several months later, when Malcolm X was assassinated in February 1965. Baraka would disavow his white, avant-garde affiliations and move to articulate black nationalism through the arts. Wilson would date his birth as an artist in relation to that death. He says of 1 April 1965, "That was the day when I made a commitment to being a writer. I spent $20 for a typewriter. . . . I didn't know how to type. I just wanted to see what AUGUST WILSON looked like. I saw it there standing up on the paper, and said, 'That's all right, man, all right'" (qtd. in Rocha, "August Wilson" 6). Not only is he paying homage to the slain Nation of Islam leader with this act but he is also responding to Baraka's call in "Poem for Black Hearts" to replace "whining and stooping" with proud emulation of Malcolm's fierce courage (6). Baraka would write overtly political plays like *Four Revolutionary Plays* or the later, Marxist-oriented *The Motion of History*, but the political thrust of Wilson's dramaturgy is more subtle. As Harry Elam has noted, white characters rarely appear in Wilson's plays, yet the effects of racism are palpable in the ways his characters seek to craft dignified, life-affirming responses to their daily challenges. The political and philosophical challenges to white hegemony can seem softened or nonexistent, given Wilson's creolizing deployment of easily recognizable cultural markers. In *Joe Turner's Come and Gone,* for example, the boardinghouse proprietors espouse a bourgeois respectability, and two of the characters are deeply embedded in Christian beliefs. Yet these values are resignified by Martha Pentecost, who urges her long-wandering husband to return to Christianity while using the Bible as though it were an African conjuring tool, and by her former deacon husband, Herald Loomis, who ultimately decides that instead of being saved by the blood of Jesus, he will bleed for himself (Richards, "Yoruba Gods"). As I have been arguing, the familiarity of signs provides a point of entry for those not steeped in black culture; the benefit for crossing into this terrain is not simply knowledge of that culture but also an apprehension of how it has influenced the mainstream and holds keys to the enactment of an inclusive America.

Bearden is another critical B for Wilson, because three of Bearden's paintings—*The Mill Hand's Lunch Bucket*, *Miss Bertha and Mr. Seth*, and *The Piano Lesson*—provide direct inspiration for characters and plot in *Joe Turner's Come and Gone* and *The Piano Lesson* (Rocha, "August Wilson" 11–12). But as

Rocha notes, Bearden's influence extends beyond these two plays. Appropriating Picasso's cubist approach that Picasso had already appropriated from West African sculpture, Bearden crafts dynamic collages of abstracted forms, flattened shapes, and shifting perspectives to narrate visions in which the mundane worlds of mothers and children, farmworkers as well as industrial laborers, hustlers, and musicians often collide with the fantastic realm of birds, African ritual paraphernalia, and Christian symbolism:

> Bearden's images are both simple and complex, and layered with meanings that can be inferred from his references to other art and cultures: Renaissance painting, modern art, African tribal sculpture, and Christian iconography. In 1977 the novelist Ralph Ellison wrote that Bearden's collages created "a place composed of visual puns and artistic allusions . . . where the sacred and the profane, reality and dream, are ambiguously mingled." (*Romare Bearden*)

Bearden himself describes his process as rooted in a blues aesthetic: "I paint out of the tradition of the blues, of call and recall. You start a theme and you call and recall" (qtd. in Rocha, "August Wilson" 12).

The playwright Wilson heard in Bearden's "call" an elevation of black life to an epic scale that he wanted to attempt in drama. Like his model, Wilson recalls the ordinary in a manner layered with the extraordinary, thereby challenging his readers or spectators to respond with an open curiosity as to how these seemingly off-center representations can inform and reconstitute the social norm.

The fourth influential B is Borges, in whose fantastic stories of gaucho life in Argentina Wilson recognized universal themes of "love, honor, duty, betrayal" (Isherwood). Wilson credits Borges with teaching him an ethics of listening when he describes Borges's technique in terms that can also be applied to his own plays. Wilson says of Borges, "With Borges, you've got all these wires carrying electrical impulses but they don't all connect up. When you encounter one of those little breaks, I think he wants you to stop and say, 'Now wait a second, how does *that* connect?'" (Rocha, "Conversation" 31).

Furthermore, scholars like Rocha and Mary Lusky Friedman have identified in the Latin American fabulist a paradigm apparent in Wilson as well. A crisis propels the hero to embark upon a journey that becomes progressively more impoverished and irreal until the hero finds himself confined. Hemmed in, he experiences a marvelous, soul-shattering experience that explodes any previous sense of self. Certainly, a number of Wilson's protagonists travel this trajectory: we need only think of Levy in *Ma Rainey's Black Bottom,* Herald Loomis in *Joe Turner's Come and Gone,* Boy Willie and Berniece Charles in *The Piano Lesson,* or Citizen Barlow in *Gem of the Ocean.*[5] Offering narrative journeys that reanimate and attempt to exorcise memory, juxtaposing realism with the mythic and regarding magic anthropologically as a complete system, Borges signifies on Western traditions. Through him, so Rocha argues, Wilson gains access to those traditions without having to genuflect as a cultural inferior ("August Wilson").

In summary, Wilson, having studied his four Bs and taken his stand on the ground of the slave cabin and urban ghetto as well as of the mainstream American theater, constructs an intercultural twentieth-century American identity that both acknowledges and redraws Du Bois's formulations, that is both rooted in and exceeds the nation-state and its ideology. As the essays in this volume demonstrate, the reward for teaching Wilson's plays is the joy of introducing students to a gifted playwright who takes them on a bracing journey toward a reconceptualization of their world.

Introduction to the Essays

The contributors to this volume teach in a variety of curricular settings, from general education courses to American drama surveys and African American theater seminars. Their strategies for teaching Wilson's plays, largely to undergraduates, have been grouped into three rubrics: "Engaging the Dramatic Mainstream," "Spotlight on Material Culture," and "African Routes."

Engaging the Dramatic Mainstream

Ayanna Thompson probes the often asserted but rarely elaborated comparison between the genius of William Shakespeare and that of August Wilson. She wisely notes that insight moves not only in one direction from the long-deceased Shakespeare to Wilson: exposure to Wilson raises significant questions as to how race, the contemporary marketing of classical texts, and theater funding shape evaluations of what constitutes good or canonical literature. Offering what at first glance seems an unlikely pairing of Wilson's *Fences* and Tennessee Williams's *Streetcar Named Desire* in a general education course, Keith Clark starts with biographical comparisons in order to focus on ways in which both plays exploit the zeitgeist of the 1940s and 1950s. When students have completed this groundwork, they are then prepared to evaluate the importance of place in relation to linguistic register and the centrality of blues music for each playwright.

Constructing her American drama survey chronologically around such familiar tropes as the father-son dynamic and intergenerational inheritance, Soyica Colbert typically includes *Fences, The Piano Lesson,* and *King Hedley II.* In contrast to sons' attempts to redeem their fathers' transgressions (in *All My Sons* or *Death of a Salesman,* for example), students observe Wilson's revisions of national mythologies, which are aimed at restoring the missing patriarch and emphasize the importance of the mother-daughter dyad for familial health. Though the three-hundred-year-old Aunt Ester at the heart of Wilson's *Gem of the Ocean* hardly seems to belong in a realistic drama, Douglas Jones offers effective pedagogical strategies that focus student attention on ordinary objects and practices, like the frequent mention of food in the play. Through assignments like collecting archival or family oral histories, students appreciate how the impossibly aged Aunt Ester is grounded in and shaped by a recognizable, material world. Their recognition of the realism of place as a determinant of character helps them understand why Wilson—as well as other artists of color—often deploy a marvelous realism, or attention to the extraordinary, in order to make hypervisible the subaltern knowledge that is denied by dominant society.

Nadel argues that Wilson's plays adhere not only to a Euro-American dramaturgical structure inherited from Aristotle but also to the musical structure of a jazz combo. With the premise that jazz and blues are quintessential American genres, Nadel reports on a classroom exercise of comparing "My Favorite Things" as sung by Mary Martin and by Julie Andrews and reimagined by the saxophonist John Coltrane. Students are thus able to understand that the blues—and Wilson's dramaturgy—is "appropriative, improvisational, and communal," dependent on a history of what preceded a given iteration and accomplished by incorporating rather than sublimating allegedly nonnormative voices.

Joan Herrington and Von Washington offer reflections on their experience directing a production of *Ma Rainey's Black Bottom* at Western Michigan University, a predominantly white, state institution with a multicultural theater program that draws black students from the suburbs as well as inner-city Detroit neighborhoods. To their surprise, the directors found that these otherwise bright, talented students knew little African American history and even less about the performance techniques of storytelling. Broadly defining *storyteller* to include musicians, poets, and public speakers, Herrington and Washington taught aspects of 1920s black cultural production and modified Anne Bogart and Tadashi Suzuki acting exercises. The essay's discussion of how students developed a vocabulary of gestures provides nondirectors with helpful ideas to make reading aloud come alive in the classroom.

Spotlight on Material Culture

In his analysis of *Two Trains Running*, set in 1969, Andrew Scheiber provides a substantive discussion of the illegal lottery system known in black communities as "policy" or "the numbers." He starts by probing students' contemporary knowledge of state-run lotteries in order to underscore the familiar before prompting them to explore how gaming functions as an "alternative economic calculus" for Wilson's characters, who are far removed from socioeconomic power. Scheiber's address of the spiritual cost of material investment productively dialogues with Colbert's essay discussed above.

Continuing the focus on the nexus of economy and identity, James Engstrom and Paul Bryant-Jackson argue the salience of urban geography for an understanding of Wilson's last play, *Radio Golf*. The authors begin with a historical geography of Wilson's beloved Hill District of Pittsburgh before delineating two competing constructions of the city—namely, a neoliberal vision in which a free-market economy and devolution of publicly funded, social services prevail and a "right to the city" concept that champions grassroots activism in its struggles to structure redevelopment so that people retain the right to occupy and use space in ways that enhance their lives. Students, armed with an understanding of late-twentieth-century urban processes, which are playing out in many cities in which they reside, can fully appreciate how Wilson was writing ultimately a history of twentieth-century America through the perspectives of its black citizenry.

Sandra G. Shannon reports on a 2011–12 Howard University interdisciplinary teaching and research project sponsored by the Mellon Foundation that brought together five two-person teams and an embedded librarian to teach the entire Wilson cycle. One result of that work is a Web site offering a wealth of overviews and bibliographic resources on topics like African systems of thought, the Great Migration, and the legacy of the Middle Passage that will satisfy novice Wilson instructors, seasoned academics, and millennial students enamored of multiple technology platforms (see http://libguides.howard.edu/content.php?pid=273384&sid=2261442).

African Routes

Harry J. Elam, Jr., offers a far-ranging reflection on his teaching approach to *Joe Turner's Come and Gone.* He effectively identifies the ritualistic dimension of pedestrian actions like Bertha's repeated offering of biscuits to her boarders; this identification helps students comprehend larger ritual moments centering on the Juba dance and Loomis's struggle to regain his metaphoric ability to stand. Readers will also find helpful resources concerning Bearden's relation to this play; the history, legend, and blues music surrounding the figure of Joe Turner; Wilson's representation of black women; and the value of in-class student performance as a way to foster dynamic communities of meaning. Like Elam, Femi Euba explores Wilson's understanding of ritual in *Joe Turner's Come and Gone.* But reading from a different scholarly archive and drawing upon his deep knowledge of Yoruba philosophy, Euba focuses upon need, sacrifice, and efficacy as well as repetitive action as central categories for the operation of ritual. The result is emphasis on Herald Loomis in contrast to Elam's concern for ritual's communal benefits. Euba's essay also demonstrates that instead of viewing Wilson's dramaturgy through the lens of a blues or jazz structure, as Nadel proposes, much productive interpretation derives from a tight focus on the hero's trajectory, understood from a Yoruba perspective, in which chance, choice, and satire operate differently from the Western canon initiated by Aristotle (see Euba, *Archetypes*).

While Douglas Jones discusses *Gem of the Ocean* in relation to ordinary artifacts characteristic of realism, Sandra L. Richards emphasizes the diaspora literacy required for one to appreciate the fantastic journey to the marine City of Bones that the protagonist undertakes. In order to help Citizen Barlow find psychic equilibrium, Aunt Ester and her helpers make use of discourses drawn from the Bible, Puritan ideology, nineteenth-century American literature, and West African cultures as they were adapted to the local ecologies of the Sea Islands Georgia and South Carolina. Students, through their research on Wilson's intertextual references, come to appreciate how the playwright creolizes dominant culture in order to raise fundamental questions concerning individual agency, responsibility, and the changing constitution of freedom and citizenship.

In contrast to Euba, Elam, and Nadel, Faedra Chatard Carpenter deploys the paradigm of fractal geometry to understand how Wilson's ten-play cycle operates internally. Fractals are constituted by the repetition of similar patterns through a constantly diminishing scale; they function like a feedback loop in which the end of one stage is the starting point for a new stage. Responding to students' initial complaints of boring redundancies, Carpenter's approach, with assignments calling for historical presentations, book reviews, and intertextual, call-and-response projects, allows students to understand the value of contrapuntal narratives within individual plays and the contrapuntal or multiperspectival dialogue operating within the entire Wilson corpus.

Focusing particular attention on the representation of women, Dana A. Williams describes strategies for using plays, like *Fences* and *Two Trains Running*, to teach dramatic structure to general education students and literary criticism to more advanced undergraduates. For majors and graduate students, Williams introduces black women's studies as a means not simply of confronting Wilson's limited repertoire of female characters but also, more important, of exposing the inattention to grounded histories and unacknowledged politics of reading that often characterize feminist and African American literary criticism.

As this overview of essays demonstrates, August Wilson's plays can be incorporated into a variety of academic settings and approached from a number of analytic perspectives. What hopefully is also apparent is his signal contribution to definitions of twentieth-century American identity. In skillfully representing the particulars of the African American experience within a collective American history, he has offered readers and spectators not only wonderful stories and memorable characters but also a challenging road map with which to rethink our past and chart new futures.

NOTES

[1] This speech can be found in *Callaloo* 20.3. There is a discrepancy in date: both 1997 and 1998 are listed in various bibliographies as the publication year.

[2] Indeed, as Keith Clark documents in his essay in this volume, Brustein has expressed disdain for Wilson's playwriting abilities, characterizing *Fences* as a "quasi-minstrelized version" of *Death of a Salesman*.

[3] In some interviews, Wilson expanded his list to include two more Bs, James Baldwin and Ed Bullins, writers whose honesty in representing everyday life he found inspirational. See Isherwood.

[4] The first two phrases found their way into music: "My Man's Gone Now" is the title of an aria in the 1935 opera *Porgy and Bess*, composed by George Gershwin with lyrics by DuBose Heyward. "Good Morning, Heartache" was originally recorded in January 1946 by Billie Holiday for Decca Records; Irene Higginbotham, Ervin Drake, and Dan Fisher wrote the song. A small beetle known as the boll weevil devastated cotton crops starting at the turn of the twentieth century, occasioning agricultural diversification in the South and black exodus to the North or the Great Migration. Numerous blues singers like Charley Patton, Ma Rainey, Bessie Smith, and Huddie William Ledbetter (aka Lead Belly) memorialized this history of devastation and of the small wreaking havoc on the seemingly all-powerful.

[5] For analyses that locate this trajectory within a different cultural universe—namely, that of the Yorubas of West Africa, specifically Wole Soyinka's deployment of the myth of Ogun as aesthetic principle—see Elam, *Past* 171–77; Richards, "Yoruba Gods."

ENGAGING THE DRAMATIC MAINSTREAM

Comparing Wilson with Shakespeare: Teaching the Politics and Practices of Race in Performance

Ayanna Thompson

In his 2002 review of *King Hedley II,* Philip Fisher declared, "If William Shakespeare had lived in black America in the twentieth century, he would have written plays like those of August Wilson." While Fisher's statement was a bold one, it was far from unique. August Wilson was, and continues to be, compared with William Shakespeare. Despite being separated by four centuries, two continents, and disparate cultural and racial backgrounds, Wilson and Shakespeare are frequently put into the same artistic universe. For instance, in her 2005 obituary for Wilson, Elizabeth Alexander claimed that Wilson "chiseled something in granite that will stand like Shakespeare" (125). Likewise, in several press releases for the 2011 August Wilson annual monologue competition in Pittsburgh, Wilson's name was coupled with Shakespeare's. According to Bill Nunn, a veteran screen and stage actor who founded the Bill Nunn Theatre Outreach Project, "I believe that the depth and breadth of August Wilson's insight is on a level comparable to William Shakespeare" (Boccella). At the competition, "[t]hey wanted to have students say August Wilson and William Shakespeare in the same breath" (Molana-Allen). To borrow Caleen Sinnette Jennings's words, "As a lover of both Shakespeare and August Wilson, I am intrigued by the comparison and the possibility of bringing the two playwrights together within the classroom" (87). Jennings provides a thoughtful way to pair certain readings from Wilson and Shakespeare, but I want to suggest ways to bring these playwrights into dialogues that challenge not only our understandings of form and content but also our common performance practices.

In some ways, Wilson himself invited comparisons with Shakespeare because Shakespeare kept haunting his discussions of theater. While he famously claimed that he did not attend the theater, let alone Shakespearean theatrical performances ("I don't go to the theater very much. Nor the movies" [Plimpton 89]; "I haven't read Ibsen, Shaw, Shakespeare—except *The Merchant of Venice* in the ninth grade. The only Shakespeare I've ever seen was *Othello* last year [1986] at Yale Rep," Wilson readily recognized that he stood on the same ground and sat "in the same chair" as classical playwrights (Savran 292). "In one guise," he said, "the ground I stand on has been pioneered by the Greek dramatists—by Euripides, Aeschylus and Sophocles—by William Shakespeare, by Shaw, Ibsen and Chekhov, Eugene O'Neill, Arthur Miller, Tennessee Williams" (*Ground* 11). Nonetheless, he derided "Cultural Imperialists," who, he claimed, "view their American culture, rooted in the icons of European culture, as beyond reproach in its perfection. It is inconceivable to them that life could be lived and enriched without knowing Shakespeare or Mozart" (29). Life could be lived quite well, Wilson intoned, without knowing Shakespeare. Yet when he described the purpose of theater, he quoted, but did not attribute, famous lines from Shakespeare's *Hamlet:* "I believe in the American theatre. I believe in its power to inform about the human condition, I believe in its power to heal, 'to hold the mirror as 'twere up to nature' [*Hamlet* 3.2.20], to the truths we uncover, to the truths we wrestle from uncertain and sometimes unyielding realities" (46).[1] In many ways, Shakespeare was very much alive and well in Wilson's imagination; he continued to occupy a seat in the theater Wilson had willingly entered. Like most Americans living in the late twentieth century, Wilson was not familiar with the particulars of Shakespeare's plays, but he recognized him as a specter—a ghost—in the theater and in the popular imagination.

The statements above may give the impression that the influence was unidirectional from Shakespeare, the forefather, to Wilson, the black "upstart Crow" (Greene 3321): from Shakespeare, "a mortal god," to Wilson, his surprising son and heir (Bloom, *Shakespeare* 3). Yet the relationship between Wilson and Shakespeare has turned out to be one that affects our understanding of both playwrights. As I wrote in a book about contemporary performances of Shakespeare, "the ghostly presence of August Wilson throughout the collection emphasizes how powerful and important his arguments about colorblind casting were and continue to be" in Shakespearean scholarship (A. Thompson, "Practicing" 19). Scholars who address the ways Shakespeare's plays are produced, performed, reviewed, and received today cannot escape the fact that Wilson has affected these practices. First, his debates with Robert Brustein, the artistic director of the American Repertory Theatre from 1980 to 2002, have shaped our understanding of the intricate relations among theater funding, racial casting, and the marketing of classical performances.[2] Because of Wilson's stance in these debates, Shakespeare scholars are much more attentive to the rhetoric of multiculturalism in the casting, marketing, and arts-funding practices of regional theaters. First, we have had to address the growth and implications of nontraditional casting in Shakespearean productions—that is, the practice of casting actors of color for roles that were originally conceived as white and written for white actors. As Peter Erickson has argued, "Despite the 1997 forum 'Beyond the Wilson-Brustein Debate,' we [Shakespeareans] are not beyond August Wilson" ("Afterword" 244). Second, there is a growing body of classically trained black actors and directors who transition regularly and smoothly between Shakespearean performances and Wilsonian ones.[3] With the completion of his ten-play cycle, Wilson's plays are now staged with a regularity that marks them as modern American classics (this in addition to a theater named after Wilson on Broadway's Great White Way!). The viewing habits of audiences and critics necessarily change as we become accustomed to the fluid movement of actors, directors, and audiences between Shakespeare and Wilson. We have learned not only to see the authors as being in dialogue with each other but also to interpret the plays, performances, and productions as existing in dynamic animation; Wilson and Shakespeare are constantly changing, evolving, and morphing because of each other.

If the dynamic relationship between Wilson and Shakespeare is increasingly recognized in scholarship and in practice, then our challenge is to impart this dynamism in our literature and performance classrooms. There are a few essays available that demonstrate how to pair certain scenes, dialogues, and monologues from Wilson and Shakespeare. For example, Philip C. Kolin provides a thoughtful analysis of the ways *King Hedley II* echoes *Macbeth*. Caleen Sinnette Jennings provides models for choral reading exercises of *King Hedley II* and *Hamlet* and demonstrates how the seemingly disparate plays' rhetoric, characters, and themes can be compared. But our pedagogical comparisons need not be limited to texts, especially since many educators employ some form of performance in their Wilson and Shakespeare classes. Taking seriously Wilson's claim that he "realized that you could arrive at the universal through the specific" (Plimpton 75), I suggest that it is time to discuss the politics of race and performance openly in the classroom. If, as Wilson argued, casting is never really color-blind in the professional theater, we must begin to question the politics of racialized readings and performances in the classroom. With this in mind, I have created three different classroom exercises that help bring Wilson and Shakespeare into dialogue about racialized performances.

Exercise 1: The Metadiscussion about Race in Performance

The first classroom exercise fosters a debate about the roles and natures of casting and race in professional theater versus classroom readings and performances. It also provides a structured forum in which to gauge the temperature of the classroom with regard to race in performance. In other words, this exercise is designed to allow the students to express their opinions freely. The challenge for the instructor is to move the free-flowing discussion from one based solely on opinions to one informed by historical, cultural, and theoretical contexts. The instructor can begin by having the students read brief position statements from Wilson, Brustein, and Timothy Douglas, a black director whose résumé consists of "50 percent dead white playwrights and 50 percent living black playwrights" (A. Thompson, "In the Blood" 148).

August Wilson

> An important part of black theatre that is often ignored but is seminal to the tradition is its origins on the slave plantations of the South. Summoned to the "big house" to entertain the slave owner and his guests, the slave began a tradition of theatre as entertainment for whites that reached its pinnacle in the heyday of the Harlem Renaissance. This entertainment for whites consisted of whatever the slave imagined or knew that his master wanted to see and hear. This tradition has its present-life counterpart in the crossover artists that slant their material for white consumption. . . . The idea of colorblind casting is the same idea of assimilation that black Americans have been rejecting for the past 380 years. (*Ground* 19, 31)

Robert Brustein

> Most American theatres today, like many American cities—indeed like many Americans—are racially mixed. Are black actors now to perform only black parts written by black playwrights? Will James Earl Jones no longer have a chance to play Judge Brack or Darth Vader? Must we bar Andre Braugher and Denzel Washington from enacting the Shakespearean monarchs? Is Othello not to be an acceptable opportunity for Morgan Freeman or Lawrence Fishburne? Will Athol Fugard be told he cannot take a colored role in his own plays? No more *Voodoo Macbeth*s or all-black *Godot*s? No more efforts on behalf of nontraditional casting and integrated theatre companies? Must history be rolled back to the days of segregation? ("Subsidized Separatism" 26–27)

Timothy Douglas

> The question that keeps coming up, especially in training centers, is when will we start mixing it up in August Wilson's plays. When will we see white people in them? My answer is: "When we have dealt fundamentally with the conundrum between the races in this country, then we can see that." But do we have to wait? Maybe we should start with the theatre, as we are meant to do, shedding light and holding up the mirror. But it is very prickly for me. I am not ready to address that yet. With that said, when I am teaching acting classes I absolutely give my white actors August Wilson. (A. Thompson, "In the Blood" 152)

Discussion Questions

What do you think the role of theater is in an integrated society? Should it mirror the racial politics of that society? Should it challenge those politics? When and why?

How do performances of classical pieces, like those by Shakespeare, fit into this debate? Why aren't there more black Hamlets, for instance?

How do culturally specific pieces, like those by Wilson, fit into this debate? Do you want to see an all-white production of *Fences*? Why or why not?

What are the benefits and risks of performing roles of the opposite race? Are they different from the benefits and risks of performing roles of the opposite gender?

Do your views change if the readings/performances are amateur ones, ones conducted in academic settings, or professional ones? Why or why not?

What needs to occur in the classroom to make cross-racial readings/performances risk-free? Or, on the other hand, is the desire for a risk-free reading/performance problematic?

If this type of metadiscussion is conducted early in the semester or year, the students will be more willing to address the politics of race in performance throughout the entire course. This metadiscussion helps situate discussions of race within discussions of performance, but the class need not be limited to discussions of race. This exercise merely provides a way to legitimize and validate the introduction of race within larger literary and performance discussions. If this exercise is used as a temperature gauge at the very beginning of a class, then it should be followed up with short readings about the history and politics of casting. The introductions to my *Colorblind Shakespeare* ("Practicing") and Brandi Wilkins Catanese's *The Problem of the Color(blind)* (1–31) provide the historical and theoretical contexts to deepen the conversations throughout the semester or year. The instructor must ensure that the students do not rely only on their opinions; they must be encouraged to interrogate their opinions through the historical, cultural, and theoretical lenses provided.

Exercise 2: Analyzing the Semiotics of Race in Performance

This classroom exercise helps students understand the fact that race not only carries interpretative meanings in performance but also impacts and alters one's interpretation of a play's entire text, performance, and production. Looking on *YouTube*, you can find a plethora of monologue performances from Wilson's and Shakespeare's plays. Find two or three short videos of the same monologues from *Fences* and *Hamlet* (these two plays are represented the most frequently on *YouTube*), choosing young actors of different races reading or performing the same lines. There are usually many offerings of Rose's famous monologue from *Fences* ("I been standing with you!" [(1986) 2.1]) and of Hamlet's soliloquy after meeting the players ("O, what a rogue and peasant slave am I!" [2.2.485]).[4] While this exercise could be conducted using clips from DVDs, the options will be limited in terms of nontraditional casting. The great variety of monologues uploaded to *YouTube* by aspiring performers provides options that are much more plentiful, diverse (including black, Asian, and Latino Hamlets and white, Asian, and Latino Roses), and up-to-date (i.e., culturally fresh and relevant).

Discussion Questions

Can you describe the mise-en-scène: setting, background, costumes/clothes, movement, lighting, music (if any), etc.? What is similar and/or different about the readings/performances of Wilson's text? Shakespeare's text?

What did you notice first about the readings/performances? How did you decide what aspects of the readings/performances were meaningful? How did you decide what aspects were not?

How does race fit into the way you analyze these readings/performances? Does race play a different role in the Wilsonian ones than in the Shakespearean ones? How and why?

After watching these videos, do you agree with Wilson that performances are never color-blind? Why or why not? (If you have not done exercise 1, you should provide a copy of Wilson's statement above.)

Are you more or less willing to engage in color-blind performances if they are created for school assignments or training purposes? Are you more willing to engage in Shakespearean performances than Wilsonian ones or less willing? Why or why not?

Do you view any of these performances as universal? How do you identify the universal? Does race impact how you define and identify the universal?

This type of exercise enables students to identify and discuss race as one of the semiotic elements at work in a production. In addition, it encourages them to think about the ways we approach Wilson and Shakespeare similarly and differently. Inevitably, discussion will enable an interrogation of the universal. I noted at the beginning of this essay that Wilson wanted his plays to "arrive at the universal through the specific." But what exactly constitutes the universal is constantly being renegotiated. Supplementing the classroom discussion with a brief essay on these renegotiations, you will be able to unpack underanalyzed assumptions about what gets labeled universal and when (A. Thompson, *Passing Strange* 68–95).

Exercise 3: The Practice of Casting

This exercise helps students formulate, articulate, defend, and put into practice their own views about casting with regard to race. First have your students read and compare one of Wilson's plays with one of Shakespeare's. Again, the essays by Kolin and by Jennings provide thoughtful ways to compare the themes, structures, and characterizations of *King Hedley II* with those of *Macbeth* and *Hamlet*. I also think an interesting textual comparison could be made between *Fences* and *Othello*. Whatever the texts employed, it is important that the class discussions enable the students to articulate the elements they think should be highlighted in a performance (themes, characters, settings, etc.). Next ask the students to create an advertising poster for the play that captures some aspects of those elements, specifically featuring images of the lead characters. You can ask the students to locate images of actors or models on the Internet by themselves, or you can provide students with a diverse selection of stock images of models.[5] Either way, the exercise is designed to get the students to articulate the themes of the plays, encapsulate those themes into visual images that are geared toward marketing, and analyze the ways that race reveals and influences our cultural practices.

Discussion Questions

Which themes did you include and exclude and why? How easy or difficult was it to condense them to static images?

Would you characterize your poster as traditional or experimental? Why? Specifically, what elements make it so?

Does race play into your poster? If so, how? How did you come to make your decisions about its representation?

Do you think your poster will be an effective marketing tool? If so, how? Did the notion that the poster was an advertisement for the play affect your decisions about race? If so, how and why?

Were your decisions different for the Wilson and Shakespeare plays? If so, how and why? What does this difference tell us about how we define theater, race, and performance?

One could achieve a similarly rich discussion about the semiotics of race in performance and marketing through an in-class performance assignment in which the students cast themselves for certain roles in Wilson and Shakespeare plays. But this casting should be done only if the dynamics in the classroom are such that all the students feel open and comfortable discussing their own races. As Karin deGravelles says in her thoughtful article about performance pedagogies for *Othello*, in-class performance assignments can be touchy when discussions about race are not carefully moderated. The poster assignment, however, removes the potential to personalize the discussions and debates.

Obviously the exercises described in this essay can be done without comparing Wilsonian and Shakespearean readings and performances; they can just as easily be done for Wilsonian texts or Shakespearean ones alone. Yet the discussions are much richer in a comparative framework because the students are forced to identify exactly how they understand and define the universal and the specific. In addition, the comparative framework enables them to place race squarely within their deliberations about what constitutes a universal and classical piece of literature and theater. After all, both Shakespeare and Wilson mastered unifying the apparently dichotomous tension between the timeless and the timely.

NOTES

[1] Wilson's unattributed quotation from *Hamlet* is not exactly verbatim. Hamlet says, "to hold as 'twere the mirror up to Nature" (3.2.21–22).

[2] August Wilson's keynote address at the eleventh biennial Theatre Communications Group National Conference at Princeton University was delivered on 26 June 1996 and printed that same year. Brustein responded to Wilson's remarks (and Wilson countered) in four issues of *American Theatre* (see Brustein, "Subsidized Separatism"). Then, in 1997, *Theater* magazine printed the debate in a special edition consisting of seven pieces (*Beyond the Wilson-Brustein Debate*). Wilson and Brustein also met for a public debate at the Town Hall in New York City on 27 January 1997.

[3] For three accounts of transition between Shakespearean and Wilsonian performances, see A. Thompson, "In the Blood"; Erickson, "From Lear's Button"; and Lennix and Fishburne.

[4] For a performance of Hamlet's 2.2 soliloquy that has received a lot of media attention, see Craig Bazan's video on *YouTube*. A young, black teenager from Camden, New Jersey, Bazan performs the soliloquy in front of an abandoned building in Camden ("Hamlet on the Street").

[5] For a selection of royalty-free images that are searchable by gender, age, and race, see istockphoto.com or dreamstime.com.

Blues Brothers: Crosscurrents in *Fences* and *A Streetcar Named Desire*

Keith Clark

For a college or high school instructor charged with educating students of multiple abilities and backgrounds, pairing and teaching the works of two such colossal and seemingly disparate American dramatists, Tennessee Williams and August Wilson, might at first seem a daunting task. One might, with some legitimacy, contend that at least the enshrined status that *A Streetcar Named Desire* now occupies brings with it a plethora of teaching tools. Witness the immensity of Williams's scholarship, along with several filmed versions and the play's ubiquity in local, regional, and Broadway theaters. Even the greenest of students has probably heard a parody of Marlon Brando's piercing, gut-wrenching "STELL-LAHHHHH!" (60). Conversely, Wilson's *Fences,* while irrefutably a classic in the African American dramatic canon, does not hold a similar place in America's collective artistic and popular imagination. Nevertheless, *Fences* is accessible on so many levels—as a racially and culturally combustible drama about the hopes, fears, and anxieties of post–World War II African Americans for whom the American dream remains a chimera and, concomitantly, as a timeless (dare I say "raceless"?) family tragedy whose themes of adultery, sibling rivalry, father-son discord, and conflicting notions of manhood that refer back to Euripides and Shakespeare as much as they do to O'Neill and Miller, transcending temporal, racial, and geographic boundaries. Thus, when I've paired *A Streetcar Named Desire* and *Fences* in my general education survey courses—catchall classes often attracting an array of students, from business or science majors grudgingly satisfying their humanities requirements, to English majors well versed in Harry Potter and Huck Finn—the plays' companionability never ceases to amaze. Unfailingly, these extraordinarily teachable dramas have yielded some of the most enriching discussions and gratifying classroom exchanges.

Despite the appearance of *Fences* in scores of anthologies since the late 1980s—and despite the play's being awarded the Pulitzer Prize—Wilson hasn't assumed a hallowed place on the Mount Rushmore of great American playwrights. Take Stephen Bottoms's observation in the introduction to *The Cambridge Companion to Edward Albee* that, "[t]oday, [Edward Albee] is frequently listed alongside Eugene O'Neill, Tennessee Williams, and Arthur Miller as one of the nation's great (white, male) dramatists of the twentieth century" (1). Bottoms at once promulgates a segregated brotherhood of Anglo-American writers while simultaneously acknowledging that the politics of literary consecration is indeed a raced enterprise. Wilson himself has what might be charitably described as a protean assessment of his place within the coterie of august American dramatists. At times, he ardently disavows being influenced by or compared with the great (white) fathers of dramatic literature: "I haven't read Ibsen, Shaw, Shakespeare. . . . I'm not familiar with *Death of a Salesman.* I haven't read Tennessee Williams. I very purposefully didn't read them" (Savran 292; qtd. in Rocha, "August Wilson" 4). Paradoxically, Wilson would praise lavishly a less-than-brotherly literary ancestor in an interview with the critic Mark Rocha: "And when I spoke with Wilson and referred to Aristotle and the Western theory of tragedy, Wilson made a point of saying he had never read the *Poetics* even though in 1990 he told the *Boston Globe,* 'As far as playwriting goes, it's Aristotle'" (Rocha, "August Wilson" 4).

Conjunctively, it would be hard to argue that Wilson's ambitious ten-play cycle or Century Cycle, his chronicling of what Wilson deems the black experience through a play representing each decade, was conceived without some knowledge of O'Neill's unrealized "cycle of plays on American history tentatively titled *A Tale of Possessors, Self-Possessed* . . ." (Shannon, *Dramatic Vision* 7). To be sure, *Fences* invariably invites comparisons with Miller's archetypal American tragedy—Rocha calls it "a deliberate point-to-point signifyin(g) parody of *Death of a Salesman*" ("August Wilson" 4), while Robert Brustein assails *Fences* as a quasi-minstrelized version of *Salesman.*[1] Certainly, the contours of Wilson's play inarguably bespeak influence, whether deliberate or subconscious: Troy Maxson, the hubris-laden patriarch with his workplace frustrations, extramarital relationship, and ne'er-do-well two sons, evokes the legendary Loman; Rose, the quintessential beset wife who gallantly elegizes Troy in the play's denouement, invariably recalls Linda Loman's noble eulogizing of her deeply flawed spouse, to whom "attention must be paid" despite his ignoble suicide. But whether Wilson's sepia tragedy of the common black Everyman is more Millerian or O'Neillian, my pedagogical concerns here are the crosscurrents between two plays that, on the surface, appear oceans apart but ultimately offer a reservoir of pedagogical possibilities.

Biographical and Historical Convergences

In juxtaposing *Fences* and *Streetcar,* students might initially iterate the stark contrasts not only between the works themselves but also between two authors who appear to them more than temporally and racially dissimilar. The most superficial distinctions are apparent enough: the vast difference in the authors' ages, signaled by Wilson's being born in 1945, the same year that Williams's first major work, *The Glass Menagerie,* debuted on Broadway; the difference in their degree of formal education, Wilson dropping out of high school in the wake of a false plagiarism charge, Williams bouncing among several colleges before finally receiving a B.A. Williams had many gay white literary forebears and peers (Walt Whitman, Hart Crane [Williams's "idol" (A. Hale 16)], W. H. Auden, fellow playwright William Inge), and not only was his homosexuality—much more so than Albee's—widely known in his heyday (e.g., his long-term relationship with Frank Merlo) but also he foregrounded sexual difference in his major plays,

Streetcar and *Cat on a Hot Tin Roof*, dramatic gambits that clearly made him an iconoclast. In contrast, Wilson's heterosexuality, evidenced in three marriages and two children, clearly informs the preponderance of his plays, their emphasis on male homosociality notwithstanding. Though he does depict one gay character (the eponymous blues diva of his first hit, *Ma Rainey's Black Bottom*), his entire canon is inexorably hetero-centered: male-female relationships take center stage alongside male-male companionate bonds in *Fences, Joe Turner's Come and Gone, Seven Guitars, King Hedley II,* and *Radio Golf.*

In terms of laying the groundwork for my class's explication of the plays, I find it immensely important to devote some discussion to Williams's and Wilson's biographies, given that the playwrights are so obviously divided by time and race. Indeed, locating the authors' commonalities provides students a gateway into the plays' crosscurrents and how such seemingly disparate dramatic classics are more kin than distant relatives. On a most rudimentary level, Williams's and Wilson's youths were blighted by an abusive and absent father, respectively. Jealous of how attached the young Tennessee (né Tom) was to his mother, Edwina, his father, Cornelius, "retaliated by calling his delicate son 'Miss Nancy'" (A. Hale 13). The mistreatment that Wilson would suffer took a vastly different but no less painful form. As the son of an African American woman, Daisy Wilson, and a white German emigrant, Frederick Kittel, Wilson and his five siblings suffered the humiliation of racial rejection and abandonment. As Christopher Bigsby ironically remarks, Kittel, "like Tom's [father] in *The Glass Menagerie* . . . , seems to have fallen in love with long distance" ("Ground" 7). Like Cornelius Williams, Kittel left his family in dire financial straits. Astute students will also note a corresponding ethnic tension in the Kowalski household, when the Polish American Stanley feels the sting of WASP-centric Blanche's anti-immigrant "Polack" taunts. As a result, both writers esteemed their mothers—Wilson so much that he embraced Daisy's racial heritage (clearly manifested in his early black nationalism and his plays' unabashed African and African American centricity), concretized in the changing of his name from Frederick August Kittel to August Wilson. Williams, too, would reject his prosaic given name of Tom in favor of the more quixotic sobriquet Tennessee, perhaps as homage to his mother's southern sensibilities. Despite the emotional lacerations left by the fractured father-son relationship, both artists would inherit their fathers' wayfaring tendencies: Williams lived in several cities and countries, including St. Louis, Key West, New Orleans, and Cuba; Wilson shuttled between Pittsburgh and St. Paul before finally settling in Seattle. Correlatively, the Midwest would figure prominently in these somewhat peripatetic writers' lives, as that region served as an incubator for their artistic gestation: Williams studied playwriting at the University of Iowa, while Wilson would accept a friend's invitation to come to St. Paul to rewrite some of Wilson's poems as plays. While attention to these picayune background details might at first seem extraneous—or excessive—juxtaposing these dramatists' biographies will help make the works' concerns with paternal legacies, psychological longing, ethnic strains, and masculine anxiety all the more perceptible.

Finally, given that poetry and drama are genres so often enmeshed (e.g., even non-English majors will be familiar with the poetry of Hamlet's or Othello's arias and may have even studied the prosody of the Bard's soliloquies), worth mentioning is how the medium of poetry served Williams and Wilson as a gateway to playwriting. Both published poems early in their careers, an important connection given that they are renowned for their protagonists' lyrical, incandescent vernacular poetry. I take care to preface our discussions of the plays by emphasizing that each begins with a poetic epigraph—*Streetcar* with lines from Hart Crane, *Fences* with a quatrain by Wilson himself on the fraught legacies fathers bequeath their sons. The dramas abound with highly emotive, rhapsodic speeches: note, for instance, Blanche's aria (scene 4) on Stanley's Neanderthal mien vis-à-vis a world where art still perilously reigns, or Troy's eloquent defense of his marital transgression through the incongruous conceit of baseball (2.1 [*Three Plays*]). Especial attention to the dramatists' ear for poetic language will augment students' understanding and appreciation of the works beyond the plays' obvious concerns surrounding financial exigency or marital turmoil.

Upon making biographical connections along with links between the playwrights' artistic apprenticeships, I've found it fruitful to steer students toward the plays' historical simultaneity as a corollary to the playwrights' personal convergences. Though forty years separate their Broadway premieres (1947, 1987), *Streetcar* and *Fences* are steeped in their historical-cultural particularities, both works in significant ways reflecting the zeitgeists of the 1940s, 1950s, and 1960s. Thus, to contextualize the class's examination of key themes, characterizations, and dramatic techniques, I inaugurate our discussion by asking the students to construct a time line of the period. I am always pleasantly surprised that, despite the chronological chasm separating children of the 1990s from the 1960s—let alone from the 1940s—students usually have a firm grasp of the historical red-letter events of the day: World War II, the integration of the armed forces in 1948, Jackie Robinson's breaking the color barrier in major league baseball in 1947, *Brown v. Board of Education* in 1954 (some can even identify the NAACP's lead counsel, who would become the first black Supreme Court justice), and the troika of radioactive raciosocial events in 1955—Rosa Parks's audacious sit, which precipitated the Montgomery bus boycott; fourteen-year-old Emmett Till's gruesome murder in Mississippi; and the Supreme Court's outlawing of Jim Crow statutes, which called for "separate but equal" public facilities (I sometimes augment discussions of this volatile period with music such as Nina Simone's rebellious anthem "Mississippi Goddamn").

In addition to these racial flash points, many students are acutely aware of the upheaval of traditional gender roles associated with the period—the emergence of Rosie the Riveter, who embodied women's breaking of the domestic bonds, only to have many of those barriers reentrenched with the war's conclusion. Thus instructors should make a concerted effort to foreground *Streetcar*'s radical dramatization of the incongruity of female liberation and the abiding cult of true womanhood that tethers women to circumscribing domestic roles. One strategy I've found particularly resonant for Generation Xers is discussing how Hillary Clinton, a contemporary iconic figure, was assailed for being insufficiently domestic during her tenure as first lady, only to become a viable and heralded candidate for the highest position in the land within a few years. This example provides a smooth segue into Williams's withering critique of chauvinism. Instructors can foreground how the issue of gender and economic oppression in *Streetcar*—Stella is economically dependent on Stanley to the extent that she endures both emotional abuse and physical violence (re "The Poker Night"), and Blanche is denied her livelihood (as a high school English teacher, no less) and thereby similarly subject to Stanley's violence—dovetails nicely with a central thematic concern in *Fences:* Gabriel's plight of being downtrodden although he is a World War II veteran.

In connecting the economic plight of white women to the lives of a black man, instructors can elucidate how issues such as gender oppression and exploitation aren't necessarily woman-specific. Troy indecorously but bluntly ruminates on the government's wanton use of Gabriel's and scores of other black men's bodies as grist for its war mill only to callously disgorge those bodies, many of which return home maimed and incapacitated for their efforts: "Man go over there and fight the war . . . messing around with them Japs, get half his head blown off . . . and they give him a lousy three thousand dollars. And I had to swoop down on that." Immediately afterward, Troy guiltily decries seizing Gabriel's pittance of a compensation to purchase a home for himself, Rose, and Cory: "If my brother didn't have that metal plate in his head . . . I wouldn't have a pot to piss in or a window to throw it out of" (128). Teachers can emphasize the interlocking oppressions that continue to beset ostensibly unalike characters like Blanche DuBois and Gabriel Maxson during a cultural moment most often associated with the collapsing of racial and gender barriers.

Finally, both plays abound with cultural-specific references—Mardi Gras, Huey Long, Uncle Remus, Jackie Robinson, Josh Gibson, Roberto Clemente—which also animate discussion of issues ranging from African American folklore to American political skulduggery to the dim prospects for black athletes in the racially segregated and economically iniquitous era that long preceded the emergence of today's athlete divas like Kobe Bryant, T. O. (Terrell Owens), and Barry Bonds. Students of the cyber age are especially responsive to research assignments geared toward unearthing political and athletic figures with whom they are unfamiliar. Such assignments will limn for students the "changing same," how issues surrounding race, politics, and sports addressed in these plays can be related to our contemporary cultural moment. Such research will reveal how bare-knuckle politicians such as Long presaged divisive figures like a George Wallace or a Karl Rove or how exceedingly gifted athletic legends like Clemente and Gibson chafed under financial and racial inequities that make the exploits and excesses of handsomely compensated ballplayers like Bryant or Owens even more unseemly and profligate.

Writing the 'Hood, Hearing the Voices

I think it is crucial for instructors not only to situate works in their distinct and unique cultural moments but also to consider the role of place and landscape, which is especially important given the rich histories of the Quarter and Hill neighborhoods, the New Orleans and Pittsburgh locales where *Streetcar* and *Fences* are respectively set. I always make students keenly aware how a work's geographic space augments and amplifies its central themes and meanings. Too often, literature instructors concentrating on place with respect to local color or regional writers limit such discussions to fiction writers such as William Faulkner and Zora Neale Hurston. But it's vital for students to apprehend the centrality of place in *Streetcar* and *Fences* as well. Williams painstakingly inscribes stage directions to capture the ambience of "the Quarter." Given that Hurricane Katrina has thrust New Orleans into the national spotlight, students might be encouraged to explore the actual places the playwright denotes: Elysian Fields, the Cemeteries and Desire streetcar lines, the L&N railroad tracks. As well, Williams's ear for the working-class argot of the Quarter most obviously emerges in Stanley's inimitable colloquialisms and figures of speech—for instance, in his unrelenting interrogation of and threats against Blanche: "You going to shack up here?" (31); "How about that? Let's have a few more details on that subjeck" (33); "What's them underneath?" (42); "You won't pick up nothing here you ain't heard before" (76); "In fact they [the proprietors at the Flamingo, the fleabag hotel that banishes Blanche for what they deem her sexual profligacy] were so impressed by Dame Blanche that they requested her to turn in her room key—for permanently!" (99). In direct contradistinction to Stanley, Blanche's heightened and richly emotive phraseology permeates the play, emblematized, for example, in her declaration to Mitch: "I don't want realism. I want magic! Yes, yes, magic! I try to give that to people. I misrepresent things to them. I don't tell the truth, I tell what *ought* to be truth" (117). To be sure, Blanche's elevation of fantasy over reality becomes a metadramatic pronouncement for Williams's dramatic objectives. Matthew Roudane incisively speaks to the author's dramatic principles:

> He sought to find the verbal equivalents for his characters' tortured inner selves, a search that led him away from the realism of Ibsen, O'Casey, (the later) O'Neill, Clifford Odets, and Lillian Hellman and toward a new dramatic form. Williams reinforced his language, moreover, by refining what he termed his "plastic theatre": the use of lights, music, sets, and any other forms of nonverbal expression that would complement the textual version of the play. (2)

More focused attention to the biography of place and the language inherent to place provides students with a more acute sense of the sinews of William's magnum opus.

Wilson, too, is a dramatist of place, not merely flavoring or overlaying his landscape with exaggerated and mimetic versions of black folk life in the name of some sort of faux verisimilitude. Sandra Shannon, a Wilson scholar, provides a concise overview of the artist as a young brother, detailing how Wilson's immersion in the community provided his artistic scaffolding:

> Without much of a fuss, Wilson moved out of his mother's apartment, took a job as a short-order cook, and began frequenting the tobacco houses, bars, and restaurants of Pittsburgh's Hill District. For Wilson, then known as "Youngblood" among the older men around him, this education was just as valuable as that provided by the system he had recently abandoned. . . . Here he listened to racy tales of love affairs and down-home blues stories, bolstered by heavy doses of braggadocio, the dozens, or just plain lies. Here in these smoke-filled watering holes where rough-edged men drank liquor, swapped tales, and laughed out loud, the adolescent Wilson found knowledge of a different sort. (*Dramatic Vision* 18)

Ironically enough, Wilson credits his cross-country trek to Minnesota as a sort of defamiliarizing event that enabled him to hone his black dramatic lexicon. While immersed in the informal pedagogical spaces that Shannon mentions, he reflects, "I didn't respect the way blacks talked"; but after relocating to St. Paul, he says, "I was removed from the black community and, perhaps as result, for the first time I began to hear the voices that I had grown up with all my life" (Bigsby, "Ground" 13). Critics hasten to point out the homosocial undergirdings of his plays, but one concurrently hears what Paul Carter Harrison calls "the oracular voice of the poet" in Rose's verbal rejoinders to Troy's overbearing voice throughout the play ("August Wilson's Blues Poetics" 302). When Troy admonishes Rose for preferring to shop at the A&P grocery store in lieu of Bella's, the local grocer to whom Troy pledges his loyalty, she retorts, "I ain't said nothing about if she got fresh food. I'm talking about what she charge. She charge ten cents more than the A&P" (110). Later, on a more consequential matter, Rose upbraids Troy for insisting that they—"we"—can work through his just-revealed adulterous act and the child that his mistress, Alberta, will soon bear: "All of a sudden it's 'we.' Where was 'we' at when you was down there rolling around with some godforsaken woman? 'We' should have come to an understanding before you started making a damn fool of yourself. You're a day late and a dollar short when it comes to an understanding with me" (163). Rose's sonorous, inflected speech, commingling the language of biblical condemnation with the vernacular practice of signifying, encapsulates Wilson's black dramatic poetics. In her taut rejoinder, she unmasks the semantic discrepancy between Troy's conveniently inclusive, collective pronoun and his exclusively phallocentric, patriarchal actions. Such language can also engender profitable discussions on the efficacy of Ebonics (i.e., Black English).

Thus, specific emphasis on the plays' oral and aural dimensions can consolidate and amplify their connections. Discerning students will see the overlapping of Williams's southern and blue-collar phraseology and Wilson's colloquially authentic, southern-hued diction. Students might further be encouraged to observe how the verbally dexterous characters in both plays reflect the works' polyphony or multiverbalness, the levels of speech ranging from Blanche's Romantic, allusion-rich language to Stanley's proletarian, unadorned phrase turnings and from Troy's black sermonic pronouncements and self-aggrandizing language to Rose's uniquely black aphoristic puncturing of his patriarchal prerogative. Both *Streetcar* and *Fences* not only contain an arabesque of linguistic registers and localized speech patterns but also are steeped in a transverbal language unique to African American and American culture: the blues.

Blues Brothers

In twinning arguably the most important Anglo-American dramatist with indisputably the most eminent African American one, I think it worthwhile to emphasize the centrality of music to their work. Students and teachers of all colors too often render musical influence as exclusively the domain of black writers, but we should resist this shortsighted, unidimensional hermeneutical practice. To be sure, Williams was at the vanguard of Anglo-American writers mining the dramatic possibilities offered by what Albert Murray, a fellow southern writer, would consider the most American of music, the blues.[2] To underscore the connection of white musicians to the blues, then, instructors might take the opportunity to expose students to recordings by artists such as Janis Joplin or Dr. John alongside recordings by more traditional blues artists as Bessie Smith or Robert Johnson.

Though it may be considered fairly pedestrian in the twenty-first century, Williams's incorporation of "The Blue Piano" as part of his play's stagecraft was a transformative moment in American drama, as he so ingeniously employed devices such as music and lighting not simply to help embroider mood but also to provide a better sense of the characters' interiority—their almost primal longings that provide the play's kinetic energy. Witness *Streetcar*'s very first scene, where Williams's stage directions help configure the aromatic milieu of the Kowalski home and neighborhood in the Quarter:

> You can almost feel the warm breath of the brown river beyond the river warehouses with their faint redolences of bananas and coffee. A corresponding air is evoked by the music of Negro entertainers at a barroom around the corner, or a few doors down the street, from a tinny piano being played with the infatuated fluency of brown fingers. This "Blues Piano" expresses the spirit of the life which goes on here. (13)

Scrutinizing Williams's punctiliously written scene descriptions opens a critical space for exploring the racial essentializing—bordering on stereotyping—involved in his delineation of setting.

Discussions of the stereotypes Williams conjures here can provide teachable moments regarding the persistence of such racial anachronisms that conflate "warm," "Negro entertainers," and "infatuated fluency of brown fingers." As well, the play's lone, nearly invisible African American character, reductively and interchangeably referred to as "Colored Woman" and "Negro Woman" in the play's opening scene, will raise some students' pique. But savvy students might notice that the omnipresent "Negro entertainers"—the combo of blues piano, trumpet, and drums—provide the musical analogue for some of the play's most sexually charged scenes (Stella's fierce embracing of Stanley that immediately follows Blanche's denigration of him as an "animal" and a "survivor of the stone age!" at the end of scene 4 (72) and Stanley's rape of Blanche in the climactic scene 10). Though the characters are white, one might legitimately wonder whether the playwright was trafficking in then-sanctioned stereotypes that rendered synonymous jazz, blackness, and sensuality. With a little digging, students will unearth that jazz originally was associated with jazzing—prostitution, which correlates to Blanche's sordid past in Laurel—and thereby often deemed whorehouse music. Thus, the racial undercurrents in *Streetcar* may spur stimulating discussions of white writers' inscription of blackness, opening an interrogative gateway to explore trenchant theoretical texts such as Ralph Ellison's *Shadow and Act* and Toni Morrison's *Playing in the Dark: Whiteness and the Literary Imagination*.[3]

In addition to raising these racially thorny concerns, I think it crucial to emphasize Williams's own blues sensibilities, evinced, for example, in his naming an early collection of short plays *American Blues* (1948). Further, in his journals he used the shorthand "blue devils" (A. Hale 17) to index his own moments of emotional disequilibrium, which sometimes resulted in hospitalization. Given the emergence of gay and lesbian historical and theoretical scholarship, students may be encouraged to examine how the proscribed status of the playwright as a homosexual in a virulently racist South gave him a unique understanding of the music's veiled and coded dimensions—its rendering musically that which couldn't be expressed publicly. *Streetcar* pulsates with blues themes—unquenched sexual yearnings, unspeakable sexual desires (specifically, homosexual ones), economic depredation. In fact, the "hot trumpet" that permeates the drama could conceivably be that of the New Orleans native Louis Armstrong. The legendary and notorious New Orleans red-light district Storyville further solidifies the jazz-sex nexus. Establishing the blues over- and underpinnings of Williams's personal life and in *Streetcar* provides a bridge to *Fences*, given Wilson's fervent extolling of the blues as the basis of his career as a playwright.

Wilson's valorization of the blues as his artistic touchstone is well documented: the blues are one of his exalted four Bs—along with the painter and collagist Romare Bearden, the Black Arts dramatist Amiri Baraka, and the

Argentine short story writer Jorge Luis Borges—the aesthetic influences and paradigms that underlie his entire oeuvre. Wilson spoke poignantly about purchasing a Bessie Smith record in 1965 (incidentally, the same year in which *Fences* ends), which spawned what Shannon aptly calls his "blues epiphany" (*Dramatic Vision* 17). Worth quoting are the dramatist's copious ruminations on the blues as "the African American's response to the world," "a philosophical system at work" and African Americans' "sacred book" (Dinah Livingston qtd. in Rocha, "August Wilson" 9). Such discussions may engender explorations of other African American writers' declarations of the blues as artistic matrix. College instructors especially might use this opportunity to introduce an array of creative writers and scholars who have drawn upon or theorized the blues—Langston Hughes, Amiri Baraka, Gayl Jones, Houston Baker, and Angela Davis, for instance. And, of course, no discussion of the blues as art form and raciocultural kaleidoscope is complete without Ellison's perpetually quoted, compelling definition: "The blues is an impulse to keep the painful details and episodes of a brutal experience alive in one's aching consciousness, to finger its jagged grain, and to transcend it, not by the consolation of philosophy but by squeezing from it a near-tragic, near-comic lyricism" (*Shadow* 78). A jumping-off point might be to juxtapose and counterpoise Ellison's and Wilson's theories of the blues as both art form and racial epistemological construct.

Denouement

In closing, I offer some specific crosscurrents, common reservoirs with respect to theme, characterization, and setting-space that offer substantive pedagogical possibilities for instructors teaching *Streetcar* and *Fences* as companionate plays. Consider these concrete points of intersection between them:

> *Patriarchal Masculinity:* The male protagonists of both plays, Stanley Kowalski and Troy Maxson, are based on men who figured prominently in the dramatists' lives: Stanley Kowalski was the actual name of one of Williams's coworkers at a shoe factory in St. Louis (A. Hale 15), and David Bedford, Wilson's stepfather, like Troy, served several years in prison for robbery and murder (Shannon, *Dramatic Vision* 92). In what ways do the characters uphold and espouse anachronistic notions of masculinity with respect to any number of concerns—gender roles, sex, politics, economics? How do these men's enactment of traditionally male rituals—drinking, card playing, and fighting—both suture male ties but also fray those ties and alienate the people around them? In what ways is their sense of untrammeled male prerogative detrimental to their own sense of self as well as their relationships with family and compatriots?
>
> *Alternative Versions of Patriarchal Masculinity:* As counterpoints to Stanley and Troy's traditional notions of masculinity rooted in power and

control, their sidekicks, Harold "Mitch" Mitchell and Jim Bono, represent versions of masculinity that don't privilege the sexualizing of women and violence. Students might be encouraged to ponder these characters' prominence and whether the reserved Mitch and Bono, unlike their more testosterone-laden buddies, reflect a more constructive, moderated notion of maleness. While perhaps only marginally successful, both contest hackneyed notions of men's propensity for sexual and gender sovereignty.

Blanche DuBois and Troy Maxson as Odd Couple: Troy and Blanche, ostensibly separated by chasms of race, place, class, and gender, are these plays' desired and desiring subjects: they are driven to satiate their needs recklessly and almost narcissistically. Students might consider how both attempt to wield power over those within their orbit in any number of ways: through verbal virtuosity in the form of storytelling as a way to self-mythologize and self-aggrandize; through their ravenous sexual appetites, which they pursue regardless of the havoc they wreak on others or themselves; and through their appropriation of memory and the past to justify their self-indulgent actions in the present.

Mental Instability and Confinement: Both Stella and Troy are increasingly threatened by their siblings—Stella by Blanche's shattering but indisputable revelation about Stanley's being not simply sexually coarse but a sexual predator who has in fact raped his sister-in-law, Troy by his mentally impaired brother Gabriel's economic independence and appreciably more convivial and nurturing relationship with Rose and Troy's own children. To remove these threats, Stella and Troy institutionalize their siblings—a particularly resonant act, given Williams's personal experiences with mental illness and confinement in his own family. Students should be encouraged to research his family history as well as Wilson's denotation of Gabriel as a "spectacle character," a figure in the African American trickster tradition whose grit and mother wit transform his mental defect into a vehicle for self-reliance and independence.[4] Moreover, more advanced students might see how the topic of mental illness interfaces with burgeoning critical schools of thought such as disability studies, creating new and nuanced critical vistas.

The Role of Setting and Dramatic Space as a Key to Meaning: In addition to the palpable importance of geographic setting, students should be encouraged to contemplate physical settings—the porch and front yard in *Fences;* the landings, bars, and the Kowalskis' asphyxiating two-room flat in *Streetcar.* How do the dramatists' choices regarding space help elucidate and buttress what the works may be saying about different forms of imprisonment or how space is often gendered? For example, Mitch's pronouncement that poker "should not be played in a house with women"

(59) at the end of the frenetic and domestically violent "Poker Night" and Troy's insistence that Rose exit the front porch and return inside the house lest she interrupt his and Bono's sexually ribald "men talk" (109) in the play's opening scene.

These are but a few intersectional linkages that can catalyze vigorous, layered conversations about two plays that may be separated by decades but are conjoined by a wellspring of common concerns.

The crosscurrents in *Fences* and *Streetcar* provide a plethora of pedagogical prospects for students of all colors, ethnicities, nationalities, genders, and sexual orientations. At such a momentous moment in American culture—from the election of the first biracial president to contentious discussions about gay marriage to equally volatile debates over immigrants and hyphenated Americans—our classrooms are more multieverything than ever, much more a pastiche than a melting pot. August Wilson may in fact have never read Williams, as he claimed in a 1988 interview (Rocha, "August Wilson" 4), but we as teachers of American and African American drama are nonetheless the beneficiaries of the artistry of two blues raconteurs whose signature plays are indelibly linked.

NOTES

[1] See Brustein's *Reimagining American Theatre* for his indictment of *Fences* as a derivative, blackened version of Miller's classic play (25–26).

[2] Following in the tradition of LeRoi Jones's *Blues People* and Ralph Ellison's *Shadow and Act*, Murray wrote extensively about the intersections between African American blues and jazz traditions and literature. See his *The Hero and the Blues* (1973) and *The Blue Devils of Nada* (1996).

[3] I appreciate the input of my friend and colleague Joy Myree Mainor of Morgan State University. In addition to reading a draft of this essay, she suggested how excursions into the sub-rosa racial dimensions of *Streetcar* open a pedagogical space for introducing critical race theory as an interpretive lens.

[4] Troy's damning role in Gabriel's institutionalization parallels a traumatic moment in Williams's life: the hospitalization of his cherished but increasingly mentally unstable sister Rose. The family's eventual decision to effect a cure by having her lobotomized is a tragedy that shattered and haunted Williams. This event recurs in some of his most acclaimed works—most profoundly in his portrayal of the mentally fragile Laura Wingfield in *The Glass Menagerie* (see A. Hale 17, 20, 26–27) and in *Suddenly Last Summer* (1958), a macabre tale of homoeroticism, (implied) incest, and cannibalism in which a perfectly healthy young woman, Catherine Holly, is committed to a mental asylum against her will by a wealthy, vindictive aunt (who also holds the specter of a lobotomy over her niece). With respect to *Fences*, Wilson delineates Gabriel a "spectacle character," upon which he elaborates: "They make me mad when I read the reviews and they would refer to Gabriel as an idiot or some other kind of description without making

reference to the fact that this man had suffered this wound fighting for a country in which his brother could not play baseball. That is the most important thing about Gabriel. Gabriel is one of those self-sufficient characters" (Shannon, *Dramatic Vision* 225). In addition to *Fences*, the issue of mental disequilibrium emerges in *Two Trains Running* (1990): See Rocha, "Black Madness."

Teaching August Wilson in an American Drama Survey

Soyica Diggs Colbert

> When the sins of our fathers visit us
> We do not have to play host.
> We can banish them with forgiveness
> As God, in His Largeness and Laws
>
> —August Wilson

August Wilson's drama functions as one of the cornerstones of the American drama survey at Dartmouth College. Although we usually read only a single work from any individual playwright, we read three of Wilson's plays: *Fences, The Piano Lesson,* and *King Hedley II.* His drama demands a larger part of the syllabus than the work of most of the other playwrights because his plays challenge, augment, and revise some of the central themes of the American dramatic tradition: the status of national traditions, the accessibility of the American dream, and relationships between fathers and sons. His work, to borrow a phrase from Cheryl A. Wall, irrevocably "worries the line" of American drama.

I coteach the American drama survey, which the English department offers as one of its largest survey courses. Most survey courses in the department contain thirty to fifty students, but the American drama one often has well over a hundred students. Over a ten-week period meeting three times a week (Dartmouth is on a quarter system), we read more than twenty plays, averaging one play per day. The course is organized chronologically, for the most part, to introduce students to the ways playwrights working in the later decades of the twentieth century refer to and revise the themes, formal attributes, and rhetoric of their predecessors. Although *Fences* was not published until 1985, we teach it in the first half of the term because of the ways it explores and explodes the idea of the American dream as an inheritance. Wilson's cycle of ten plays—one for each decade of the twentieth century—exemplifies the process of passing down, both within a play (for example, the cultural practice of singing that the protagonist of *Fences* Troy passes down to his children) and between plays (for example, the machete that a main character in *Seven Guitars* leaves behind when he dies to King in *King Hedley II*). Wilson's drama questions the emphasis within the American dramatic tradition on monetary legacies; the question of who and what must be lost in order to reap financial inheritances is one of the driving concerns of *The Piano Lesson.*

Moving chronologically through the twentieth century, the American drama survey could explore familial dynamics in the first half of the course before considering how individual, national, political, and cultural identities function in the plays of the second half of the course. For example, one could organize the term through discussions of the following texts:

Eugene O'Neill, *Desire under the Elms* (1924)
Langston Hughes, *Mulatto* (1935)
Susan Glaspell, *The Inheritors* (1921)
Tennessee Williams, *Glass Menagerie* (1944)
Arthur Miller, *All My Sons* (1947)
Arthur Miller, *Death of a Salesman* (1949)
August Wilson, *Fences* (1985)
Lorraine Hansberry, *A Raisin in the Sun* (1959)
Eugene O'Neill, *Long Day's Journey into Night* (1956)
Tennessee Williams, *Cat on a Hot Tin Roof* (1955)
August Wilson, *The Piano Lesson* (1990)
John Guare, *Six Degrees of Separation* (1990)
Cherríe Moraga, *The Hungry Woman* (2001)
August Wilson, *King Hedley II* (2005)
Suzan-Lori Parks, *Topdog/Underdog* (2001)
Tony Kushner, *Angels in America* (1993)

At Dartmouth most students arrive well prepared to excel academically and to cultivate their critical reading, writing, and speaking skills. As a part of our course goals we also teach students to situate texts within literary and cultural traditions, historicize texts and understand them as historical objects, and recognize their ongoing political, social, personal, and cultural implications. Nonetheless, the American drama survey presents particular pedagogical challenges within the context of a humanities class at the college because literature classes are usually small and driven by conversation versus lecturing. In order to cultivate the students' close reading skills, we assign a number of short response papers that ask students to focus on a key theme that emerges in one or more of the plays (for example, we may ask them to compare the ghosting quality in *The Piano Lesson* with the ghosting in *Long Day's Journey into Night*). The papers enable students to develop a critical vocabulary about the newly assigned play. Students post them to *Blackboard* before class, and then we incorporate the students' observations into the lecture, emphasizing how their production of knowledge shapes our learning community.

By the time we read Wilson's *Fences,* we have already taken up the question of the familial dynamic in several plays, particularly that of fathers and sons. Both Eugene O'Neill's *Desire under the Elms* and Langston Hughes's *Mulatto* depict the dissolution of the family, which points to powerful domestic ideals that haunt relationships between fathers and sons and require sons to negotiate the legacies their fathers have left for them. In introducing the first of Wilson's dramas, we focus on how his plays depict the father-and-son relationship as a central theme of the American dramatic tradition. Wilson's drama calls for the "reordering of the problematic father figure" (Elam, *Past* 130). As Harry J. Elam, Jr., explains while quoting Charles R. Lyons:

> "The problematic father becomes a staple of American realism as evidenced by *Long Day's Journey into Night, All My Sons, Death of a Salesman* and *The Glass Menagerie.*" In each of these plays the stability of the family, the sons in particular, is threatened by the earlier transgressions of the fathers. The common narrative result is the fragmentation and dysfunctionality of the family unit. The family members must suffer psychologically as well as materially as a result of the father's actions. (130)

But while the sons are called to redeem the lost fathers in *All My Sons, Death of a Salesman,* and *Long Day's Journey into Night* in order to figure out a way to incorporate the father's legacy into the family's life moving forward, Wilson's plays "do not attempt to absent the father or to vilify him for the family's tragic demise. Instead, even as they reveal the faults and frailties of the father, the underlying objective is to reconcile and restore the position of the patriarch within the fabric of the family, precisely because the father seems so apparently lost" (130–31). Moreover, to present the relationships of fathers and sons does not necessarily imply that the playwright must reinforce a patriarchal structure. In many ways, Wilson's *Fences* struggles with concepts at the core of a patriarchal order of kinship.

Fences depicts the life of Troy Maxson, a sanitation worker obliged to care for his wife, Rose, and son, Cory. All the while, he longs for a greater sense of purpose, which was denied him when the color line prevented him from trying out for major league baseball in his youth. Troy satisfies his longing for something more than the doldrums of a job with little chance of advancement and the monotony of domestic life by having an affair that results in the birth of his daughter, Raynell. The play uses the imagery of the angel of death and the conflict between Troy and other characters—Rose; Cory; Troy's brother, Gabriel; and Troy's best friend, Bono—to communicate the protagonist's dissatisfaction with life and simultaneous wish to care for his family in the only ways that he knows how. *Fences* maps Troy's conflicted motivations intergenerationally, which adds richness to Wilson's tragedy. Yet while Troy provides financial support for his family, his emotional unavailability and resistance to Cory's pursuing his dreams drives a wedge between him and the ones he loves. At the same time, Troy offers playful modes of engagement with his family, such as the weekly ritual of storytelling with Rose and Bono or the songs that he teaches Cory and Raynell, activities that render him a charismatic and sympathetic character (for more on ritual in black theater and performance, see Edwards, Harrison, and Walker; Richards, "Yoruba Gods"). Troy's persistent struggle to live a fuller life finds a fitting dramatic end in the final scene of the play, which depicts the other characters' readying for his funeral and reflecting on his legacy.

In our class and online discussions of *Fences,* we ask students to consider the singing in the final scene or Troy's battle with death as modern-day rituals that inform the generational shifts in Wilson's play and in American drama. By asking the students to write about one scene or image, we encourage them to think specifically and in depth, while opening conversation about the play as a whole. In class we ask them to consider the relation between their response papers and Troy's characterization throughout the play. The papers that analyze the final scene of *Fences* usually interpret his children's singing the song he taught them as a moment of cultural transfer that extends his legacy beyond his death. The papers that examine Troy's battle with the angel of death often relate his mythmaking to his desire to forestall dying and "go on for it" instead of simply subsisting ([Plume] 70).

Analysis of the play in the classroom, which predominantly takes the form of a lecture but does incorporate some question-and-answer time, teases out some of the implications of the students' response papers and calls attention to other major themes in the play. For example, we begin by noting that in *Fences,* Wilson's play for the 1950s, time seems to be up in Troy's relationship with Bono, Rose, Cory, and Gabriel. Instead of shifting with the sands of time, Troy fights as if he's in quicksand to maintain the status quo of his relationships, only to find himself gasping and alone. We ask students to consider why he chooses to repeatedly describe his battle with death, and we ask them to incorporate their responses into the lecture. When Troy tries to cheat death, he actually ends up cheating himself and his loved ones. His inability to negotiate the realities of the moment (i.e., the changing status of his relationships with Bono and Rose, Cory's opportunity to play college football on an integrated team, and the aftermath of Troy's manipulation of Gabe) limits his interactions with his family.

As the responses to the question about the final scene of the play reveal, although Troy refuses to make the most of his time with his family, he does leave a fruitful legacy for his children. While material inheritances preoccupy Miller's *All My Sons,* Hansberry's *A Raisin in the Sun*, and O'Neill's *Long Day's Journey into Night,* storytelling becomes Troy's legacy and marks Wilson's aesthetic difference. The opening scene introduces the audience to a weekly ritual among Troy, Bono, and Rose. Every Friday, Troy receives his pay, stops by the local bar to flirt with his girlfriend, Alberta, returns home with Bono for a drink, and then launches into a story.

Although the generational conflict between Troy and Cory that develops around the son's desire to play football is one of the driving forces in *Fences,* when Troy assumes the role of storyteller, he directs attention away from his conflict with his son. The first story that he tells, which amounts to over two pages of text, captivates his audience. After reading through the long passage in class, we ask students about Rose's role in this ritual. They often observe that she periodically interjects comments but does not have the ability to alter the direction of the narrative. Troy unilaterally directs the conversation and therefore enacts agency over his life that has been denied in other arenas. Even as he attempts to reshape the past and future, he must contend with the fact that becoming a major league athlete, an opportunity absent to almost all black men in his youth, by the 1950s has become an opportunity absent only to black men over age forty.

At the end of the class session on *Fences*, students should note that Troy has several conversations with Cory throughout the play, but the father does not perform as a storyteller for Cory in the way that he does in the opening scene—although the father does teach him songs. Unlike some of Wilson's other characters, including the mythical Aunt Ester, Troy does not articulate the transformative power of his narration. Only in his death does Cory recognize that the true force of Troy's power resides in the intergenerational transfer of the daily rituals he performed, like singing his signature song, and not in his claims to a self-generated power to conquer death. Troy's belief in his own individual strength and his anxiety about its waning set up the competition between him and his son and motivates his desire to have an affair.

Troy does not narrate stories for Cory, but he does share the intimate details of his life with Lyons, which suggests that he interprets this ritual activity not as part of his legacy to impart knowledge to his children but instead as a means to relate to his adult child. In class, we call students' attention to the way that storytelling exemplifies Wilson's aesthetic, which incorporates the performance of the daily rituals of black life. His use of quotidian cultural practices transforms the theater into a ritual space that negotiates the transition from the physical to the metaphysical. For example, Rose's periodic insertions in Troy's depiction of his first battle with death creates a ritual quality in that the rhythm of the characters' language resembles a familiar dance that is performed again and again to ameliorate the rigors of a long workweek. As the play indicates in the stage directions, "*Though she* [Rose] *doesn't drink, her presence is an integral part of the Friday night ritual*" (5). Instead of offering new information, the storytelling among Troy, Rose, and Bono seeks to affirm for them what is already known, to draw them closer together through a familiar practice.

Although Troy denies Cory the ability to inherit his role as patriarch and to explore his athletic potential, he does leave him with a sustaining mode of performance. In the last scene of the play, Cory returns to pay respect to his father even though he does not plan to attend the funeral. Cory explains to Rose:

> The whole time I was growing up . . . living in his house . . . Papa was like a shadow that followed you everywhere. It weighed on you and sunk into your flesh. It would wrap around you and lay there until you couldn't tell which one was you anymore. That shadow digging in your flesh. Trying to crawl in. Trying to live through you. Everywhere I looked, Troy Maxson was staring back at me . . . hiding under the bed . . . in the closet. I'm just saying I've got to find a way to get rid of that shadow, Mama. (96–97)

Rose responds by pointing out the ways the family structure encouraged Troy's parental practices. She comforts her son and convinces him to come to the funeral. She gives him the language to contextualize his relationship with his father when she says:

> You can't be nobody but who you are, Cory. That shadow wasn't nothing but you growing into yourself. You either got to grow into it or cut it down to fit you. But that's all you got to make life with. That's all you got to measure yourself against that world out there . . . he meant to do more good than he meant to do harm. He wasn't always right. Sometimes when he touched he bruised. And sometimes when he took me in his arms he cut. (97)

Rose points out that Troy's abrasive touch does not disqualify it as an embrace. Although she does not dismiss Troy's actions, she provides a context for Cory to reevaluate them. Alternatively, Raynell reminds him of a critical practice. When Raynell begins to sing, Cory quickly joins in a duet of a song Troy taught them. Their duet "conveys the importance of legacy but also the potential for growth and progress" (Elam, *Past* 75). Troy used different methods with the adults and children in his life, but his use of ritual served to draw his loved ones closer and soften the sting of his embrace. In the final scene, Cory retrieves his inheritance—a model of action that he may translate to fit a new social and historical context.

In the second half of the course, when we return to Wilson's drama, we call attention to how *The Piano Lesson,* like *Fences,* is preoccupied with remains. *The Piano Lesson* troubles the son's exclusive claim on the legacy of the father and asserts the central role of the mother in the process of passing down the legacy, a worrying of the patriarchal line that Hansberry also enacts in *A Raisin in the Sun.* In a determined resistance to the singularity of a leading role, Wilson's *The Piano Lesson* emphasizes the equal importance of Boy Willie and his sister Berniece. Written for the 1930s, the play depicts their struggle over a family heirloom, the piano, which the final scene interrupts dramatically with the incursion of a ghost. In order to exorcise the ghost, Berniece must play the piano. Her ability to make use of the piano allays Boy Willie's desire to sell it, and he leaves, warning that if she stops playing the piano, he will be back. Her victory at the end of the play did not take place in the original production, which emphasized the siblings' equality by ending ambiguously, with the fate of the piano still up in the air.

Calling attention to the plays' production histories in class is important because it allows students to see that Wilson's drama actively revises the emphasis on material advancement as fundamental to the American dream. Before offering information about production history of *The Piano Lesson*, we often ask students to write a response paper that makes an argument for who should keep the piano, telling them to consider how references to the American dream, either directly or indirectly, serve as an organizing theme of the course. We then note in class that the changes Wilson makes to the play, which appear in the final published version, seem to favor Berniece, who symbolizes the past, rather than

Boy Willie, who is willing to leave the material remains of the past for progress's sake. While students may disagree with Wilson, the assignment helps them see the value of engaging with theater history when writing about a play and the way that textual evidence must be used to support an argument.

The legacy that their father, Boy Charles, leaves traps brother and sister in an equation of human value with material property. They must work through how to form a different relation to the past and future through an inherited object. In order to claim their inheritance, they must let go of the dead even when the remains of the past serve an objective purpose. The piano carries the genealogy of the entire family by producing music, which is key to Wilson's aesthetic. Wilson explains in an interview with Sandra Shannon, "the music has a cultural response of Black Americans to the world they find themselves in. Blues is the best literature we have" ("August Wilson" 121). The blues, one of Wilson's major influences, take painful situations and transform them into expressions of joy. Ralph Ellison writes:

> The blues is an impulse to keep the painful details and episodes of a brutal experience alive in one's aching consciousness, to finger its jagged grain, and to transcend it, not by the consolation of philosophy but by squeezing from it a near tragic, near-comic lyricism. As a form, the blues is an autobiographical chronicle of personal catastrophe expressed lyrically. ("Richard Wright's Blues" 78–79)

Although Berniece does not sing a blues song at the end of the play, her return to music marks a way to narrate a new chapter in her story that keeps the legacy of her mother and father alive as it allows her to move forward. Her playing of the piano also acknowledges the cultural inheritances mothers leave to their daughters—note that the play emphasizes that Berniece's daughter too plays the piano. Wilson therefore revises the nature of inheritance and the order of succession, which reconfigure value in the American dramatic tradition. He demonstrates the value of leaving behind cultural practices and not just money and calls attention to what women as well as men leave for their children.

Berniece's musical exorcism reorganizes the broken lines of kinship depicted in Wilson's *Joe Turner's Come and Gone* because it challenges the legacy of slavery, which left black people kinless and without history. The reclamation of the piano as a mechanism that enables liberation allows Boy Charles to live on and offers Boy Willie and Berniece freedom from the historical burden his insurgent act imposes. As in *Fences,* Wilson offers a mode of practice that enables future generations to live with the legacy of the father while forging their own modes of meaning making. His drama transposes the material inheritance central to the work of his predecessors into a practice that frees black people's value from property and offers a way for sons and daughters to work with inheritances instead of simply accepting or rejecting them. *The Piano Lesson* is an ideal example of how Wilson signifies on the theme of inheritance in American drama through the transformation of the status of the piano from an instrument to an artifact marked with carvings to a ghostly heirloom to a mechanism for insurgent practice. The morphing of this material object serves as a metaphor for the type of practices that may also transform the seemingly static racial signifier of the black body, a question Wilson takes up in *Joe Turner's Come and Gone* and continues to explore in *King Hedley II*.

King Hedley II, Wilson's eighth play, nicely rounds out the trio of Wilson plays in our American drama survey. It recalls the themes of the evasive American dream of intergenerational financial prosperity and the influence of the family's past generations on future generations as it engages with the themes of chance, apocalypse, and the end of history that preoccupy playwrights including Tony Kushner (*Angels in America*), Suzan-Lori Parks (*Topdog/Underdog*), and Sam Shepard (*True West*). At the same time, that *King Hedley II* builds on themes in Wilson's drama makes possible the final written assignment of the course, which is to pick a major theme and show how two or more plays exhibit it. This assignment increases students' understanding of the American dramatic tradition. In *King Hedley II*, written for the 1980s, Wilson incorporates characters he first imagined for *Seven Guitars* in order to extend the cycle's consideration of the failures and possibilities of black kinship relations. When we teach *King Hedley II,* we focus on two questions. First, how does King fulfill the role his name confers? Second, how does the fulfillment of his role address the concerns of an arbitrary world that, unlike the plays of Kushner, Parks, and Shepard, has no decipherable purpose?

The eponymous protagonist lacks a clear familial genealogy. Although King believes that a man named Hedley, who is a character in *Seven Guitars,* is his father, he learns at the end of *King Hedley II* that his biological father was actually a man named Leroy. Similarly, although King knows that Ruby is his biological mother, her absence throughout his childhood causes him to exclaim in a conversation with her, "My mama dead. Louise my mama. That the only mama I know" ([2005] 12). His claim that his great-aunt, who was his primary caregiver, is his mother challenges the authority given to the biological ties of kinship that have inspired many tragic scenes of betrayal (consider Joe Keller's motivations in *All My Sons* or Walter Lee's choices in *A Raisin in the Sun*) depicted in the first half of our course. Yet even with his seemingly more fluid notions of kinship, King predicates his future on the birth of his child, saying, "Now Tonya pregnant. It's like I finally did something right. . . . I don't want him to grow up without nothing" (24). Additionally, he takes great pride in receiving Hedley's bloodstained machete, cherishing it as a family heirloom. He boasts, "This my father's machete. Stool Pigeon give it to me. Say this the machete that killed Floyd Barton. This the machete of the Conquering Lion of Jude. This is mine" (63). The line of kinship King draws from Hedley to himself and then to his unborn child suggests that the child ratifies the value of the parent's life. Unfortunately, as the still bloodstained machete testifies, the legacy that King confirms is one of violence and misunderstanding.

When the play opens, King has just been released from jail for murder. As a felon, he has difficulty finding legitimate employment, so he sells stolen refrigerators with his friend Mister and plans to rob a jewelry store so that they can get enough money to open a video store. Wilson artfully ties their illegal practices to conversations in the play about playing by the rules. At one point King complains about his friend's being unfairly denied a government contract. He asserts, "You got the lowest bid, you supposed to get the contract. They set up the rules and then don't want to follow them themselves" (10). His lament of social injustice continues when he tries to retrieve photographs with his receipt in hand and the clerk tells him that the pictures are lost. Ruby's longtime lover, Elmore, tries to offer King another way of understanding the rules:

> The way you keep your dignity is to make your own rules. If you want to beat the system you got to step outside of it. You got to make your own rules. You ain't doing nothing but breaking their rules. That's what the problem is. They hustling you and you don't know it. See, if I break a rule it be my rules. That's the only rules I can break . . . 'cause that's the only ones I live by. (57)

Although King imagines himself an outlaw, a transgressive figure who lives and will die negotiating the underworld, the brief moments in which he communicates his hopes and dreams reflect a deep investment in the same values of parental succession that animate the American dream.

Just as the final scene of *The Piano Lesson* serves as a rich point of entry to the play, the final scene of *King Hedley II,* in which King dies, works as an excellent point of departure in teaching the play. King dies in an attempt to right the wrongs of his biological father by denying Elmore's ability to determine King's legacy. His refusal to play by Elmore's rules enables King to make his own rules. In the penultimate scene of the play, Elmore reveals to King, "Leroy was your daddy" (97). After learning of his parentage, King leaves and returns with the $50 that Leroy owed Elmore. King asserts, "Now we straight on that. But see . . . my name ain't Leroy Slater, Jr. My name is King Hedley II and we got some unfinished business to take care of" (99). Once again rewriting his genealogy, King claims Hedley as his father in order to place himself in a radical genealogy. In analyzing this scene with a class, it is important to draw student's attention to the way Wilson's cycle of plays restructures the role of inheritance in American drama through an act of naming (similar to the way Troy leaves his children a song and a lesson instead of money) and therefore renders the American dream more flexible. In *King Hedley II,* King's assertion that "My name is King Hedley II" seems to produce the same result as traditional modes of kinship relationships, but the final scene of the play reveals the radical difference that King's act of naming makes.

King challenges Elmore to a game of chance, craps. Before Elmore arrived, Ruby warned King not to gamble with Elmore because Elmore would take all of King's money. Nevertheless, the obstinate son challenges the man who doubled his paternal loss. They begin to play, and King loses. After Elmore wins all the money, King realizes that Elmore "switched the dice" and conned him (101). Enraged, he kicks Elmore, knocks him down, and holds the machete to his throat. But King spares his life, refusing to repeat the legacy of murder that Hedley left. King refuses his deadly inheritance and therefore once again places himself in a self-authorized genealogy. Once he releases Elmore, they face off, and Ruby, rushing out of the house to stop the confrontation, accidently shoots King. King falls to the ground, and his blood saturates the grave of Aunt Ester's cat. "As the lights go down on the scene, the sound of a cat's meow is heard" (103).

The final scene reconfigures the notion of patriarchal sacrifice as it suggests a way to engage with the past that accounts for the precarious nature of the present. *Fences, The Piano Lesson,* and *King Hedley II* depict different forms of inheritance and offer innovative ways to engage with the past. The productive space that the plays provide does not depend on the sacrifice of the son or the father but instead on a fruitful coming together of parents and children. Through his engagement with key preoccupations of the American dramatic tradition and his notably different way of negotiating social and cultural vestiges, Wilson furthers the tradition, and his plays are indispensable in an American drama survey.

Person, Place, and the Ordinary in August Wilson's *Gem of the Ocean*

Douglas A. Jones, Jr.

One of the most compelling and instructive aspects of August Wilson's ten-play cycle is how it uses the ordinary to tell its stories and give an account of twentieth-century African American history. Within their respective plays, mundane objects such as a smudged shoe, a ham, or a handful of seeds propel dramatic action and signify broader processes of personal and collective striving.[1] Wilson himself recognized the significance of the ordinary to his dramaturgy, and he strove to endow it with a kind of aesthetic dignity:

> Despite my interest in history, I have always been more concerned with culture. . . . I am not a historian. I happen to think that the content of my mother's life—her myths, her superstitions, her prayers, the contents of her pantry, the smell of her kitchen, the song that escaped from her sometimes parched lips, her thoughtful repose and pregnant laughter—are all worthy of art. ("Note")

That these sorts of cultural materials captivated Wilson not only clarifies his keen interest in the ordinary but also helps make sense of the most frequent setting in the cycle: the home.[2]

The recurrence of the home and, more broadly, domestic relations in the plays helps establish Wilson as a playwright committed to the aesthetic and signifying principles of modern dramaturgy. Una Chaudhuri, a drama semiotician, argues that the "privileged setting of modern drama is the family home," especially in realism (6). Within the realist imagination, which strives to describe the world as it is, the home is paramount because its specific, material environment accounts for characters' nature and their subsequent actions. At the same time, realism's emphasis on the institutions and processes of everyday life allows playwrights to make art out of the ordinary in extremely legible and meaningful terms precisely because they are ordinary. Wilson's turn to realism, therefore, accords with his interest in common people. Studying his dramaturgical formations strengthens students' understanding of his treatment of African American life.

Although Wilson expands the conventional borders of realist drama (e.g., his use of lyrical dialogue or inclusion of a ghost as a tangible presence), one underlying structural assumption throughout the cycle helps situate the plays within the canon of modern drama: namely, place is indispensable to the "dramatic logic" in that it is "not contingent but determining" (Chaudhuri 80). Wilson's *Gem of the Ocean,* which premiered on Broadway in 2004, is particularly illustrative in this regard. It is an especially useful text with which to teach a number of the assumptions, possibilities, and limitations of realism. This essay offers an approach for teachers and students to analyze how one of those principles of realism, the interdependency of person and place, regulates the poetics of *Gem of the Ocean* and, by extension, the entire cycle.

Set in 1904, *Gem of the Ocean* tells the story of Citizen Barlow, a recent transplant from Alabama to Pittsburgh who seeks to redress the "hole inside" him that forms after another man dies for his crimes. To do so, he calls on Aunt Ester at her home, 1839 Wylie Avenue, because members of the Pittsburgh Hill District community tell him that she "wash[es] people's souls" (20). Although characters in three other plays of the cycle talk about Aunt Ester, *Gem of the Ocean* is the only one in which she actually appears.[3] Wilson calls her "the most significant persona of the cycle." He continues, "The characters, after all, are her children. The wisdom and tradition she embodies are valuable tools for the reconstruction of their personality and for dealing with a society in which the contradictions, over the decades, have grown fiercer, and for exposing all the places it is lacking in virtue" (Preface [2005]). To substantiate her historical, cultural, and dramaturgical matriarchy, Wilson dates Aunt Ester's birth at 1619, when British colonists first established slavery on the North American mainland. As she wryly tells her protégé, "I'm getting old. Going on three hundred years now" (*Gem* 43).

Of course, a three-hundred-year-old Aunt Ester flouts the tenets of strict realism. Students immediately recognize this, so it becomes an opportunity to discuss not only why Wilson decides to anthropomorphize the black presence in North America but also how that choice questions and perhaps reworks the rationalist assumptions that inform realism itself. I've found it useful to discuss Aunt Ester as an example of Wilson's turn to marvelous realism, a mode of representation that seeks to expose the extraordinary in ordinary life by materializing the immaterial, the supernatural, and the magical.[4] The objective of the marvelous, especially among writers of color, is to endow hyperperceptibility to forms of political, cultural, and historical thought and praxis that traditional, hegemonic representational frames frequently ignore. Once students understand the aesthetic and ideological intentions of the marvelous, they begin to see how it constitutes its own kind of real within the logic of the performance or text, a real that works to disrupt the dominant cultural imaginary.

Wilson makes Aunt Ester flesh because she is to be construed as "real." Thus I ask students to take account of her basic human processes as they read the play. They most frequently list that she eats, sleeps, tires, recovers, nurtures, envies, and even flirts. Enumerating these actions helps them ground Aunt Ester as mortal rather than as the supernatural figure she is intimated to be elsewhere in the cycle. In this way, the class recognizes that she is not simply a symbol of the black presence but a realist character with the same potential for action as that of the other characters. Any power she holds—including that to "wash people's souls"—is not magical but derives from the material world of the play. Thus a close reading of Aunt Ester and her physical and emotional life throughout the play demonstrates how the persons of realism, even the most marvelous, are fundamentally products of their place.

Exploring character formation in *Gem of the Ocean* leads to a focus on the play's material conditions and contexts, in particular that of 1839 Wylie Avenue. Students already familiar with the cycle frequently point out the home's mythical status. But in *Gem of the Ocean,* Aunt Ester's house is far more than symbol; it is the physical environment where people are made. Put another way, in realism "the home is a space of obligatory self-fashioning" (Chaudhuri 8). To impart this formal principle, I ask students to consider how the home is framed throughout the play: How does Wilson describe it in the stage directions? How do the characters interact with the physical structure? In what ways do entrances and exits signify beginnings and endings in action or changes in character?

One particularly useful way to begin these discussions on the relation between place and person in the play and, more broadly, in realism is to direct students to Citizen Barlow's opening relation to 1839 Wylie Avenue. In the prologue, he asks Aunt Ester for her help, but she tells him to come back in four days, because then she can take care of him. Instead of returning at his appointed time, Citizen Barlow decides to stand directly outside her house and wait. As Aunt Ester's gatekeeper relates at the beginning of scene 1, "He still standing there. He been standing there since he left out of here yesterday. . . . He went right out there and stood across the street. If he go somewhere he come right back. He been out there every time I look" (*Gem* 9). Later that evening, Citizen Barlow sneaks into the house through an open window and immediately implores Aunt Ester for her help. What students should recognize is the play cannot begin until he is positioned in the home. In discussions, moreover, it is important to remain mindful of the ways in which Aunt Ester's home is more than just the play's setting—it is a very specific place that facilitates very specific action and character formation. In other words, 1839 Wylie Avenue accounts for the particular poetics of *Gem of the Ocean.*

As if to redouble our focus on the home, Aunt Ester instructs Citizen Barlow, once he becomes her boarder, to help Eli build a rock wall around the back of the house. As Wilson explores in his play set in the 1950s, *Fences,* these protective barriers not only keep out but also keep in. Given Citizen Barlow's fixation in the first scenes of the play and the broader mutualism between person and place that animates modern drama, I ask the class, What is inside 1839 Wylie Avenue that requires protection? Students' responses range from the more momentous objects, such as Aunt Ester's bill of sale and the masks that facilitate the journey to the City of Bones, to the more mundane, such as the stove and domestic utensils like pots and dustpans. I find it useful to discuss these categories on their own terms because, taken together, students frequently minimize the everyday objects as simply domestic trappings and less consequential to the play. On the contrary: these objects symbolize the historical resources of care and comfort that sustained African Americans as they navigated the uncharted waters of freedom in the late nineteenth and early twentieth centuries.[5]

One of those resources was food. Because cooking and eating occur so frequently in *Gem of the Ocean,* I dedicate a large portion, if not all, of a class period to the importance of these practices to African American social and political culture. (For insights into this relation, I suggest Psyche Williams-Forson's incredibly rich text, *Building Houses out of Chicken Legs: Black Women, Food, and Power,* and recommend assigning sections of it to upper-level courses.) To deepen students' understanding of the importance of foodways to African American life and why food figures so centrally in *Gem of the Ocean,* not to mention the entire cycle, I ask students to cull recipes of traditional African American dishes such as fried chicken and collard greens. I point them toward the period's black newspapers (e.g., *The Christian Recorder* [1861–1902]) and cookbooks (e.g., *Good Things to Eat: As Suggested by Rufus* [1911]). I also suggest that, if possible, they interview cooks who might maintain such recipes as part of family lore. What these oral histories and primary materials show students is the social sustenance that foodways have afforded African Americans since slavery. That is, students learn that Wilson's representation of cooking and eating is not incidental but, rather, a signifier of how African Americans have used the most limited and ordinary of resources to foster personal and collective agency.

Honing in on the historical registers of seemingly commonplace actions and objects in *Gem of the Ocean* facilitates a smooth transition to explore the climax of the play, in which Wilson transforms and manipulates the ordinary to render Citizen Barlow's journey to the City of Bones. When students first read this scene, many of them feel jolted, asserting that it feels unreal in an otherwise real play. In response, I remind them that the play is not real but operates within the conceits of realism. It is vital to orient the discussion in such a way that the class remains focused on how Wilson uses the principles of realism to actualize the conceptual City of Bones. Not only does this approach force students to grapple with the play on its own dramaturgical terms but also it deepens their understanding of the interdependency between person and place that typifies modern dramaturgy.

To begin, it is essential that students take note that Aunt Ester shows Citizen Barlow where the City of Bones is located on a map. That the map is sewn into a quilt situates Citizen Barlow's encounter with the City of Bones (and ours) in the realm of the ordinary. From the time of slavery, the quilt has played a significant role in African American life as a space of personal and collective expressivity; in fact, it was often one of the few sites where slaves and their descendants could archive their experiences. As such, the quilt becomes an ideal topic for outside research because this craft shows students the ingenious ways that African Americans have recorded historical thought and praxis. I have students, in small groups, collect images of at least five different quilts from the nineteenth and early twentieth centuries. I ask each group to focus on the aesthetic qualities and on how the quilts tell stories. Students frequently comment that the quilts are repetitive and off-kilter and may contain secret or coded messages (see Tobin and Dobard). Overall, I want the class to discover how the quilt has been "illustrative of a particular way of seeing, of ordering the world" (Brown, "African-American Women's Quilting" 926).

With this in mind, we turn to consider what the quilt tells us about how characters in *Gem of the Ocean* see and order their world. The main point that I think students should recognize is that the characters believe in the continuity between the earthly realm and the spiritual realm. To explore this continuity, I introduce Wole Soyinka's theory of the chthonic realm, which, in Yoruba tragedy, is understood as real. As such, it is unlike that in Greek tragedy, which was built on the "principle of illusion." Soyinka writes, "Yoruba tragedy plunges straight into the 'chthonic realm,' the seething cauldron of the dark world-will and psyche, the transitional yet inchoate matrix of death and becoming" (*Art* 28). The plunge into the City of Bones evokes this very matrix: it is the journey to the site where the dead of the Middle Passage became the founding architects of the City of Bones. These dead but living inhabitants of the center of the world resurrect the dead Citizen Barlow into the living Citizen Barlow who leaves Aunt Ester's house anew.

Students should also note the crucial role of ordinary objects to this interworld connectivity. Like the communicants of Yoruba tragedy, the voyagers in *Gem of the Ocean* carry ordinary materials with them as they travel from realm to realm. I frame our exploration of these objects around three main considerations: How do these objects function in both worlds? In what ways, if any, do they signify as historical markers? How do they accord with the dramaturgical assumptions of the play, such as the relation between person and place?

These questions are useful anchors in discussions because they keep the class focused on the narrative, historical, and formal significance of the climax rather than on its unreality, as students often categorize it upon first reading. For instance, the boat, the eponymous "Gem of the Ocean," carries the voyagers from 1839 Wylie Avenue to the City of Bones. It is not a large vessel but a small document folded into the shape of a boat that Citizen Barlow holds. The document is Aunt Ester's bill of sale. I bring in images of several bills of sale of slaves so the class understands the ordinariness and ubiquity of these bills. Consequently, students should recognize how Wilson's use of the document is far more than symbolic of black bondage and the slave trade: it is evidence of how such bills did, in fact, carry Africans to the New World. As the historian Ira Berlin argues, "[I]f slavery made *race,* its larger purpose was to make *class*" (5).

Exploring the use of objects in the climactic voyage to the City of Bones, in addition to its historiographic value, deepens students' understanding of the expansiveness of realism, showing students that attempting to reveal the world as it is does not mean simply staging what is immediately perceptible. To demonstrate realism's potential in this regard, I have students compare Citizen Barlow's journey with the end of act 1 of *Joe Turner's Come and Gone,* Wilson's play for the 1910s that premiered on Broadway in 1988. *Joe Turner* recounts the existential odyssey of Herald Loomis, the tortured protagonist who wrongly served seven years of gang labor for the state. At the end of the first act, Loomis brazenly challenges God because God allowed Loomis, who was a deacon in the church, to waste his life through illegal capture and servitude. In the midst of his apostastic declaration, the demons of his past transfix him, and he recounts the marvels he has seen: "I done seen bones rise up out the water. Rise up and walk across the water. Bones walking on top of the water" ([1988] 53). This is clearly a vision of the Middle Passage, and Wilson situates Loomis's personal tragedy within a trajectory of collective African American trauma and historical memory.

Gem of the Ocean, too, uses the Middle Passage to explore the relation between history and individual self-making. But if Loomis's vision is illustrative of the ways in which "*Joe Turner* pushes against conventional limitations of realism as it incorporates African-based symbolism and ritual," as Harry Elam rightly argues ("Teaching" 582), then Citizen Barlow's journey to the City of Bones in *Gem of the Ocean* suggests that Wilson embraced realism's dramaturgical principles with greater force in his second, fuller rendering of the Middle Passage. Instead of being a kind of possessed vision, Citizen Barlow's plunge into history is more present in its immediacy and materiality. Students take note, for instance, that when Citizen Barlow sees the gatekeeper, Garret Brown, the man who died for his crimes, we see him too: the character Solly Two Kings wears a mask of Brown as he exists in the City of Bones. I have my class focus on how the mask, along with the profusion of other objects, allows for the action to be experienced firsthand rather than related secondhand. From there, we continue to think about why Wilson might have chosen to stage the Middle Passage with ordinary objects.

Students' answers vary, ranging from the view that Wilson was interested in creating ritual to speculation that he sought to complement his discursive rendering in *Joe Turner* with a more material one. Regardless of their responses, there are two key takeaways for students: one, the choice reflects Wilson's belief that the effects and consequences of the Middle Passage are not past but very much present and part of our everyday lives; two, the scene evidences the ways in which realism operates as a capacious form of representation that depicts the world at its most marvelous and most mundane. Wilson recognized and used the fullness of the form to delineate Citizen Barlow's journey to the City of Bones and, more broadly, to fulfill the animating ideological principle of the entire cycle: ordinary people, with their ordinary places and objects, are agents of history and "are all worthy of art."

NOTES

[1] These specific objects figure prominently in the plot and politics of *Ma Rainey's Black Bottom, Two Trains Running,* and *King Hedley II,* respectively.

[2] Six of the ten plays take place inside or around the home. Of the four that do not, one of them, *Jitney*, is set at a family business, and the central plot of another, *Radio*

Golf, concerns the fate of 1839 Wylie Avenue, the home that physically and symbolically appears throughout the cycle.

[3] Characters in *Two Trains Running*, *King Hedley II*, and *Radio Golf* discuss Aunt Ester.

[4] Another striking example of marvelous realism in the cycle occurs at the climax of *Piano Lesson*, when Boy Willie physically wrestles with the ghost of Sutter, the man whose land Boy Willie's family toiled on as slaves. For more on the mode of marvelous realism and its aesthetic and political criticism of conventional realism, see Zamora and Faris.

[5] For a good source on the importance of ownership and domestic wares among slaves and their descendants, see Penningroth.

August Wilson, Jazz Structure, and the Historical Record

Alan Nadel

One goal that I make crucial to teaching August Wilson's work is to help students understand the ten-play cycle as a record (or CD) album that attempts to orchestrate and arrange the American twentieth century as ten versions of African American blues played by a jazz combo with one to three singers. In the introduction to my 1994 collection of essays on August Wilson, I wrote:

> Because these plays all resemble structurally a jazz set as much as they do a Euro-American play, we are confronted not with protagonists and antagonists but rather with the tension of interpretive energy, as a community of players play off one another's solos. If they tend at times to play variations on recognizable themes, the synergy of the interaction creates unexpected and exciting results. The interactions are exciting, not in the way a tragic death is, but in the way a Duke Ellington or John Coltrane finale is. The disparate strains, the subversive chord structures, the competitive rhythms, having been given their freedom from the copyrighted version and the initial collaborative circumstance, remarkably unite, in spite of and because of their freedom and individual power, to create an unimagined and, even at the outset of the number, unimaginable new version. (Introduction [*May*] 5–6)

The best template for understanding this approach can be found in *Ma Rainey's Black Bottom,* where the various character types that inform Wilson's orchestrations are directly identified with musical instruments. In the earliest Wilson plays (in order of composition), *Jitney* and *Ma Rainey,* the character types instrumental in producing the dramatic performance are the warrior, the historian, the earnest young man, the trickster, and the pragmatist. With *Fences,* in the figure of Gabriel, Wilson adds to the combo the man not quite right in the head, and in *Joe Turner* he completes the group with the magician-healer and a spectrum of female soloists, enabling the full array of Wilson's styles and arrangements. These compositions, in effect, offer a rich verbal history of that twentieth-century art form, the blues, as an alternative to authorized white twentieth-century American history.[1] Thus the ten-play cycle reconnects the styles of African American blues to the events and traditions that produced those styles. Because the blues are appropriative, improvisational, and communal, moreover, these styles facilitate both the creation and reconfiguring of a community in constant tension with the historical conditions and aesthetic paradigms that produced that community.

Throughout Wilson's work, as Harry Elam incisively points out, music, most particularly the blues, "functions as both metaphor and metonym, as vehicles for cultural transmission and remembrance" (*Past* 29). From this perspective, an approach to Wilson can be developed through careful attention to one play, through a comparative examination of two works, or through a term-length academic seminar devoted to the entire Wilson canon. The goal would be to identify Wilson's sense of the dramatic as that which is produced by a community whose rights and actions can be delimited by specific rules, conditions, and practices but never determined by them. Wilson's drama constitutes the intersection of theater history and African American history, the blues serving as the paradigm for the negotiation of that intersection.

It is impossible to divorce blues and jazz from the history that produced it, just as it is impossible to divorce Western theater from the Aristotelian ideas about leadership, ethics, and the Greek state—that is, to divorce those ideas from the historical moment that informed Aristotle's poetics. To put it another way, the blues record for Wilson is the historical record, a fact that, in this age of the iPod, the download, the mix, and sample, may be so prevalent for our students as to be completely invisible.

In an essay on the African American writer John A. Williams, I once wrote that history is an intersection of time and place at which an accident is happening ("My Country"). I go on in that essay to elaborate some of the issues at stake in such an intersection and accident, especially those concerning who gets to write the accident report, for, as I have argued elsewhere, history belongs to whoever owns the erasers (*Invisible Criticism* xiii). That is to say, we cannot construct a history until we clear away the opaqueness, confusion, and chaos out of which accidents occur. Similarly, in our culture we cannot resolve the accident until we impose narratives of cause and effect, extracting from the accident its accidentalness, identifying the victims, and determining the conditions of culpability and liability. In this context, we could say that all historians are ambulance chasers. But then, as we know all too well, for people in some neighborhoods the ambulance never arrives; those people remain the unaccounted casualties of history or, to put it another way, the casualties of historiography, the process of writing history. History performs acts of inclusion and exclusion that have profound social consequences.

When Toledo, in *Ma Rainey's Black Bottom,* wins a bet about the spelling of the word *music*, for example, he cannot collect because everyone else is illiterate. "I done won the dollar," he states, in a way that articulates the quintessential problem of history: "But if don't nobody know but me, how am I gonna prove it too you?" ([Plume] 28). This is, of course, the same problem that Troy Maxson, in *Fences,* has with baseball records, and it is the problem represented by the records that Floyd Barton, in *Seven Guitars,* never gets to record in Chicago.

The problem of history, in other words, lies in making and keeping records, in producing the ledger, determining which voices and arrangements to include, and, particularly, determining who retains the rights. The issue of rights, especially, provides the source of drama in a blues context, one configured and delimited by communal adaptation. Henry Louis Gates, Jr., has identified the critically joking mode of African American discourse, called "signifying," with the jazz tradition by citing the saxophonist John Coltrane's adaptation of a Richard Rodgers melody: "Another example of formal parody is to suggest a given structure precisely by failing to coincide with it—that is, to suggest it by dissemblance. . . . A stellar example is John Coltrane's rendition of 'My Favorite Things' compared to Julie Andrews' vapid original" (*Signifying Monkey* 243). The original rendition of "My Favorite Things" however, came not from Julie Andrews, who starred in the film version of *The Sound of Music,* but from Mary Martin, who played Maria on Broadway—a point that is significant, because the film version of *The Sound of Music* adapts the Broadway play and score to stress its vapidity. Thus the Broadway show, eclipsed by the immensely popular film, ceases to be the reference for the original. The song merges in the public imaginary with the cinematic version, whose vapidity already hints of unintentional parody. Coltrane's version is quite another thing. One of the landmark recordings of postwar American jazz, the Coltrane version, parodic implications notwithstanding, is a multifaceted and dramatic intervention in the history of American music.

I begin my classroom investigation of Wilson's drama, therefore, with the recordings of "My Favorite Things." Playing the Martin, Andrews, and Coltrane versions in succession, I start my discussion of Wilson by getting the class to compare the three versions. I have very little formal musical training and try to structure the discussion such that it will be open to students with none. At the same time, I invite those who have a sophisticated knowledge of music to enlighten us about subtleties we might otherwise miss, so long as they do so using terminology that is generally accessible.

It is important, I think, to approach the comparison from a variety of perspectives. Starting with the Martin and Andrews (film soundtrack) version makes clear how the film studio production values provide a grandiosity that runs counter to the more personal, intimate status of the voice in the stage production. Both, however, privilege individual voice over communal activity, with the chorus and the orchestration subordinated to the centrality of the soloist and the lyrics, so as to render those versions radically different from Coltrane's. Not just the absence of lyrics but also, and more important, the presence of the other musicians—McCoy Tyner on piano, Elvin Jones on drums, and Jimmy Cobb on bass—turns all the solos into contributions, so that it is impossible to isolate a solo as the piece's raison d'être. Listening carefully, we not only hear each member of the group but also how much each solo depends on the other players to frame, introduce, inspire, and accent what might at first sound like a solo performance.

It is important for students to see, moreover, how fragile that relation is. Without the tight orchestration of the stage version and especially without the overproduced electronic discipline of the film version, the soloists in the Coltrane version, it becomes clear, always teeter on the verge of spinning out of control, of dissolving the communal association. The drama in the Coltrane version, therefore, does not come from the articulation of a central lyric, emphasized harmonically and rhythmically by every section of the orchestra and by every subordinate voice in chorus. That is, it comes not from the lucid explication of one powerful story but from the competition of several voices called forth in a specific historical moment. The historical moment in Coltrane's adaptation of "My Favorite Things" is the moment in which Coltrane attempts to reclaim, at first through incisive shifts in emphasis and then through radical extrapolation, the African American roots of the American musical theater. He is thus making musical history through the work of performative historiography, one that evokes, in fact requires, Martin, Andrews, Rodgers and Hammerstein, the American musical theater, and the Anglo-Euro operetta as much as it does vaudeville, burlesque, Dixieland, the copious forms of nineteenth-century African American song and dance, and the minstrelsy that exploited it.

Understood in this way, Coltrane's "My Favorite Things" becomes a useful heuristic for analyzing Wilson's plays. I suggest, for instance, that the students go through a play by identifying the solos and duets and, as well, the way in which each of the solos and duets is orchestrated within the scene, so that they can see how Wilson works to undermine the idea that individuals are merely accompaniment for one or two privileged soloists. If one theme of *Joe Turner's Come and Gone,* which resonates throughout Wilson's work, is that each person has to find his or her own song, then we can see how in the arrangement of a scene or an act or a play Wilson, like Coltrane, refuses to deny any character, any member of the play's community, the expression of his or her solo.

Coltrane is equally useful in helping the students understand Wilson's sense of resolution. In the Aristotelian model, an overarching curve of action places the tragic hero into an economy whereby the hero's life is exchanged for an insight, the absence of which produced the hero's tragic flaw. The communal dimension of this trajectory comes from the way the chorus participates in the economies that define the hero's fall and the way in which the hero becomes the representative of the community. This kind of resolution requires that the material life of the community be subsumed by the symbology of the hero, but such a process replicates the process of American history and American drama that has reduced to symbolic status the material lives of minority populations.

Listening to the resolution of Coltrane's "My Favorite Things" makes clear how vital each instrument, each interpretation is to the power of the performance. Similarly, not one of Wilson's plays revolves around a single person's goals. As *King Hedley II* makes clear, the consequences of Floyd Barton's death in *Seven Guitars* have as much to do with the man who killed Barton, the women who loved him, and the neighbors who befriended him as it does with his musical career cut short. Aunt Ester is both the functionary for the members of her community and, as *Gem of the Ocean* demonstrates, an agent with her own goals and desires. While the drama of *Joe Turner's Come and Gone* seems to focus on the history and intention of the mysterious stranger Herald Loomis, by the end of the play his exorcism is part of an elaborate reorientation of all the boarders at Seth Holley's boardinghouse. The point is that the resolution relies upon the contributions of and effect upon the community.

Perhaps no play better illustrates the musical composition inherent in Wilson's drama than *The Piano Lesson.* Focused as the play is on the history, meaning, and fate of a piano, it makes the production of music central to the desires of every character, including Sutter, the white man whose family formerly owned both the piano and the ancestors of Boy Willie and his sister, Berniece. Each of the scenes, moreover, elaborates on the disparate goals of the members of the community, such that it is difficult to privilege one player over another. Boy Willie's desire to buy back the land on which his ancestors worked as slaves is neither superior nor subordinate to Berniece's desire to preserve the piano as the only relic of her family's history, as both accomplishment and suffering. Lymon's desire to start over in the north is just as important as Boy Willie's desire to go back south, and the play makes it impossible for us to privilege Lymon's loyalty to Boy Willie over his attraction to Berniece, or vice versa. Even Avery's Christian vision of the church he is founding cannot be ignored, as it is his performance of the exorcism at the end of the play that is crucial to the dramatic resolution (in the same way that, in *Fences,* Gabriel's delusional playing of a trumpet without a mouthpiece opens the gates of heaven for Troy).

The Piano Lesson develops around a number of musical moments, including Berniece's finally playing the piano during the exorcism, that produce dramatic resolution by incorporating rather than subordinating the disparate voices of the community. The first, which occurs in act 1, scene 2, starts when Boy Willie, Lymon, Doaker, and Wining Boy are sitting around the kitchen table talking about the possibilities or impossibilities for a black man in the South, where the white law always subjugates black labor and black property to its ends.[2] Thus by the standards on the southern work farm Lymon is considered lazy because he refuses to submit to the forced labor that results from the collusion of the business community and the law enforcement system to make black criminality a function of white supply and demand. As Wining Boy says, "Mr. So and So, he sell the land to you. And he come to you and say, 'John, you own the land . . . but them is my berries.'. . . And he go and fix it with the law that them is his berries. Now that's the difference between the white man and the colored man. The colored man can't fix nothing with the law" (38 [1.2]).

In such a system, Boy Willie's aspirations to own land and be a successful farmer seem dubious to Lymon and Wining Boy. Wining Boy's parable, in other words, points both backward and forward—back to the history of forced labor that delimited black aspirations in the South and, in fact, in the whole nation for over three hundred years and forward to the fixed legal game that repairs the damage to white economy and property at the expense of black humanity. In terms of the play's structure, that historical condition makes the personal quest of Boy Willie—to sell the piano and use the money to buy the land—impossible. It suggests that there is no legal remedy for historical injustice or for the material conditions it has produced.

Boy Willie therefore privileges the extralegal: "I don't go by what the law say. The law is liable to say anything. I go by if it's right or not. It don't matter to me what the law say. I take and look at it for myself." He need not be more specific to evoke the aura of violence that surrounds the idea of a black man who puts himself outside the parameters of white Southern law, who says, "I go by if it's right. . . . I take . . . for myself" (38–39 [1.2]). Doaker's presence makes the aura of violence all the more cogent because, as he will shortly reveal, he has witnessed the long history of bloodshed that led to Boy Willie's father's decision that it was right for the father to have the piano and to take it for himself.

These circumstances would appear to bring the play to an impasse, in that Boy Willie seems helpless because he may not acquire the piano and, more important, because he may never be able to acquire with the piano what rightfully should be his. Should he try to take the property, he will only perpetuate the violence that denied it to him in the first place. This impasse is broken by the music that emerges around the kitchen table as first Boy Willie, then Wining Boy and Lymon, and finally Doaker start singing, "O Lord Berta, Berta," using hands, feet, utensils, pans, and the tabletop to create an improvised accompaniment, while "[t]hey sing in harmony with great fervor and style" (39).

Careful attention to this moment, in the light of Coltrane's "My Favorite Things," can help students see not only how the blues are used to dramatic effect in Wilson's drama but also how, understood historically, they are inherently dramatic, for the circumstances that produce this performance encapsulates the history of the blues. Like the blues, Boy Willie's situation is the product of a set of historical conditions that exploited people as though they were property and frustrated their aspirations through a fixed legal and social system. The blues as an art form express the frustration by converting it into aesthetic and—very important for this discussion—communal accomplishment. The blues thus create a community out of shared, thwarted, or deferred aspirations; it is the art of keeping alive the dream that the official laws and unofficial social codes struggle so relentlessly to smother. The blues thus provide people with a common identity, even though those people need not necessarily have common goals.

Under the influence of Wining Boy—who repeatedly brings music to life, even at the point where Berniece is on the verge of shooting Boy Willie—the blues in this instant in the play do the work of the blues in general. They fix with music what "the colored man can't fix . . . with the law" (38). If in some of Wilson's plays crisis is averted and in others not, the tradition of creative survival persists in the form of the blues, which, I want my students to understand, in Wilson's hands is always at the soul of drama. The drama thus emerges from the danger involved in attempting to create a space for the simultaneous and finite recognition of a community's infinite potentials. But what alternative, from Wilson's perspective, would not replicate the exclusionary practices of history that his ten-play cycle is attempting to address? I want to make a larger point, suggested by this quick taxonomy: structure, development, and resolution in each play and in the entire cycle have to be understood as those terms work in music, not as they apply to traditional—and, especially, Aristotelian—drama. History—despite the implications of some traditions of historiography—is not the work of a handful of privileged people, for whom the rest of the world serves as sidekicks and extras. The energies of communities, societies, or nations are always the product of that large mass, that critical mass necessary for a body to be recognized as a community, society, or nation. And that mass is not a fixed unit, a painted backdrop for the stage of history. Rather, it is the ever-changing set of arrangements and rearrangements of melody, harmony, and rhythm.

NOTES

[1] The most instrumental work articulating this position is *The Blues People*, by LeRoi Jones (Amiri Baraka). See also: Baker, *Blues*; Harrison, "August Wilson's Blues Poetics"; Ellison, "Richard Wright's Blues"; Murray, *Hero* and *Stomping*.

[2] The video of the television production of *The Piano Lesson* is very helpful in demonstrating how the music effects a physical and psychological change by combining improvisation with harmony, originality with tradition, to alter the state of a community on the verge of crisis.

Telling the Story: August Wilson's Challenge to Young Actors

Joan Herrington and Von Washington

> In the African tradition, theatre begins with the incantative voice of the storyteller (griot), the poly-rhythms of the musicians, and the gesticulate responses of the body, all orchestrated to bring spiritual enlightenment to mundane experience.
>
> —Paul Carter Harrison

The plays of August Wilson are striking for their rich characterizations, the rhythm of the dialogue, and the inspiring retelling of the African American legacy. But what lingers so powerfully after a performance of *Ma Rainey's Black Bottom* or *Two Trains Running* or *Gem of the Ocean* is the spectacular storytelling. This is the special gift that Wilson gives to his audience and the special challenge his work presents in its call for actors and musicians who are also gifted storytellers.

When we began our production of *Ma Rainey's Black Bottom* at Western Michigan University, we were confident in our ability to produce it well. This explosive drama, centering on the legendary blues singer Ma Rainey and the musicians in her band, examines the depth of exploitation and the consequences of the tolerance of injustice. Within our predominantly white university, the Department of Theatre has a multicultural theater program with a sufficient pool of trained actors to cast the play with talented, committed students. These students come from a wide array of backgrounds, ranging from integrated suburbs to inner-city Detroit.

While the program is exclusively undergraduate, its expansive training prepares its students to successfully engage a range of dramatic literature. Early in rehearsals, however, it became clear, from the blank look on the face of the actor playing Toledo and from his decision to disengage from the text, that he had no idea what his character was trying to say or how the actor was supposed to say it. He knew his character was part of Ma Rainey's band, and he knew the details of his character from the information in the script, but he was at a loss when the dialogue did not live within the immediate exchange of one character with another.

This actor's disengagement immediately highlighted one of the main problems facing educators who teach and direct African American students confronting plays that focus on the African and African American experience: the students know very little about their own history. Even in today's so-called inclusive environment, the schools they attend do not provide an adequate educational focus on the African or the African American experience in the world.

Thus, African American students often begin the rehearsals of a play that is deeply embedded in their cultural history at a disadvantage when compared with other students who have been exposed to the history of their ancestral groups while attending schools with an emphasis on Western civilization. Many African American students have not been given the educational opportunity to study life as it pertains to them. As a result of this oversight in education, college productions of Wilson's plays must often begin both with a history lesson that goes deeper than one actor's looking into the background of his or her character and with an introduction to the art of storytelling.

In act 1 of *Ma Rainey's Black Bottom,* Toledo tells his fellow musicians, "Now, I'm gonna show you how this goes . . . where you just a leftover from history." He proceeds to challenge them to recognize the plight of the colored man resulting from his forced service throughout American history. Early in rehearsal, we thought that the actor playing Toledo had just not yet connected to the material and that in short time it would open a window in his head and heart, memory would flood back to provide an understanding of the scene, and we would be in full flight. Toledo continues:

> Everybody come from different places in Africa, right? Come from different tribes and things. Soonawhile they began to make one big stew. You had the carrots, the peas, and potatoes and whatnot over here. And over there you had the meat, the nuts, the okra, corn . . . and then you mix it up and let it cook right through to get the flavors flowing together . . . then you got one thing. You got a stew. ([*Three Plays*] 46–47)

The young actor spoke the lines, but he gave no indication that he understood what Toledo meant by saying, "Now, I'm gonna show you how this goes. . . ." He continued to recite the lines but made no attempt to *tell* the story. Obviously the young actor knew that the lines belonged to his character and that he was responsible for delivering them in the moment; however, he was clearly uncertain as to how he should approach the material.

The moment exemplified that even though Wilson is keenly aware of the place of African Americans in American society, many of our young (and not so young) actors are not. With a double strike, Toledo and Wilson reminded us that, in many cases, the study of African and African American life is also a leftover or, more accurately, a left out in the American educational system. As Zora Neale Hurston wrote, "'I, who am borne away to become an orphan, carry my parents with me. For Rhythm is she not my Mother and Drama is her man?' So he groaned aloud in the ship and hid his drum and laughed" (29).

As rehearsals continued, it became clear that this young actor (and, in our experience, many others) had had no educational opportunity to study his place in this world from which Wilson takes his cues. He had not been provided with the history of Africans or African Americans; his American history classes had not taught him about the melting pot. Toledo was saying that there is information to be given through performance, but our young black actor, though intelligent and educated, did not have that information, unlike Toledo, who is thoroughly knowledgeable of the subtleties associated with the African American experience.

It is in moments like this that August Wilson brings his audience closer to him. He challenges African Americans to become knowledgeable about their past and to tell this past as their African ancestors were able to do. To become a good storyteller, one must know the idioms of a people—the language or dialect of this people, the way in which the words of a particular language are joined together and presented to express thought. Perhaps more relevant to us in terms of missing education was the fact that this actor's literary and dramatic training had not included exploring the African or African American art of storytelling. He was training to perform onstage, whereas we needed him to learn to perform in the living room, on the back porch, outside the barber shop, on the street corner. At this point we were reminded of Babatunde Lawal's comments in his essay "The African Heritage of African American Art and Performance":

> Because of the dynamic and expressive nature of the spoken word, many African cultures ignored the art of writing until fairly recently. In precolonial Africa, myths, folktales, proverbs, legends, and history were transmitted orally from one generation to the next by guilds of professional historians and poets. These professionals are known as griots. (40)

As the griots and those familiar with their work traveled to the new world, they brought with them their storytelling to ensure that they did not forget their past, to ease their minds in times of oppression, and to maintain in a foreign land a cultural connection to their home. Thus, early on and continuously in African American culture, storytelling served a vital role in daily life. Both in the old-time black Gospel song and in black street vernacular, "gittin ovuh" has to do with surviving. While the religious usage of the phrase speaks to spiritual survival in a sinister world of sin, its secular usage speaks to material survival in a white world of oppression. Since men and women live neither by bread nor spirit alone, both vitally necessary acts of "gittin ovuh" challenge the human spirit to "keep on pushin'" toward "higher ground." In black America, the oral tradition has served as a fundamental vehicle for "gittin ovuh." That tradition preserves the Afro-American heritage and reflects the collective spirit of the race. Through song, story, folk sayings, and rich verbal interplay among everyday people, lessons and precepts about life and survival are handed down from generation to generation (Smitherman, *Talkin and Testifyin* 73).

The stories told were a familiar combination of tales brought across the ocean and new stories of life in America, and the event of their telling was not limited to the storyteller. As the tale was woven, the audience could respond, join in, add a note, laugh, and cry out, ensuring a communal experience. Indeed, the value of storytelling to the community is evidenced in its continuity from the plantations into the early churches, where the preacher shared both stories from the Bible and stories from the street and the congregation provided chorus, correction, affirmation, and extensive participation. The act of testifying enabled parishioners to be storytellers, sharing personal tales in an act of healing. Stories were told outside barbershops, at family picnics—anywhere African Americans gathered to reinforce their history and sense of community. Over the second half of this century, however, particularly as African American families became fractured and African American neighborhoods became integrated, fewer stories were told.

So, with this generation for whom this oral tradition is largely absent—who are educated to be so deeply dependent on the art of writing and who are socially dependent on the art of texting—the challenge is great. While many elements of Wilson's plays demand attention during rehearsal and performance, one key to a successful production is the devotion of a significant amount of time to exploring the craft of storytelling. Many colleges and universities across America teach the craft of acting from a Eurocentric perspective—that of Konstantin Stanislavsky and his descendants—but it is rare that actors are taught the craft of storytelling as practiced by Africans and handed down to African Americans. It involves the ability to share the story by using dialogue, character, movement, music, dance, costumes, props, and much more. The storyteller must establish an effective rhythm and a relationship of engagement with those who are listening that moves them past the role of traditional audience. More elusive, perhaps, but crucial is the ability to hold a story in one's heart and mind such that its teller is both a master of spoken word and a guardian of tradition.

The griot, one of Wilson's primary dramatic tools, emerges in character after character. Wilson clearly follows the legacy of the great griot artists who influenced his work. As Eleanor Traylor notes:

> The oral traditions of Black slaves in America provided the motif and substance of the only distinctively indigenous American dramatic form. When, in the first two decades of the twentieth century, those traditions, embellished by the genius of Negro composers, librettists, dancers, actors, musicians, and arrangers, appeared on the professional stage, an authentic Afro-American theatre was born. (45)

So it was in the show we had selected, *Ma Rainey's Black Bottom.* Throughout the play, Ma Rainey and her band members use narrative stories and reflective dialogue to hold the attention of the audience for long periods of time—time that some critics of Western dramatic practice argue would be better used to move the plot along.

There was a time when people who grew up in the African American community had experienced this storytelling, because narrative dialogue was expected in lives throughout the community and delivered with appropriate intention, style, and content. In other words, one had to perform while telling a story, or nobody would stay to listen. Because that time is past, we cast our play with young African American actors who had limited knowledge of their history and no knowledge of the art form required by Wilson to share it.

How were we to overcome this challenge and teach storytelling while teaching and directing Wilson? There were six basic goals we needed to achieve:

- to provide appropriate history lessons and to enable the actors to appreciate the importance of the art of storytelling
- to prepare the actors to use their entire body as an expressive storytelling tool
- to broaden the onstage horizons of the actors beyond the fourth wall so that the story is fully shared with a community
- to develop a stronger kinesthetic response in the storytellers so as to increase the impact of the telling of the story during performance
- to teach the actors to find the rhythm of the story and to bring themselves to it (as opposed to bringing their own rhythm to the story)
- to prepare the actors onstage to participate in the telling of the story through the establishment of a call-and-response relationship with the storyteller

Teaching appropriate and specific history can be approached from many paths, and, depending on the selected Wilson play, the options vary. But incorporating these lessons, assigning readings, engendering conversation about the key moments in history so brilliantly captured by Wilson must be a part of the rehearsal process. Additionally, time should be devoted to including in these history lessons an introduction to blues music, the plays of Amiri Baraka, the paintings of Romare Bearden, and the fiction of Jorge Luis Borges—Wilson's primary, acknowledged influences.

To help the entire cast understand Toledo's "Now, I'm gonna show you how this goes . . . where you just a leftover from history," we chose two expansive texts to provide needed overview and perspective—Lerone Bennett's *Before the Mayflower* and John Hope Franklin's *From Slavery to Freedom.* To help capture the slave experience, keenly influential in many Wilson works, we watched the PBS series Slavery and the Making of America. Then, to bring us closer to this particular play, we shared *I'll Make Me a World*, a documentary focusing on twentieth-century African American art and sharing stories of great musicians, dancers, poets, and painters.

We encouraged the actors to study the history of the blues, moving from the early instrumental blues of the 1910s to the national phenomenon that appeared in the 1920s. We brought them early blues from such greats as Mamie Smith, followed its influence on jazz, and proceeded to the music of Bessie Smith and Billie Holiday. We read plays by Baraka (aka LeRoi Jones) and short stories by Borges and studied the collages of Bearden, particularly those that directly influenced other Wilson works—for example, the *Millhand's Lunch Bucket* on *The Piano Lesson.*

Part of this history is the place of storytelling and the central role of the griot in community life. In his book *Griots and Griottes,* Thomas Hale states, "the African griot performs as genealogist, historian, praise-singer, mediator, interpreter, witness, warrior, and more." Without the griot, whole cultures would have been lost. "Entire complex cultures have been carried down through the centuries by the spoken word. The tradition of storytelling is one of the most ancient in African culture; this tradition is rich with many stories, songs, poems, and religious and tribal custom due to the diversity of people living in this vast continent" (15). Within this history we studied storytellers in many artistic traditions—musicians, poets, novelists, and great public speakers.

Once the students understand the key role of storytelling in this history, they can begin to embrace its demands. Lawal writes, "For the professional poet or storyteller, oration is a form of performance. The speaker is never stationary but acts out the narrative using intonation, chants, and mime" (40). Indeed, effective storytelling involves the entire body. The challenge of bringing young actors to this place is great: not only has storytelling not been a part of their cultural upbringing but also their very acting training may stand in the way. For young acting students, well versed in realistic behavior and schooled as much from small-format television as from their acting classes, the fear of being too theatrical looms large. The fear is an ironic dilemma for an actor who has chosen to work on the stage but endemic nonetheless in this generation of young performers.

There are many approaches that can address this problem. In our experience, enabling actors to use their body as an expressive instrument is a crucial first step. An exercise we have used in rehearsal involves the creation of a vocabulary of gestures. It can be helpful to begin their work with texts the actors already identify with storytelling (e.g., Aesop's fables) and to progress from there to actual production text. The actors are divided into small groups, provided with a story, then asked to select words from the story that have particular resonance and to create a gesture that accompanies each word. The gesture should not illustrate the word but express its resonance. Many actors will gesture only with their arms and hands but should be encouraged to use their whole bodies. The actors then present their work to one another, accompanying the speaking of their words with the gestures.

It is very important to engender a spirit of support and enthusiasm for the individual work, as some actors may feel awkward at first. Each group then selects a few gestures that it finds particularly meaningful in terms of the story. This selection should not be a process of intellectual debate but instead focus on those gestures that evoked feeling or were visually stimulating. From this exercise, a vocabulary of gestures is defined that this group will use when telling their story to the rest of the company. Each actor tells a piece of the story, using the defined gestures as he or she chooses and adding others as inspired. This exercise can be repeated over several days until the actors begin to use their bodies expressively and, equally important, to enjoy doing so.

In an extension exercise borrowed from director Anne Bogart, the scale of the gestures can be explored. Moving around a circle, the gesture created by one actor is made progressively larger by successive actors until it is barely within their physical capability to embody it. This exercise is repeated with several different gestures. Then the opposite is done; a gesture is begun at one point in the circle and made smaller as it progresses, until it is barely perceptible. This work enables the actors to begin to consider when and how to use larger and smaller gestures for effect.

The exercise of generating the gestures was then undertaken with Wilson text selected from plays on which we were not working. We made this choice because it enabled the actors to work as one on a story that did not belong to any of their individual characters. There are many Wilson stories, and we worked with a few, including Bynum's story of meeting the Shiny Man on the road from *Joe Turner's Come and Gone* or Troy's story of facing down death in *Fences*. We chose stories that did not represent emotionally climactic moments for the characters, as our purpose was to focus on storytelling and not character development.

Finally, the actors worked on the stories within *Ma Rainey*, each selecting one, and we encouraged them to start with a story that offered a good opportunity to work with physicality, such as Cutler's tale of Slow Drag dancing or Slow Drag's story of Eliza selling his soul to the devil. Continuing to work in small groups, the actors chose words from the text, accompanied them with gestures that had particular resonance individually and within the context of the play, and presented their choices to one another. The exercise was repeated over time. Then the actors were challenged to use the gestures in a rehearsal of the play. To the selected gestures they could add new ones that were inspired in the rehearsal. It is an exciting moment when the first actor truly makes the investment and commits to expressing the essence of his or her story with his or her body. The other cast members are often surprised at how effective these theatrical choices can be.

For an actor exclusively versed in traditional fourth-wall performance, the art of extending the audience beyond those on stage is a vital part of training for a Wilson play. The actor must come to understand that the community extends beyond the footlights. For many, mere permission to speak beyond the proscenium can facilitate the change. For others, having an audience in rehearsal and challenging the actors to speak to people in the audience at the same time that they address their fellow characters can be a simple solution.

But merely speaking to these listeners is not enough. If the storytellers are to be effective, they must have a visceral relationship with those to whom they are telling the story; in other words, there must a kinesthetic connection through which the storyteller can gauge the impact of the story and adjust the telling appropriately. Such adjusting was particularly important in the emotionally charged stories—Levee's telling of the rape of his mother, for example. We approached this challenge from two perspectives. First, we worked to create in the actors the ability to respond instinctively to their surroundings. There are many training methods that develop this ability. We began with some very physical exercises borrowed from Bogart's viewpoints training. One example is a simple challenge called "three up, two down," in which five actors are onstage, three standing and two close to the ground. Moving constantly, participants must maintain this arrangement through instinctual physical response, moving and rising or dropping as inspired by the energy of those around them. We continued with variations on this exercise throughout our early weeks, undertaking daily physical work that enabled the actors to respond instinctively. For example, we did an exercise where two actors hold a pole between their chest bones (inspired by the training of Tadashi Suzuki). The object is to move around the space without dropping the pole. The listener inspires the movement, and it is the responsibility of the storyteller to make the immediate physical transitions necessary to accommodate the listener and ensure that the pole is not dropped.

Following a series of such introductory physical exercises, we returned to the text of the play. As we had done previously, we began with stories that the students associated with storytelling. The initial challenge was to tell a story the listener knew while retaining the attention of the listener. As the exercise progressed over time, we used stories borrowed from other Wilson plays; this choice was made to motivate the actors themselves to be storytellers before we asked them to become their characters as storytellers. Finally we turned to the stories in *Ma Rainey*, asking Ma to weave the stories of her difficult life or Cutler to tell of the humiliation of Reverend Gates. We encouraged the listeners to move when the story was no longer engaging, particularly when they felt that the body of the storyteller was no longer speaking to them. The storyteller was thus forced to move and make changes in physicalization and energy in order to reengage the listeners. Then we made the exercise more subtle, forcing the storyteller to determine for himself or herself if the listeners had disengaged. Finally we asked the storytellers to make that determination with closed eyes, in this way challenging them to connect more fully to their audience.

Telling one's own stories and telling Wilson's stories are aligned but not the same. Wilson's words present very specific rhythmic challenges. Although early in rehearsal we have actors tell their own personal stories to practice the art, we were concerned when they brought their own specific rhythms to their characters. For assistance, we turned to the inspiration to which Wilson turned. As he noted, "Anything you want to know about the black experience is in the blues. The blues is The Book—it is our sacred book" (Interview [Herrington]). We brought in the music and asked the actors to respond to it as they told their stories. The choices are many, but we worked with, for example, Muddy Waters's "Mannish Boy" for Slow Drag's story of the juke joint in New Orleans and with the music of Bobby "Blue" Bland for Levee's description of his mother's rape.

We then had the actors themselves select different blues pieces to accompany their stories from *Ma Rainey* and consider which music was a good rhythmic match for which story. We examined the musical quality each character brought to the play—in the text, in the defined movement, and in the approach to the music the character played—noting such elements as the African rhythms that pervade Slow Drag's tones or the nonbelligerent nature of Cutler. In conversation, we paralleled Wilson's work to the music, noting their shared qualities of metaphor, lyricism, and loose organization. We found the soulfulness of the blues and the repartee of jazz in each story and brought to the actors a variety of examples, ranging from the Delta blues singer Jimmy Rushing to John Lee Hooker.

Our final lesson of engagement was for those onstage who heard the stories. Inherent in these stories is the call-and-response form, in which the caller puts forward the song and the chorus responds and agrees underneath. Young actors are deeply invested in making discoveries in the moment and allowing every moment to be fresh. But if the stories that Wilson's characters tell are new in their details, the story is often familiar too, at least to some in the room. Tim Shepard, a historian, notes:

> Oral African storytelling is essentially a communal participatory experience. Everyone in most traditional African societies participates in formal and informal storytelling as interactive oral performance—such participation is an essential part of traditional African communal life, and basic training in a particular culture's oral arts and skills is an essential part of children's traditional indigenous education on their way to initiation into full humanness.

This participation has held true for African Americans for hundreds of years on new soil.

How were we to breed such familiarity and participation in an actor born in 1991? One way was to have all the actors onstage tell these stories. Each rehearsed some of the stories in the play that were spoken by other characters—particularly those we identified as representing a history that several on the stage shared, either personally or culturally: a personal connection engendered a need for the story to be told. We also worked with the dropping and joining of stories, whereby one actor would start a story but could stop at any time, requiring another actor to pick it up immediately. This exercise created an attentiveness that we felt was key. Finally, we asked the actors to create soundscapes to accompany the stories of others. Like the early gesture work, the idea was not to illustrate the sounds referenced in the stories but rather to find the resonances in the story and express them orally but not verbally.

When the stories were returned to their rightful characters, we asked the other actors to share by allowing a story to live in them while it was told, perhaps by adding modest sound, by speaking along at certain moments, or by responding aloud at other moments. The level of engagement was tremendous, and a dynamic energy was created that truly enabled the story to live in this community. Additionally, the oral responses assisted our actors in their preparation for verbal response from the audience—something Wilson plays often inspire and something young actors may not have experienced.

African culture has been a way of passing the traditions and beliefs of a particular society from one generation to the next. It has also been used to maintain traditions, codes of behavior, and social order. "African tales are told and retold under the shade of a tree or around a village campfire, passing on the history, philosophy, and moral laws of the people" (*African Tales*). And Wilson's tales are told and retold on stages across the world. It is an extraordinary opportunity to bring his work to a young artist and to bring that young artist to Wilson's work. The benefits extend far beyond newfound actor training and a great performance. Perhaps for Hurston and for us, these young artists can stop being orphans. Perhaps, like Wilson and his griots, each can become a master of words.

SPOTLIGHT ON MATERIAL CULTURE

The Logic of Chance: Blues and Policy in August Wilson's *Two Trains Running*

Andrew Scheiber

> What if history was a gambler, instead of a force in a laboratory experiment . . . ?
>
> —Ralph Ellison, *Invisible Man*

Students encountering August Wilson's *Two Trains Running* are often fascinated by the illegal lottery—known historically as policy—that dominates so many scenes in the play. Many students are curious about the vernacular culture of gaming evoked by Wilson's characters, particularly its elements of numerology and dreamwork; and some are scandalized by the antithesis it poses to the mainstream American ideology of work, thrift, and economic calculation. But through their participation in policy wagering, Wilson's characters enact and articulate a vision of personal destiny that embraces the play of chance and the irrational and provides an alternative economic calculus that reflects with greater experiential accuracy the realities of people living outside the main currents of social power. This essay explores how one might teach Wilson's play as a dialogue between the dominant, Enlightenment-driven model of economic engagement and the alternative and subversive culture of gaming and chance embodied in the characters' participation in policy.

"It's the same thing as putting money in the bank"

The gaming culture evoked in *Two Trains Running* provides a significant pedagogical point of entry to the deeper, more challenging issues raised in the play. Majority-culture or upper-middle-class students in particular may bring to the table a problematical tendency to see gambling among people with scarce resources as a cause of, rather than a response to, their impoverished circumstances. But the proliferation of state-run lotteries and tribal casinos has mainstreamed gambling in recent years and made some of its appeals more familiar to a broad segment of the population. In addition, the near meltdown of our financial institutions in 2008—not to mention the recession that followed—has underscored for many the fragility and questionable operations of the formal economy.

I find it useful as a prereading exercise to tap into students' recent experience or awareness of such trends and events. The exercise typically takes the form of a dual writing prompt. The first part of the prompt addresses student perceptions and attitudes toward state-run lotteries and other mainstreamed forms of gambling; the second asks students to reflect on their experience of what we might call the work-and-invest model that characterizes the formal economy. The first part of the prompt involves questions such as the following: "Do you play the lotto [or whatever it might be called in one's particular state]? Do you have family members or acquaintances who do so? Explain or analyze the appeal of this activity." Responses to such questions often yield helpful parallels between the experience of the students and the world of policy; for instance, numerology almost invariably manifests itself in these discussions, as birthdates frequently figure in the selection of numbers for students or for their acquaintances who play the state-run systems.

In the second half of the prompt, I ask students to reflect on their experience in the work-and-invest sector of the economy: "Do you feel you are fairly paid for the work you perform for your employer? Are there other satisfactions besides material ones that come from paid work? How is paying money for a particular good or service different from buying a lottery ticket? What is the risk that you won't get your money's worth? How about investing in the stock market or putting money into a 401k retirement plan? How do the risk calculations change as one moves from the exchange economy to the gambling or the gaming economy? What are the different satisfactions of using one's money in these various ways?" And recent history has added potency to a final question I usually include in this half of the prompt: "Discuss an experience in which your faith in the economy was shaken. How did you or people you know react to this?"

I then ask students voluntarily to share what they've written in these responses, either orally in class or by posting to an online discussion board. The views that typically emerge from this exercise correspond roughly to the range of economic philosophies expressed or enacted by the characters in Wilson's play. While most students seek the safe ground of a middle position that is relatively uncritical of both recreational gambling and engagement in the work-and-invest economy, there are some who articulate oppositional sentiments: some students disdain gambling as a sign of moral or psychological weakness; others take the view that the official economy is itself a rigged game, played for the benefit of the wealthy few. (The emergence in recent years of the ninety-nine percent movement has spurred an increasing number of responses in the latter category.)

For many students the effect of this assignment is to close some of the perceived distance between the presumed rationality of the market and the supposed irrationality of the gaming economy. At this point it may be useful to explore the distinctive history and practice of the game policy as it functioned in the African American community. This is a fascinating topic on its own terms, the more so once students realize that policy operated on the same random-draw system many state-sponsored lotteries use today. The overview I offer is brief, but I have found sufficient to help students grasp the historical background to Wilson's play without completely distracting them from the study of the work.

Though the details varied somewhat from city to city and from decade to decade, policy operated as a lottery in which "gambling bettors placed their money on one or more numbers that they hoped would be among those picked in a drawing of twelve numbers between 1 and 78" (Haller 719). Bets were taken by policy agents at various locations in the community (usually legitimate businesses like restaurants and barbershops) and recorded on slips that were delivered to a central location where the daily numbers were randomly selected (sometimes by the spinning of a roulette-like wheel, as depicted in Ralph Ellison's "King of the Bingo Game"). So-called numbers runners were responsible both for collecting the betting slips and returning payouts to the holders of any winning numbers (Haller 720).

In the interwar period in particular, when employment and other avenues of economic opportunity were scarce in black urban neighborhoods, policy offered a simple, ubiquitous, and inexpensive form of economic engagement, with a chance for a high rate of return that, however long the odds, seemed a fair match for the rates of return faced by blacks in the formal economy. Aside from the opportunities they offered bettors, policy operations were integral institutions in the community, providing jobs and access to capital that mainstream industry and banking were typically not able—or not willing—to extend to the African American population. As the boxer Joe Louis noted in his autobiography, community-minded policy entrepreneurs "got as much respect as a doctor or lawyer" (29–30; qtd. in Wolcott 47).

Once presented with such information, students are generally ready to acknowledge the viability, even the necessity, of an alternative to an economic model whose rewards are by and large inaccessible to those living on the margins of power. It's more difficult to get them to see the alternative rationality that Ann Fabian describes as governing the policy model: "To bet on dreams and hunches against very long odds was not simply a rational response to a closed economy but was the means of opening the closed economy to the play of imagination—play based on a distinct vision of human nature and its expression in the market" (138).

Play, of course, is usually taken as the opposite of *work*, just as *imagination* is often seen as opposed to *reality*, and therein lies the crucial distinction (for most readers and viewers of Wilson's play, at least) between policy's ludic ethos of risk and the contrasting model of entrepreneurial individualism, with its values of thrift, effort, and accumulation. Students often express an initial preference for work and reality over play and imagination, on the grounds that the former represent a more productive or practical set of values than the latter, at least in material terms. But in the very first scene of *Two Trains Running*, the denizens of Memphis's diner engage in a debate that casts doubt on this valuation, at least as far as the economically marginalized black community is concerned. Risa, one of Memphis's waitresses, sees policy as a sucker's game: "I don't know why people waste their money playing numbers. Time you hit you just getting back what you put in." But Wolf considers the numbers a good investment, especially compared with what he sees as the rigged game of the formal banking economy. For him, playing policy is "the same thing as putting money in the bank. This way you might take out more than you put in . . . but Mellon ain't gonna let you do that. The numbers give you an opportunity" (3).

This perception—that "opportunity" in the conventional economy is reserved for someone else—underwrites many of the reasons given for playing the lottery, both among Wilson's characters and actual people interviewed by historians and other researchers.[1] Entrenched patterns of racialized economic disinvestment and the memory of the 1929 stock market crash (strikingly recollected in Holloway's tale of how the Prophet Samuel parlayed Aunt Ester's wisdom into a close acquaintance with Andrew Mellon [26]) provided a reasonable basis in experience for seeing the hidden hand of capitalism as dealing uncertain cards from the underside of the deck—in comparison with which the daily lottery drawings provided transparency and the perception at least of better odds.

In order to help students grasp the logic of chance embodied in policy play, it is often necessary to help them recognize more fully the ways in which the formal economy can fail to deliver on its promise of greater individual and collective felicity. While the financial dislocations of recent years have made it somewhat easier than before to engage students on this point, it still helps to begin with some purposeful brainstorming on matters internal to Wilson's play. To this end, I sometimes ask students to rank the main dramatis personae along two scales—one assessing which characters seem happiest or most emotionally healthy, the other evaluating the characters in terms of the degree to which they espouse or practice the values of the formal work-and-invest economy. Interestingly, two characters typically appear simultaneously near or at the bottom of the first scale and near or at the top of the second: the financially successful funeral home director West and the deeply damaged Hambone.

Hambone's story is emblematic of the way in which Wilson's black characters are marginalized by the functioning of the formal economy. After entering into a contract for painting the fence of Lutz, the white butcher, Hambone discovers that the interpretation of the terms of the contract—and thus the value placed on his work—is entirely the prerogative of the white employer. After being paid with a chicken in lieu of the ham he believes he has earned, Hambone becomes almost maniacally obsessed with this injustice, obsessively repeating, "I want my ham!," throughout the scenes in which he appears. In discussing him, we often revisit student responses to the prereading prompt, especially the part that asks the student, "Discuss an experience in which your faith in the economy was shaken. How did you or people you know react to this?" For many students and their families these experiences have involved the abrogation of contractual agreements by employers in both the private and public sectors—a betrayal of fair play and trust as well as a threat to one's livelihood—or the loss of retirement or college funds in an exploded investment bubble. Hambone may have the appearance of a madman, but he is a walking example of how the insults of what passes for the normal and reasonable status quo can drive a sane person crazy.

In parsing such economic realities, students are often able to see that West, the well-to-do undertaker, represents the opposite danger: the spiritual cost to a black man (perhaps to a white man as well) of accepting as rational a definition of existence in terms of profit-and-loss calculation. West speaks for the entrepreneurial model of industry, thrift, and the accumulation of wealth by any means necessary; his parsimony and his penchant for cutting corners in the name of profit are subjects of frequent discussion in the diner. Even the entrepreneurial Memphis finds West's focus on the bottom line too much, speculating that West disposes of bodies so he can resell the same coffin twice (7). Still straddling the fence between policy's economy of chance and the entrepreneurial model fully embraced by West, Memphis places his bets with the justification that he doesn't want to be like the undertaker, who has "been wearing the same pair of shoes for three years" (11).

In terms of the ranking exercise mentioned above, Holloway often appears in the inverse position with respect to Hambone and West: he is near the top in terms of his emotional and spiritual health, yet near the bottom in terms of his identification with the market assumptions that drive Hambone mad and make West into a ruthless, spiritually desiccated miser. He also tends to figure prominently in another ranking exercise I often ask students to perform: to rank Wilson's dramatis personae according to who they think most fully articulates the playwright's own sentiments or convictions.

Anyone familiar with other works by Wilson will recognize that Holloway's historical consciousness and trenchant analysis of the workings of cultural and material power establish Holloway as this play's wise elder figure, a role played elsewhere by characters such as Toledo in *Ma Rainey's Black Bottom.* But even students who are unfamiliar with Wilson's other works or with his artistic agenda find themselves drawn to Holloway without quite knowing why. I sometimes ask them to identify passages that seem to them to express in miniature the larger worldview of the play, and more often than not they find that such passages prominently feature Holloway dispensing lore or wisdom. For instance, it is Holloway who tells the story of the fateful encounter between Hambone and Lutz and who offers an appreciation of how Hambone's madness, seen another way, stands as a criticism of an unjust status quo. As Holloway wryly tells Wolf, Hambone "might be more in his right mind than you are. He might have more sense than any of us" (29). More important, Holloway delivers the crucial speech about "stacking niggers" (34–35), which stands as a condemnation of how the work ethic honored in the conventional economy masks the historical and ongoing extraction of surplus value from black bodies.

The opposition between the assumptions of the formal and the informal economies (policy play standing as a synecdoche for the informal economy) provides a wonderful window for student discussion of the economic aspects of social and psychological life and in particular how one's position in structures of power—including that of race—affect one's economic assumptions and behavior. Such an important and meaningful discussion can be facilitated through a combination of directed, experience-based brainstorming and well-focused research into some of the historical and cultural contexts in which the characters and events of Wilson's plays are embedded. Regardless of the philosophies they express, Wilson's characters are all torn between the desire to affirm their identity as economic actors in terms of their own shared cultural experience and practice, on the one hand, and their aspiration to participate successfully in a larger economy that marginalizes them, on the other. Their complex negotiation with these opposing economies is one of the main dramatic engines driving the talk and actions of this play.

"Take twenty dollars and throw it in the river"

Most of my prereading strategies for and initial discussions of Wilson's play aim at uncovering and questioning the unexamined beliefs and pieties that have accrued around the operations of the formal economy and modern market society in general. This demystification is important, I think, in clearing the ground for a fuller apprehension of the cultural-racial concerns that are central to Wilson's work. What remains, then, is to engage students in a discussion of how the economic aspects of policy play might point us toward other realms of value.

The initial brainstorming exercise described above often produces accounts of various practices that students have observed in themselves or others while engaging in state-sanctioned lottery play. It is common for them to use terms—*ritual*, *lucky numbers*, and so on—that suggest the irrational or transrational factors that determine their betting behavior. The use of the word *ritual* provides an especially handy opening to talk about the possible meaning or significance of such habitual but seemingly irrational behavior. A little probing of the various possible definitions of *ritual* generally allows students to note the word's association with ceremonial or religious forms and thus to see that the everyday and secular sport of lottery wagering, whether it is policy in *Two Trains Running* or the more familiar (to most of them) state-run lotto, can be invested with some of the properties of religious or cultural belief. I expect them to describe such beliefs as magical or superstitious—but after discussion of cases like Hambone's there's usually one in the class who will ask whether there isn't something similarly magical in the rational proposition that hard work leads to just rewards.

This acknowledgment of the ritual elements of play—in both policy and in more contemporary manifestations of the random-draw lottery—can provide a helpful transition to another body of secondary source material that is important to an understanding of *Two Trains Running*. Wilson's commitment to black cultural nationalism is a matter of record (for evidence of this, his manifesto "The Ground on Which I Stand" is probably most accessible for students), but students are often surprised and interested to find that in Native American as well as African American literature games of chance function as "ritual site[s] where the forces of assimilation are contested" and "provide a framework to assign value and difference" (Pasquaretta 21). Wilson's evocation of policy is part of this larger phenomenon; through policy, Wilson expresses his long-standing emphasis on the recognition and preservation of distinctively African American cultural forms and practices, particularly with respect to the roots of those forms and practices in the southern past and beyond. Policy play, especially with its adjunct of vernacular dream work, functions as a synecdoche of the larger body of folk wisdom and practice that Wilson regards as fundamental to any healthy projection of modern black identity.

As with the economic history of policy, the cultural origins of policy are of instructive interest to students, and here again a little research can go a long way to alert them to possible subtexts to Wilson's play and help them productively engage those subtexts. (For useful sources that are accessible to advanced student readers, see Haller; Lears.) Still more interesting, and possibly bearing more profoundly on Wilson's concerns in the play, is the similarity of policy gaming to some of the West African practices of divination, in which combinations produced by chance (through the casting of shells, nuts, or other objects by the priest) are invested with significant, even prophetic, meaning for the individual supplicant. Yoruba practice, for instance, involves the casting of sacred palm nuts onto a divination tray by a priest, or *babalawo*; the resulting configurations point toward corresponding verses containing "exemplary myths" from the Ifá (the set of sacred Yoruba texts), from which the supplicant is to make sense of his or her circumstances or to derive or interpret an appropriate course of action (R. Thompson 34–36).

Such divination practices, which Henry Louis Gates, Jr., aptly describes as "a marvelous combination of geomancy and textual exegesis" (*Signifying Monkey* 10), find their inverse image in the traditions of vernacular interpretation that sprang up around policy gambling. Dreams, commonly regarded as extrarational auguries of the future anyhow, became texts to be interpretively mined for winning policy combinations, thus helping bettors improve their odds. This interpretive practice was assisted by so-called dream books, which helped players translate dream images into particular number sequences. Students can easily investigate samples of such dream books, as many from the 1920s and 1930s have been published online, and there are any number of sites where such texts continue to be marketed in tandem with other divination supplies.

As students will discover with even the most casual research into this subject, female clairvoyants play a central role in this divination tradition. These women are frequently identified as the authors of dream books or as suppliers of other goods to be used in discerning or improving one's fortunes. This discovery helps illuminate the importance of Aunt Ester, a local seer who embodies the ancestral African culture that is vestigially present in policy and other practices depicted in the play. She represents the past that Wilson's characters must reclaim, as evidenced in her urging Memphis to "pick up the ball" (84) and confront the painful memory of the land and the life he abandoned at knifepoint in the South.

But more important for this particular approach to Wilson's play is that Aunt Ester eschews the hoarding and accumulation of wealth and instructs her supplicants to do likewise. When Memphis protests that he's never seen Aunt Ester "change nobody's luck. . . . If it was as easy as that we'd all be rich," Holloway corrects him: "There you go talking about being rich. . . . Aunt Ester don't buy into that. She don't make people rich" (25). Indeed, her typical advice to her supplicants—"take twenty dollars and throw it in the river" (98)—requires them to abandon the logic of the exchange economy in much the same way that policy betting does. Her advice requires, at least in financial terms, either destroying rather than increasing value or transferring it from one person to another; thus she evokes what Georges Bataille once characterized as an ethics of "waste" (see Fabian 137–38), which stands in stark contrast to the imperatives of accumulation in modern capitalist societies.

The characters' responses to Aunt Ester's methods fall along a spectrum, from West's outright rejection (76) to Sterling's desperate assurance that "I'll throw twenty dollars in the river if it help me get a job" (78). Not surprisingly, most of my students, when asked to place their own responses on a scale between West's and Sterling's, incline toward West's more pragmatic and skeptical position. They tend to regard her spiritual technology as superstition, and throwing money away seems to them foolish and scandalous.

But when the question is rephrased in more neutral terms—"Is there a value in parting with your money without the assurance of consequently receiving something of value in return?"—many students respond in the affirmative, noting that such otherwise irrational behavior can be justified on the grounds of generosity, charity, faith, or a pay-it-forward view of human felicity. Some even recognize Aunt Ester's prescription as a form of ritual, in which the twenty dollars becomes a sacrificial offering to the god or gods whose favor the supplicants are beseeching or as a way, as one of my students wisely put it, of "putting money in its place" so that other concerns—presumably cultural and spiritual ones—can take precedence.[2]

Putting money in its place, I would propose, is the insight that Wilson's play is designed to spark in us—an insight equally suggested by the long odds of policy, in which the satisfaction of playing is a more frequent return than the satisfaction of a big payoff, and in Aunt Ester's "throw twenty dollars in the river." As if to underscore the validity of her sacrificial advice, Memphis receives an unexpected windfall when he forgoes his legal wrangling and follows her instructions: the city offers him $10,000 more for his property than he was prepared to demand. This windfall is a clear inversion of the results obtained by Hambone for his own attempt to market his labor power in the formal economy of work and investment, and it suggests that for the dispossessed of Wilson's play the best odds lie in the transvaluation of capitalist exchange required in order to accept both Aunt Ester's advice and the long odds of policy.[3]

Memphis's unexpected payoff is perhaps a necessary dramatic gesture to tell twenty-first-century readers that Aunt Ester's methods are not to be dismissed as superstition, but it is in some ways a distraction from the more fundamental point here, which is the importance of attending to ancestral wisdom, even (or especially) when that wisdom points away from the rationalist materialism that threatens to dissolve the ties of memory and the bonds of community. Aunt Ester's discipline involves what the formal economy would regard as a scandalous abuse of money, but its proper function is to break the spell of capital and to concentrate people's attention on other mysteries and realms of value.

Teaching *Two Trains Running* through a consideration of policy is not merely an exercise in historical context. While the actual history and practice of policy gaming appeal both to our curiosity and desire for romance (as with many institutions and groups associated with an illegal, underground economy), in Wilson's play policy is a dramatically and symbolically charged element of his larger argument regarding African American cultural recovery and self-determination. Both an alternative to market ideology and a mocking travesty of it, policy engages the reality of the present as well as black cultural memory in a way that the workings of the formal economy fail to do.

What I hope that students will draw from this approach is not just a sense of Wilson's criticism of dominant-culture assumptions about economics, culture, and history in America but also a sense of how cultural practices like policy might provide a matrix of resistance for those consigned to the margins of national life. But students should also be cautioned against essentializing or overromanticizing these practices of resistance: the way forward cannot be an off-the-shelf formula such as one might find in a dream book. "Picking up the ball," as Aunt Ester urges Memphis to do, involves not just going back for the ball but carrying it forward as well.

Trudier Harris has written that Wilson himself "is constantly revising the folklore, reinscribing it with features that enhance his own purposes" (62); so too must his characters, who inhabit an African America in transition between increasingly attenuated residual traditions and a future struggling to be born. The bridge that will carry one over must necessarily be a product of bricolage, something new constructed out of the materials one has inherited, and its footings must first be planted not in reason and calculation but in the extravagance of hope, the litheness of the interpretive impulse, and sturdiness in the face of chance and loss that are the characteristics of the player par excellence.

NOTES

[1] Indeed, Wolf's comments are nearly identical to those documented in one study of policy betting in interwar Detroit. As one subject reported, "Number gambling is really not gambling. . . . You've got a good chance of winning, and if you do win you're sure to get your money. That's more than you white folks can say about your gambling" (Carlson 154; qtd. in Wolcott 62).

[2] One shouldn't base a lesson plan on the expectation of such a brilliant student remark, so sometimes I use a free-write or discussion board prompt such as the following to elicit an insightful comment: "How would we choose our actions differently if success depended on the way one prayed or approached the gods rather than on the way one worked, saved, or invested?"

[3] Interestingly, Aunt Ester's instructions conform to those of a popular mid-twentieth-century dream book documented by Fabian. Its author, one "Harlem Pete," urged upon his readers the efficacy of the gambler's looseness with money: "If you want to be rich, Give! If you want to be poor, Grasp! If you want abundance, Scatter! If you want to be needy, Hoard" (152).

Spatial Politics and Memory: The Urban Geography of August Wilson's *Radio Golf*

James Engstrom and Paul K. Bryant-Jackson

> From the 1920s on, blacks and whites flocked to the bars and night spots in the Hill that attracted some of the nation's finest jazz musicians. Marie's and Lola's, small and stuffy clubs, provided spots for late-night jam sessions, and helped make Pittsburgh a center for nurturing internationally known musicians. Jazz notables born, reared, or nurtured in Pittsburgh included Billy Strayhorn, Kenny Clarke, Art Blakey, Earl ("Fatha") Hines, Roy Eldridge, and Leroy Brown, in addition to such notable musicians as Lean Horne, Mary Lou Williams, Louise Mann, and Maxine Sullivan. Mary Dee, a popular disk jockey in the 1950s, labeled the intersection of Wylie Avenue and Fullerton Street as the "Crossroads of the World."
>
> —Laurence Glasco

> YOUNGBLOOD: They gonna tear the whole neighborhood down.
>
> DOUB: They supposed to build some houses. That's what they need to do.
>
> TURNBO: They supposed to build a new hospital down there on Logan Street. They been talking about that for the longest while. They supposed to build another part to the Irene Kaufmann Settlement House to replace that part they tore down. . . .
>
> BECKER: They *supposed* to build some houses but you ain't gonna see that. You ain't gonna see nothing but the tear-down. That's all I ever seen.
>
> YOUNGBLOOD: That's all there is to see.
>
> —*Jitney*

> The resurgence of gentrification following the economic depression of 1989–1993 . . . will not mean the end of the revanchist city and the instigation of a kinder, gentler urbanism. The more likely scenario is of a sharpened bipolarity in which the white middle-class assumptions about civil society retrench as a narrow set of norms against which everyone else is found dangerously

> wanting. . . . "Extermination," George Custer declared in 1865, eleven years before his last stand in the Dakotas, "is the only true policy we can adopt toward the political leaders of the [Sioux] rebellion." . . . The "regeneration" of the *fin-de-millénaire* city is premised on a similar act of extermination.
>
> —Neil Smith

From his first sketches of *Jitney* (1978) to creating *Radio Golf* (2005) in the final year of his life, August Wilson wrote passionately about that which he knew and loved and for which he had great concern—the Hill District in Pittsburgh and the urban condition in the United States. Consequently it is not surprising that his Pittsburgh Cycle invites interdisciplinary and multidisciplinary interpretations of the experiences, emotions, and dilemmas he reveals in written word and on the stage. Certainly one can employ traditional methods of dramatic criticism and literary analysis to examine the poetry of his language, his interest in orality as an African American tradition, his incorporation of music, and his finely drawn characters. On these measures alone, the broad appeal of his plays is understandable. But Wilson's works, more than those of most other playwrights writing during the last thirty years, yield additional insights that come by stepping beyond the traditional bounds of dramatic criticism and literary analysis. In fact, Wilson has often been referred to as a historian as much as a playwright, not only because his plays span every decade of the twentieth century but also because he effectively incorporates history into the center of his dramas (Bogumil, *Understanding*; Elam, *Past*; Shannon, *Dramatic Vision* 3–16, 195–96).[1] While Wilson himself has acknowledged the profoundly historical elements of his work, he has also declared that he was only indirectly interested in history and mainly as a lens for examining culture, particularly the survival of a specifically African American culture as a unique and distinctive phenomenon (Shannon, *Dramatic Vision* 202–03).

In this essay we investigate the inherently geographic nature of Wilson's work. Through his ten plays, in addition to constructing a cultural history of African American life in the twentieth century, we propose that Wilson has written an urban geography. We suggest that geography, with its emphases on spatial relations and the importance of place, is a useful tool for investigating his work. In particular, urban geography and contemporary urban theory can excavate and illuminate many of the experiences, challenges, issues, and perspectives of his characters. While many students are not familiar with the rich intellectual tradition of geography, we propose that place and geography perform an active role in his dramas, thereby shedding further light on more commonly employed constructs of dramatic literature and theater criticism. Therefore Wilson scholars can benefit from a basic introduction to certain concepts in urban geography and urban theory. Most important, urban geography can inform a reading of his last play, *Radio Golf*, which takes place in the 1990s, the final decade treated in the Pittsburgh Cycle, as this play reflects significantly the contemporary debates and conceptual frameworks of urban geography and urban theory. In fact, we maintain that the central conflict in this play concerns two competing and opposing visions of urban futures.

Christopher Rawson describes Wilson's Hill District as an

> archetypical northern urban black neighborhood, evolving over both historic and imaginative time, a construct of frustration, nostalgia, anger and dream. The real Hill was once a city within a city, with a proud history of art, sports, and journalism. Then, it was torn apart by the urban renewal in the 1950s and by the fires of 1968. Now, as if in cosmic compensation, the Hill lives on in Wilson's imagination. (4)

Although the Pittsburgh Cycle is a narrative about a specific neighborhood, its lessons and tragedies resonate with many audiences. Ultimately, the cycle and its cultural ramifications can be viewed as applicable to a larger spectrum of the African American urban experience, particularly in the cities of the Northeast and Midwest.

People who become familiar with Wilson's plays soon learn that Wilson did not write them in a clear order of historical chronology. In his later plays, he sets out to reveal and explicate the interconnections of people and places by frequent referrals to people, experiences, and places in previous plays (Seidler). In many ways, *Radio Golf*, which focuses on the Hill District of the 1990s when it appeared poised on the cusp of redevelopment and gentrification, is a culmination of this process of remembering. The connections with and meanings of not only that neighborhood but also specific buildings within the neighborhood come to play an important role in the transformation of the main character, Harmond Wilks, as he begins to comprehend and embrace a particular vision of urbanity.

In this essay, we briefly present a historical geography of the Hill District and introduce a conceptual framework for understanding two competing visions of the urban: a neoliberal urban vision and a "right to the city" vision. These visions have been articulated in the academic arena by urban geographers and other scholars interested in documenting and explaining contemporary urban change. We discuss these visions and their theoretical underpinnings by focusing on *Radio Golf*. We provide examples where these contrasting urban visions are embodied in the human drama of the play, both among the five characters and as an internal conflict within Wilks. Finally, we discuss a strategy for introducing urban geography and urban theory to students of theater and dramatic literature in a way that will spur dialogue about the play, engage students in thinking about Wilson's plays in explicitly geographic terms, and hopefully increase their overall appreciation of his work.

The Hill District

While many observers characterize Wilson's plays as presenting a universalizing portrait of African American life (Kenny Leon qtd. in Elam, *Past* xvi; Gantt), all but one of his plays take place in one neighborhood in one city. The settings of the plays within that neighborhood are varied—houses, apartment buildings, yards, bars, restaurants, cabstands, and—in the case of *Radio Golf*—a real estate office. The plays are peppered with references to schools, community centers, and tuberculosis sanatoriums. These offstage places ground his plays, contribute to their highly evocative quality, and add a geographic specificity that isn't always present in contemporary drama. It is instructive to briefly trace the history of the Hill District to understand how and why the neighborhood was at a particular juncture in the 1990s of *Radio Golf*. Pittsburgh's human and physical geography as well as broader national processes of urban change are essential to understanding the neighborhood's evolution.

The Hill District was advantageously located just east of downtown Pittsburgh, offering dramatic views of the city, and as early as the 1820s it began developing as an affluent neighborhood (Glasco). By the 1850s, as the housing aged and the city grew, the Hill began attracting European immigrants, first from Ireland and Germany, then by the turn of the century primarily from southern and eastern Europe. As early as the 1880s, African Americans began moving to the area, but it was not until World War I that African Americans from the South, seeking to escape an oppressive cultural climate and pursue economic opportunities, began moving to the Hill in large numbers. In the first half of the twentieth century, the Hill remained a racially integrated poor and working-class neighborhood. It also developed into a vibrant business and entertainment district. African Americans frequented the movie theaters and jazz clubs located in the neighborhood, and the *Pittsburgh Courier*, an important African American–owned newspaper, was published from offices located in the Hill District. During this period, African Americans gradually made inroads into industrial work, and many neighborhood residents worked in nearby steel mills and other industrial venues.

The white population gradually moved out during this period, however, and by the 1950s the neighborhood was almost exclusively African American. By this time the housing stock had deteriorated considerably and the neighborhood had become increasingly overcrowded, as discrimination prevented African Americans from finding housing in most other parts of the city. In the late 1940s and 1950s, the city's first public housing was built on the eastern edges of the Hill District, offering some neighborhood residents an opportunity to improve their living environments. Then, in the late 1950s, as in many American cities, large-scale urban renewal projects were implemented that permanently changed the neighborhood. The entire area referred to as the Lower Hill, closest to downtown Pittsburgh, was demolished, displacing 8,000 people to build a civic arena and a surrounding sea of parking lots. Promises were made to make housing available elsewhere in the city, but for the most part these promises did not materialize. Riots in the 1960s brought further devastation, and further disinvestment, neglect, and redlining continued to depopulate the area (Trotter and Day 144–47, 163–66). By the 1980s several square blocks were completely abandoned, and on most other streets pockets of housing alternated with empty lots and boarded-up buildings. Many of the businesses on Centre Street, the main commercial vein, also were boarded up or torn down. The population of the neighborhood declined from 50,000 in 1950 to less than 15,000 in 1990 (Singh), with a high percentage of remaining residents living in poverty. Whether emanating from the African American community, the mainstream media, or government reports, discussions of urban renewal in the Hill almost universally categorized it as a failure (Fitzpatrick).

The Hill and Urban Theory

By the 1990s, however, discussions about the Hill increasingly were framed around words such as *renovation*, *redevelopment*, and even *gentrification*. Urban theory provides an explanatory framework for understanding nascent neighborhood change in the Hill District at this particular moment in the 1990s. In particular, it presents an argument that American cities, Pittsburgh included, were remaking their governance structures to align with a neoliberal vision of the city that could respond more effectively to structural economic changes.

The basic argument about the rise of neoliberal urban governance structures goes as follows. As the United States transitioned to a postindustrial economy, partially as a response to globalization, cities throughout the country were faced with the disappearance of much of their tax base (Gallaher; Harvey, *Brief History* 47–48, 59–60, 73). As opportunities in manufacturing declined, reduced employment opportunities led to the increasing impoverishment of central city dwellers. African Americans, who in many cities had only recently gained access to well-paying manufacturing jobs, were particularly hard hit by these changes. Pittsburgh provides one of the most dramatic examples of this process of deindustrialization, as one steel mill after another shuttered its doors and opportunities in industry disappeared. The decline of jobs in the steel sector was especially precipitous in the 1980s, and the last steel mill in the city of Pittsburgh shut its doors in 1998.

From the 1950s through the 1970s, many urban governments in the United States spent significant resources on social services and efforts to improve the lives of their increasingly impoverished populations, as housing policies favoring middle-class home ownership triggered white flight to the suburbs. The construction of public housing and even massive demolition of housing such as occurred in the lower Hill District, while sometimes characterized as well-intentioned, were often ill conceived and ended up harming poorer citizens more than helping them (Teaford, *Rough Road* and "Urban Renewal"). The riots of the 1960s presented a challenge to city governments, but during this period many antipoverty agencies were formed that provided a variety of social services through a combination of federal and local monies. Nevertheless, some neighborhoods scarred by riots never recovered. By the 1980s many cities in the United States were turning their attention away from this service-oriented approach. A new ideology, which we can categorize as neoliberal urban governance, began to take hold. What processes triggered this change of focus?[2]

As cities began to engage in competition to attract multinational corporations and young, educated people that Richard Florida refers to as the "creative class" (*Cities* and *Rise*), such efforts also involved not only offering companies tax breaks but also remaking the image of the city by providing attractive urban environments to people who worked in the corporate offices and new entrepreneurial enterprises that formed the basis of the new postindustrial economy. Any city that did not pursue these strategies was in danger of falling behind, so cities had no choice but to adopt them, even if this meant allocating fewer funds for traditional social service and antipoverty programs. An important element in remaking a city along neoliberal lines involved supporting gentrification of specific neighborhoods that had a strategic presence or geographic visibility, neighborhoods where gentrification was not only possible but also deemed by politicians and policy makers to be necessary. By the 1990s, the highly extolled public-private partnership had become the raison d'être of urban governance throughout the United States. Public-private partnerships involved attracting private real estate interests in risky redevelopment projects, often in poor neighborhoods, with a promise of government grants or subsidies to improve the developers' chances of profitability. Many of these public-private partnerships involved support for projects aimed at gentrifying key neighborhoods.

Neil Smith, a geographer, explores what he describes as a capitalist imperative at work in urban gentrification and redevelopment ("Gentrification" and *New Urban Frontier*). He argues that capitalism is continually in an act of creative destruction and that in the urban real estate market a process of property and neighborhood devaluation occurs until a "rent gap," which is the gap between actual land value and the value that a property would have after redevelopment or renovation, becomes large enough to make the property, and perhaps by extension an entire neighborhood, profitable again. However, such neighborhoods often contain a stigma of poverty or a long-standing association with nonwhite racial groups. (Nonwhite neighborhoods in the United States have a long history of being the victim of policies that resulted in their devaluation both economically and socially.) Private real estate interests typically try to garner funding or government subsidies to reduce the risk involved and to improve chances of making a profit. Local governments, seeking to increase their tax bases and improve the image of their cities, are often more than willing to provide generous support to the developers. Although Pittsburgh had lost most of its manufacturing base, it was somewhat successful in remaking its economy and its image as a city where health care and education were the driving forces of the "new economy" (B. Jacobs 9–10, 91–92; Streitfeld). Therefore it is not surprising that Pittsburgh, along with almost every other major American city, has provided financial and political backing for urban redevelopment projects (Crowley).

While the neoliberal vision has been adopted by almost every city in the United States and many urban areas in other parts of the world, it has also been subject to trenchant criticism. Opponents of neoliberalism recently have begun to articulate an alternative. In contrast to the neoliberal vision, the "right to the city" vision starts with the premise that everyday citizens, as users of urban space, should have greater decision-making authority on matters that affect their lives. The French philosopher Henri Lefebvre articulated this concept in *The Production of Space* (1991). Lefebvre contends that the everyday spatial practices of urban inhabitants should be given priority over the abstract neoliberal perspectives of urban space held by planners, developers, and city governments. These perspectives marginalize the users of urban space such as those embodied by Wilson's characters.

Lefebvre's ideas disseminated during the last decade of the twentieth century and galvanized what might be called an emerging "right to the city" movement. David Harvey, a geographer, has been particularly active in the articulation of this vision in academic circles throughout the English-speaking world and more recently with activist groups in the United States. Unlike in the United States, where the neoliberal vision of the city has been almost universal during the last thirty years, in some European and developing countries, particularly those where left-wing and labor perspectives traditionally have exerted a stronger political influence, alternative urban visions, in which citizens have more decision-making power, are being adopted, thanks to Lefebvre's concepts. Finally, reaching globally, in 2009 UNESCO published a document entitled *Urban Policies and the Right to the City* (Brown and Kristiansen) detailing citizen-oriented efforts in exercising their "right to the city" in several cities throughout the world. Even in the United States, where the neoliberal vision still reigns, a Right to the City Alliance connecting community organizations in eight metropolitan areas has recently formed (http://righttothecity.org).

One of the contentions of the Rights to the City Alliance is that while urban power brokers continue to target historic neighborhoods, often with large nonwhite populations, grassroots efforts can be effective in stopping or at least modifying redevelopment efforts (Singh). The "right to the city" movement focuses not just on participation but also on the appropriation of urban space, in other words "the right to access, occupy, and use space, and create new spaces that meet peoples' needs" (Brown and Kristiansen). Although such groups often are up against entrenched and powerful economic and political interests, the neoliberal vision can be challenged through a variety of actions such as lawsuits and public protest. In some instances, redevelopment projects have been stopped or modified significantly in response to the needs and desires of marginalized urban populations.

But redevelopment and gentrification are not ubiquitous; the specific conditions that make a part of a city likely to be upgraded are not present everywhere.

An examination of the geography of Pittsburgh is instructive in revealing why the Hill District in particular was ripe for revitalization. Pittsburgh is located at the confluence of three rivers. Downtown Pittsburgh is at the western tip of the east side of Pittsburgh, where the land comes to a narrow point; it is surrounded on two sides by water and cut off from the south and north of town, which can be reached only by a series of bridges. To the east of downtown, however, and comprising almost the entire area as it fans out, is the Hill District. This neighborhood of abandoned streets and dilapidated buildings did not present an attractive face to health care workers, students, Web designers, and bohemians looking for a place to live. Yet the location, less than a mile from downtown and with dramatic views of it, still beckoned. In the terminology employed by Smith, the rent gap of the area had reached a point where the area had been devalued to such an extent that it was primed for the redevelopment and gentrification that meant a rise in profitability for developers and increased city tax revenues. The events that transpire in *Radio Golf* can be explained by this inevitable process of urban capitalist real estate development.

Radio Golf

Let us now apply this new understanding of late-twentieth-century urban processes to *Radio Golf*, the Hill District in 1997, and the people who inhabit this play. At the beginning of the play, the protagonist is a real estate developer who grew up but no longer lives in the Hill. He and his business partner, Roosevelt Hicks, a banker, enter the office of Bedford Hills Redevelopment, Inc. (Bedford Hills is a real estate moniker used to describe the area while avoiding any reference to the Hill and the negative connotations the name implies.) Wilks and Hicks, both active agents in the neoliberal development of Bedford Hills, are anxiously awaiting the City of Pittsburgh to declare a section of the Hill District blighted so that they can receive $5 million in federal redevelopment funds for their mixed-use development project. The plans for the project include a 180-unit apartment building and several businesses, including a Starbucks, Whole Foods, and Barnes and Noble (*Radio Golf* 11–12). Wilson pointedly chooses these three companies as prototypical representations of late-twentieth-century yuppie consumer capitalism.

Wilson purposefully employs the jarring image of blight in conjunction with this storied African American neighborhood. How could declaring a neighborhood blighted be a good thing? Yet in the context of Wilks and Hick's role in the redevelopment of the neighborhood and the potential personal gain involved, it is a contradiction with which these two men must come to terms. Hicks addresses his anxiety about the city's decision by saying, "How are we going to do this [the redevelopment project] if we don't get the fed money?" Wilks, a bit more optimistic, responds, "What are you worried for? The feds are ready to fund the project. And the city's not going to mess that up. They're not going to pass up five million dollars even if it is for minority redevelopment. They're going to declare it blighted" (11–12). He goes on to say, "City council has to go through all that bureaucracy. But the blight will come through. Any fool can look around here and see that the Hill District's not fit to live in." Later in the play, he declares, "Sometimes you got to prime the pump. That's what gets the motor of big business going. The blight's good for everybody. It'll come through" (47). Finally, when the positive word comes from city hall, Hicks yells, "Blight! Blight! Blight! Blight!" (49), and then they break into a chorus of "Hail, Hail, the Gang's All Here."[3] As the play proceeds, however, we see that Wilks and Hicks come to terms in quite different ways with the contradiction of having the neighborhood declared blighted.

Wilks and Hicks both appear to be somewhat cut adrift from their African American roots. In discussing the social structure bearing on the characters of Wilson's plays, Harry Elam states that white hegemony is often not visible but is always present (*Past* 152; see also Üsekes). Although most characters in Wilson's other plays live in an entirely African American environment, white hegemony nevertheless makes itself known through actions such as police brutality and labor violence that may have a large impact on the characters even if it takes place offstage. In *Radio Golf*, however, three of the five main characters—Wilks; his wife, Mame; and Hicks—seem firmly entrenched in the black middle class and are willing participants in the mainstream economic and social structure. Wilks's roots are local—he grew up in the Hill and inherited his father's real estate business—but he has not lived in the area for more than twenty-five years. Well-connected and with political as well as economic ambitions, he is about to announce his candidacy for mayor of Pittsburgh. Hicks works for Mellon Bank, founded by Andrew Mellon, a leading early-twentieth-century Pittsburgh robber baron, industrialist, and philanthropist who briefly served as secretary of the treasury but resigned facing impeachment. Hicks has developed a close relationship with a white businessman of questionable ethics to obtain assistance in financing the purchase of a local radio station. Mame, a public relations executive, is seriously being considered for a top position in the governor's office. Hicks and Wilks are both devoted golfers, and their participation in the sport reveals their desire for inclusion in the world of the white movers and shakers of Pittsburgh. Mame makes reference to an expensive Cuban cigar that her husband purchased on a trip to Costa Rica, revealing the couple's comfort with being cosmopolitan world travelers. So in this play, white hegemony is not just present but visible through these educated, successful, and ambitious characters' connections to the larger world outside the Hill.

Wilson also makes a point in the speech of these three main characters. Almost all Wilson's characters in his previous plays were poor or working-class and spoke in an urban vernacular that Wilson uses to great effect (Cook). On the other hand, most of the conversation among Wilks, Hicks, and Mame is laced with the jargon of urban redevelopment terminology, as if to make a point that the romance of the colorful language of the urban vernacular has been squeezed out of the very way they communicate. Their neolanguage is now laced with words like "bureaucracy," "redevelopment," "demolition fees," "infrastructure," and "groundbreaking ceremony."

Early on, we see that Hicks and Mame seem completely comfortable with their embrace of the neoliberal urban vision. They have no familial connection to the Hill District and view the proposed redevelopment solely as a potential avenue for economic gain. Wilks appears to be conflicted, however, and holds some opinions that are not completely consonant with the neoliberal vision. While he has not lived in the neighborhood for many years, he does have a strong family connection to his grandfather and his father. His father was a successful neighborhood businessman during a time when avenues for attaining middle-class status were found only within the black community. As revealed in *Radio Golf* and *Gem of the Ocean*, the play written just before *Radio Golf*, his father and grandfather may not have been nice people, but at least from his father he learned that serving the community and achieving financial success did not need to be mutually exclusive. So even though Wilks has partially embraced the neoliberal vision, he also perceives himself to be an altruistic businessman with a genuine interest in improving the community. However, it is not long before the contradictions in his thinking are revealed. Eventually, he experiences an identity crisis and then a transformation when he realizes that the neoliberal vision that he has embraced and is acting out comes at a high price, perhaps a higher price than he is willing to play.

The two other characters in the play, introduced after the middle-class milieu is clearly established, serve as intruders into this hegemony and as reminders of the long, conflicted history of the Hill District and—for Wilks in particular—as links to his family and perhaps through blood memory to more ancient connections to African Americans and Africans. Sterling Johnson, a self-employed contractor and handyman, and Elder Joseph (Old Joe) Barlow enter Wilks's office, and over the course of the play it is revealed that the connections between these characters and Wilks are deeper than first imagined. These two new characters speak more like the characters in Wilson's other plays. Their language is infused with a poetic black vernacular.[4] The following passage taken from Old Joe's initial meeting with Wilks in the real estate office exemplifies Wilson's use of language to contrast the class positions of the characters in *Radio Golf*:

> OLD JOE: Everybody knows Wilks Realty. Right up on the corner there. I used to know your daddy. I ain't gonna say nothing about him. My mama told me if you can't say something nice about somebody don't say nothin'. Your daddy was a big man like you. He didn't have no truck with the little man. He always drew a line like that. He put the little man on one side and the big man on the other. My mama say everybody on the bed or everybody on the floor. (26)

A large part of the conflict in the play revolves around an abandoned house at 1839 Wylie Avenue. (Interestingly, while many of the places in Wilson's plays are real locations in the neighborhood, 1839 Wylie Avenue is imaginary, actually existing as an empty lot in the Hill District today, although it is located near the center of his life during much of his childhood and early adulthood.) Hicks and Wilks plan to tear the house down in order to build their new project. In *Radio Golf,* initially, we do not know the significance of this house, but in the sweep of the Pittsburgh Cycle we know that it carries tremendous historical and symbolic significance.

In *Radio Golf,* we gradually come to know that Old Joe Barlow actually owns the house, but the house was sold illegally to Harmond Wilks Realty and subsequently to Bedford Hills Redevelopment, Inc. Back taxes were owed on the house, which made it eligible for sale, but no public notice was given, as required by law, when the house was sold at a public auction. Mysteriously, Wilks finds out that the taxes on this house were paid by his own father for many years while members of Barlow's family were living in it. Old Joe complains that he didn't know that he had to pay taxes on the house, as they were secretly being paid by Wilks's father. Wilks admires the structure and architectural details of the house and perhaps feels some closer tie to it that he cannot yet explain. At a point later in the play, he says to Hicks, "You should feel the woodwork. If you run your hand slow over some of the wood you can make out these carvings. These faces. An old language" (62).

As the play continues, the relationship between Wilks and Old Joe Barlow becomes clear. Wilks's grandfather, Caesar Wilks, was half brother to Black Mary, Barlow's mother, who lived at 1839 Wiley Avenue. The relationship between the grandfather and Black Mary is explored in *Gem of the Ocean,* which takes place entirely inside this house. The house as a place of great symbolic significance resonates from the beginning to the end of the Wilson century. Furthermore, while an encounter is only obliquely alluded to, we can assume that another character in *Gem,* Citizen Barlow, bore a son with Black Mary—namely, the Old Joe of *Radio Golf.* In drawing these connections, Wilson is highlighting the intertwined symbolism of home, place, and family.

Johnson provides a less directly familial but perhaps even more symbolically important connection to 1839 Wylie Avenue. He informs Wilks that Aunt Ester lived in this house and that he went to see her in 1969 for spiritual guidance, a scene chronicled in *Two Trains Running.* Aunt Ester is a seer figure who is referenced in several of Wilson's plays, appears in *Gem of the Ocean,* is an off-stage character in *Two Trains Running,* and dies in *King Hedley II* in 1987. She is said to be 289 years old in *Gem* and dies in *King Hedley* at the age of 366, and is according to Wilson the most important character in his Pittsburgh Cycle (Caywood and Floyd; Wilson, Preface [2005]). Even though she is not present in most of Wilson's play, she performs the role of a wise sage and "conjurer" who offers spiritual sustenance and enlightenment to those who seek her counsel, evoking the power of Ashe (Elam, *Past* 186). The house at 1839 Wylie Avenue carries the traces not only of the migrations of African Americans from the South to northern industrial cities such as Pittsburgh but also, through Aunt

Ester, of their past: slavery, the Middle Passage, and Africa. The home of Aunt Ester is imbued with a West African cosmology that is always "in the process of stretching back to Africa and into the future" (xix) where "the past, present and future coexist and continually interact" (8).

When Wilks finds out that Old Joe is the rightful owner of the house, he offers compensation of $10,000 and insists that the house still needs to be torn down. However, Old Joe refuses the payment and wants to stick with the plan of fixing the house up so his daughter can live in it. Wilks quite readily agrees and quickly redraws plans for the development that saves the house. Upon seeing the new design plans, however, his partner strongly reacts, telling Wilks that "that old man is crazy" and that Old Joe's ownership of the house could all be explained away by a "technicality" (48). In the following dialogue, we see Harmond Wilks beginning to transition away from Roosevelt Hicks's neoliberal stance and taking small steps to reveal his more inclusive right to the city sympathies:

> (*Harmond unwraps the parcel. It is a new rendering that features a photograph of 1839 Wylie preserved with the complex built around it.*)
>
> ROOSEVELT. What the fuck is that?
>
> HARMOND. It's a relatively easy adjustment. See . . . we pull back the south wing . . . all we lose in the long run are thirty-two parking spaces.
>
> ROOSEVELT. What the fuck is that ugly-ass house sitting there for?
>
> HARMOND. Mr. Barlow wouldn't accept the payment for his house.
>
> ROOSEVELT. So what? He didn't take the money proves he's crazy. Put the ten thousand back in your pocket where it belongs.
>
> HARMOND. He won't accept compensation because the house isn't for sale. We have no choice but to build around it. We don't own the house.
>
> ROOSEVELT. Harmond, where you at, man? That's a dead issue. I don't care now if the Pope owned it. Come Thursday that house is history . . .
>
> HARMOND. I have a lot invested in it too. We can still do the plan. We're just altering it. We can't tear down a house we don't own. It's the law.

The Transformation of Harmond Wilks

The last third of the play portrays Wilks's transformation, which begins when Hicks informs Wilks that the development plan is unraveling. The end of the play charts Wilks's evolving comprehension of the power of place, memory, and identity as he grasps the importance of 1839 Wiley Avenue. He thereby gains an integrity that is consonant with the "right to the city" vision. His efforts to save the house involve far more than upholding his legal obligations. The house begins to represent his own family's history and the cultural memory of thousands of African Americans, including Aunt Ester, who have imprinted their lives on the Hill District. The symbolic weight of this house is just too great to be swept aside in the name of neighborhood redevelopment. Wilks's transformation includes his beginning to see the danger in carrying through a neoliberal urban vision. He is also coming to understand the neighborhood as a lived space, in which community and community relationships are more important than economic profitability. Ultimately, Wilks sees the meaning of the right to the city and that embracing this vision is not without a cost and will involve a struggle.

There are moments in the play that reflect a "right to the city" worldview. The first can be captured in the dialogue of and about Old Joe and Sterling Johnson. Embedded in the dialogue is the notion of a spatial practice, highlighting the ways that everyday activities create an emotional connection of people with their neighborhood and city. Hicks enters the real estate office flustered and incredulous. He says that he encountered a man (Old Joe) painting an abandoned house:

> HARMOND. Why is he painting the house?
> ROOSEVELT. He says it's his property. . . .
> HARMOND. Did he stop painting the house?
> ROOSEVELT. When I left he was sitting down resting. Had the paintbrush in his hand. . . . I told him I was gonna send the police to make him stop. He just started laughing. (17)

A second juncture centers on Sterling's story about a "fried chicken place around the corner." Sterling informs Wilks that on "Saturday night the line would stretch clean around the corner." Silencing these spatial practices has had a long history in the Hill, often with tragic human consequences. Old Joe states, "They tore that [place] down. June 28, 1974. Miss Harriet closed her restaurant for the last time and walked straight from there to the hospital. They didn't know what was wrong with her. . . . She died three or four days after that" (43). He goes on to relate a similar story about a "Sam Green, a black man used to own a grocery store down on Fullerton Street." Arrested in a white neighborhood for "looking suspicious," they "[h]ad to haul him away in a straitjacket" (57). The point of these stories is that local business people who served the community in the past, who were valued by the community, and who were life forces in the community were swept aside by an abstract vision that turned lived space into property viewed only in terms of future capitalist real estate development. Old Joe says that the tests revealed "she had a broken heart" and then adds that her place was torn down and nothing has been built there for the last twenty years (43–44). Similarly, the Green story hinges on success or positive community networks and patronage in one neighborhood and suspicion in another.

A final confrontation that reflects a spatial practice invoking the right to the city occurs as the impending destruction of 1839 Wylie Avenue looms. With two bulldozers parked in front of the house, Mame describes the scene. This moment in the play represents the tension between the two contrasting visions. She reports to Wilks and Hicks what she sees as a "party," unable to recognize it as a community rally organized to liberate 1839 Wiley Avenue from the bulldozers:

> MAME. There's a bunch of people up there too. They're passing out these flyers. (*Reads from the flyers.*) "Come one, come all. Paint party, 1839 Wylie Avenue. Thursday, ten A.M." That's just what they're having . . . a party. Got music blasting. Got the barbeque cooking. Kids running around. Looks like the Fourth of July." (71)

The conflict over the house at 1839 Wylie Avenue, the efforts by Wilks to save the house through redesign of the redevelopment project, Old Joe's hiring Sterling to paint the house so his daughter can live there, and the neighborhood house-painting party all represent small-scale but concrete examples of how this "right to the city" movement occurs through the actual spatial practices of urban citizens. Wilson places Wilks within the flow of historical events, past and present, and so Wilks's private transformation must be also seen as a community act. Finally, this act of claiming community is one Wilson desires for all communities at the end of the twentieth century.

On a material level, Wilks loses a great deal. A newspaper article raising allegations of "backroom dealings" involving real estate property in the Hill dashes his mayoral candidacy (74). The entire redevelopment project is in jeopardy. His partner, Hicks, threatens to buy him out of the development company so the original plans can proceed. Finally, although Mame appears willing to stand by her man, she has forfeited her chances of obtaining the job as the governor's press representative because of bad publicity surrounding Wilks's real estate deals. It is clear that she is deeply disappointed in her husband.

At the end of the play, it is uncertain whether the house at 1839 Wylie Avenue will be demolished. Perhaps Wilson ends the play in this way in order to force the audience to ponder the potential loss of the house and the significance of that loss. He raises the question whether indeed those claiming a right to the city can ever be successful in standing up to powerful political and economic interests. However, it is quite clear that on a personal level, Wilks has declined the Faustian bargain and will be able to maintain his pride and integrity no matter how uncertain the future. In a final gesture, he picks up a paintbrush and exits, on his way to join the house-painting party. For Wilks, his place-based connections to the Hill District and his obligations to his familial memory, to Aunt Ester, and to Africans and African Americans everywhere, prove more compelling than his desire for economic gain. He comes to realize that his participation in the neoliberal urban vision would come at too high a price.

Urban Theory and August Wilson in the Classroom

An application of urban theory to Wilson's emphasis on place as a connection among past, present, and future deepens the experience of reading or viewing *Radio Golf*. In this last section, we provide some guidance on how these ideas can be introduced to students. Some students, especially those who are familiar with Wilson's other plays, may find the subject matter and the characters of *Radio Golf* disconcerting. Indeed, some critics argue that *Radio Golf* is Wilson's least accessible and least poetic play.[5] In one of the strongest criticisms, David Rooney ruminates that "something is missing from the central character, his shifting moral compass seemingly ruled not by inner workings but by narrative necessity." But we maintain that although the conflict in the plot may have been triggered by the circumstances surrounding Wilks's lack of ownership of the house at 1839 Wylie Avenue, Wilks is simultaneously experiencing an inner conflict that moves beyond his response to narrative circumstances. Applying the concept of contrasting urban visions adds a level of complexity to his transformation and character that some critics may have missed.

Professors and students of theater and dramatic literature do not need to become experts in urban geography and urban theory to apply their insights to *Radio Golf*. Exposure to a handful of readings can suffice in facilitating a discussion of the primary internal conflict detailed in this essay. In addition to readings, some provocative study questions can be assigned to facilitate a discussion on the urban and how Wilson addresses questions related to alternative urban visions. We suggest assigned readings for students. Comprising no more than fifty to seventy-five pages, they can provide an introductory framework for these conceptual debates.

For a generalized exposition of the postindustrial transformation, the rise of neoliberal urban policies, and the role of gentrification in these policies, Neil Smith's "New Globalism, New Urbanism: Globalization as Global Urban Strategy" serves as a good introduction. Laurence Glasco's "The Hill and the African American Experience" and Glasco and Rawson's *August Wilson: Pittsburgh Places in his Life and Plays* provide a brief but concise history of the Hill District that places the play in its specific geographic context.

The instructor must also provide the students with material that shows the articulation of the two urban visions. Academic writing defending neoliberal urbanism is not very common, but the neoliberal perspective has been actively promoted by a few American think tanks. A typical and effective exposition of the think-tank perspective is Myron Magnet's introduction to *The Millennial City: A New Urban Paradigm for Twenty-First-Century America*. A number of other essays in that book, all of which endorse free-market approaches to urban governance and a withdrawal from municipal government concerns with social welfare, could be assigned to provide a similar argument. Finally, a short planning or policy document espousing a neoliberal viewpoint would be an effective way of introducing the language of urban neoliberalism echoed in the language of *Radio Golf*'s three middle-class characters. The "right to the city" vision is concisely encapsulated in "Whose City Is It Anyway?," a brief polemic that provides a history of neoliberal urbanism in four paragraphs as well as a call to action against its excesses (Lipman). The previously mentioned "The Right to the City," by Harvey, is a short but theoretically sophisticated discussion that not only presents the conceptual underpinnings of this vision but also reveals its inherently oppositional nature. Chapter 3 of the UNESCO report *Urban Policies and the Right to the City* (Brown and Kristiansen 13–17) offers a briefer and less theoretically dense exposition of the ideas and so would be particularly appropriate for lower-level students. Finally, "Anti-Gentrification Rebels" (Singh) is a four-page article describing two examples of the "right to the city" movement in practice, including one example from Pittsburgh's Hill District, where local activists (including Kimberly Ellis, Wilson's niece) and residents successfully blocked a proposal for a new civic arena that would have involved further demolition in the lower blocks of the neighborhood.

In addition to these readings, study questions should be distributed in order to facilitate class discussion. (For a set of these questions, see the appendix to this essay.) First, instructors should take some time to ensure that students understand the basic conceptual framework of the two opposing urban visions. In this discussion, instructors may need to clarify the difference between neoliberalism as a free-market economic perspective and the common use of the term *liberal* in American politics. Next, as a simple introductory question, students should be able to identify which characters represent the two opposing visions. Students then will be asked to identify specific examples in the plot that demonstrate those visions. A more complicated question is the internal transformation of Wilks. He represents the most interesting entry point into these urban visions, given his internal conflict, which is absent in the other characters. As the play proceeds, students will identify events or statements that point to contradictions within him and portend a shift in his viewpoint. Finally, instructors should turn the students' attention to the events at the end of the play that reveal the transformation of Wilks and his embrace of the "right to the city" vision—his rapid acceptance that Elder Joseph Barlow is the rightful owner of the property, his rapid redrawing of plans to save the house at 1839 Wylie Avenue, his refusal to capitulate to Hicks's and Mame's admonitions not to change any of the redevelopment plans, and his ultimate decision to join the house-painting party in a direct act of opposition, even if the consequences include his being shut out of the development's potential profits and the jeopardizing of his mayoral candidacy. (At the end of the play, Wilks is very clear in his intent to side with the neighborhood residents in asserting their right to the city. His act of picking up a paintbrush and putting on war paint—an obvious allusion to the similar plight of Native Americans' having their land confiscated—indicate that he has undergone a rapid but radical change.)

Another helpful exercise would be for students to identify specific places within the Hill District and discuss their importance to the characters and plot and how they represent the symbolic significance of place. Students attending universities in metropolitan areas can also be asked to identify communities in their own region where similar processes of gentrification and redevelopment are occurring and what conflicts have arisen in these communities.

In a creative or practice-oriented classroom, instructors can move beyond the text and class discussion. Students can be grouped according to place (region, city, state) and instructed to create a project that performs that place. In their creations, they should be sensitive to the current narratives around that particular place. The salient narrative may revolve around something other than gentrification and redevelopment. For example, it could be about a suburban area experiencing a dramatic increase in the immigrant population, a small town with few and declining job opportunities, or even a natural disaster such as a devastating hurricane or tornado. Instructors should encourage students to include several forms of artistic expression, including music, poetry, visual arts, and sections of novels. While such a detailed investigation of concepts of place and community would not be appropriate for general survey or theater appreciation courses, using *Radio Golf* to stimulate a process of creating a performance in an acting class or theater practicum might serve as an effective foundation for an entire teaching unit.

In upper-level or graduate classes where students are familiar with Wilson's other plays or where Wilson's work is treated in a broader context, the themes in *Radio Golf* that connect to previous plays can also be introduced. Wilson explores themes of urban policy in relation to urban decline and renewal in *Jitney* and *Two Trains Running.* In *Jitney,* an unlicensed cabstand is threatened with demolition, and in *Two Trains Running* the city wants to tear down a restaurant for an urban renewal project. (In *Radio Golf,* redevelopment is a real possibility, while in the plays set in earlier decades it is uncertain that any rebuilding will follow the demolition.) The symbolic significance of 1839 Wylie Avenue as ancestral home is clearest in *Gem of the Ocean,* the only play to take place within that house. However, the importance of home and place in the urban environment are woven throughout the fabric of the entire Pittsburgh Cycle, including but not limited to the boardinghouse in *Joe Turner's Come and Gone,* Troy's fences in *Fences,* and the gathering places and homes in *Jitney* and *Two Trains Running.*

Wilson's Pittsburgh Cycle provides an opportunity to investigate the trajectory of urban America, the frequently harmful influence of urban policy on inner-city neighborhoods, the importance of place, and the spatial practices implicated in making a place. Through his characters, Wilson investigates how African Americans have reacted individually and collectively to their changing communities throughout various stages of dynamism, upheaval, and decline. It is in *Radio Golf,* however, when the Hill District is in a nascent stage of gentrification, where contemporary issues regarding the possible futures of urban America take front and center stage.

Although we have presented the conflict of *Radio Golf* in the context of two competing urban visions, the neoliberal vision and the "right to the city" vision, in practice they are open to blurring and negotiation. Indeed, Wilks's suggested redesign of the redevelopment project is an attempt to integrate these two visions. Wilson, however, is very clear regarding his sympathies: the neoliberal vision has been a detriment to urban neighborhoods and an assault on African Americans. Although in *Radio Golf* the redevelopment might bring long-needed economic development to the Hill, Wilson mourns that in a neighborhood that has already lost much of its poetry, language, and song, further improvement will only erase any remaining memory from the Hill District and render it soulless.

Three of the main characters in *Radio Golf* represent an upwardly mobile African American middle class that Wilson did not portray to any great extent in his previous plays. These characters present a challenge to an audience who may expect the rich language of the urban vernacular embodied in almost all Wilson's other characters. Understanding the characters in *Radio Golf* in the context of contemporary American urbanism can enrich the understanding and the appreciation of this play for readers and audiences. At this particular juncture in history (1997) and in Wilson's life (2005), Harmond Wilks is placed very intentionally at center stage in this drama. Just as Wilson interrogates the Faustian bargain that Wilks ultimately declines, Wilson also challenges the audience to interrogate their own duplicity or active participation in an urban vision that he believes can only lead to a loss of community. He also challenges audiences to consider whether those claiming the "right to the city" can be any match for the powerful structural economic forces and accompanying forms of urban governance that work against democratic participation in urban life.

NOTES

[1] Bogumil examines how Wilson used oral tradition with the intent of exploring the mythical dimensions of the past rather than creating objective historical accounts. Elam revisits the major issues, ideas, and arguments within the Wilson canon, placing particular importance on the historiographical concept of "blood memory" (xvii–xviii, 175, 188, 202–06). Shannon examines how Wilson employs credible historical situations to inform contemporary audiences about the struggles of African Americans and examines the effect of racism on the lives of African Americans during various periods of United States history. All three authors share an interest in the importance of memory in his plays and of his desire to examine the historical contexts that helped create African American culture.

[2] The term *neoliberalism*, as it has come to be understood in the last twenty-five years, is primarily an economic concept. The neoliberal perspective proposes that a free-market economy that avoids excessive regulation and promotes free trade is essential to the

success of a country, region, or city. In an increasingly globalizing economy, adopting free-market principles becomes even more important as countries compete with one another in a global marketplace. The rule of the market as operated by private companies and businesses is viewed as promoting the greatest efficiency and wealth for the most people (Mudge). American students who are not familiar with this term often misinterpret its meaning, as they primarily encounter the word *liberalism* as a political construct. While liberal American political philosophy may incorporate notions of individual rights, American liberal political philosophy also argues for a strong government presence and intervention not only in the economic arena but also in the social arena and usually voices support of policies of income redistribution and programs that serve the less fortunate. Proponents of the neoliberal economic philosophy, however, would generally argue that funneling resources for social programs is an unnecessary use of government money and a drain on the economy, in that it diverts capital and human energy away from market activities. The use of the term *neoliberal* in association with urban governance strategies followed the turn toward neoliberal economic strategies, which were on the rise in the 1980s (Hackworth 10–12, 26–27). Local urban governments increasingly structured their policies, budget priorities, and decision making to complement and support, rather than contradict, the neoliberal economic policies. This meant turning away from previously implemented service-oriented strategies that assisted or at least paid lip service to the needs of poorer and more vulnerable residents. Instead governments pursued urban strategies that privileged the actions of the private real estate market. It would be a mistake, however, to equate the decline of government resources away from social services with embracing a philosophy of complete retreat from public funding. In fact, an integral part of the neoliberal urban governance strategy involved providing extensive public subsidies to private developers undertaking both large- and small-scale redevelopment projects.

[3] The use of "Hail, Hail, the Gang's All Here" is curious, and to the best of our knowledge Wilson did not discuss his use of this song. The words were written in 1917 by D. S. Esrom to a melody originally written by Arthur Sullivan in 1879 for the comic opera *Pirates of Penzance*. The song became popular and was frequently sung in group settings. Wilson frequently used the blues in his productions as a way to emphasize the connection of the blues to African American history and culture. Perhaps in choosing this popular mainstream song rather than using the blues, he was highlighting the upper-middle-class status of Wilks and Hicks and the lack of connection to their cultural roots. "Hail, Hail, the Gang's All Here" also was used as a fight song by college football teams. Wilks and Hicks were roommates at Cornell University, and one review suggests that "the blues and gospel from Wilson's earlier work has been traded in for Ivy League harmony" ("*Radio Golf*").

[4] For further information on the rules that govern speech, see Finegan and Rickford; Smitherman, *Talkin That Talk*.

[5] Complaining about the original New Haven production, Ben Brantley, a *New York Times* critic, wrote that the "characters have never seemed more in danger of being songless" and that "the play itself falls prey to an addling preoccupation with the mechanics of business." David Rooney in *Variety* states that in employing the stilted language of real estate developers, the play resorts to "sacrificing much of the singing lyricism and quasi-mythic qualities that give Wilson's best works their incomparable bluesy texture and piercing depth."

APPENDIX: SUGGESTED QUESTIONS FOR CLASSROOM DISCUSSION ON OPPOSING URBAN VISIONS IN AUGUST WILSON'S *RADIO GOLF*

1. What places in *Radio Golf* are important to the plot or help create a sense of place in the play? Why are these particular places important?
2. What is neoliberalism? Describe the neoliberal urban vision.
3. Describe the "right to the city" urban vision.
4. Which characters in the play represent and embody these two visions?
5. Identify specific passages or interactions between characters where the neoliberal vision is represented.
6. Identify specific passages or interactions between characters where the "right to the city vision" is represented.
7. What clues do we have that Wilks is experiencing an inner conflict between these two urban visions?
8. What actions in the play point to his transformation from one urban vision to another?
9. (Optional). Are there neighborhoods in your city or metropolitan area (or where the college or university is located) where similar conflicts over gentrification and redevelopment have occurred? What has been the outcome of these conflicts?

Lesson Plans for the Millennial Student: An Interdisciplinary Course Inspired by the Plays of August Wilson

Sandra G. Shannon

> Under no circumstances should a student text or talk on his/her cell phone during regular class time. . . . Students are expected to remove all Bluetooth devices upon entering the classroom. . . . Students may not come to nor sit through this class with headphones in his/her ears . . . Students may use open laptop computers for note-taking purposes only.

Over the last decade, standard operating procedures in my classes have involved setting parameters for students whom researchers have recently dubbed "the millennial generation" or those who entered college after the year 2000.[1] On day 1 of each semester, members of this eternally wired population who enter my classes have been invariably met with a litany of dos and don'ts on proper classroom etiquette. My opening-day ritual of calling attention to a host of zero-tolerance measures, such as those listed above, proved to be a feeble attempt to preempt any possible misuse of an ever-encroaching cache of communication devices smuggled into or blatantly displayed in the learning space. Less than one week into the semester, these students manage to adopt a host of ingenious ways to circumvent these policies and to avoid detection. With cell phones and laptops in their usual inconspicuous positions, many apparently saw then and still see now no wrong in dividing their attention between engaging the course content and finagling with their devices. When discovered and subsequently exposed, many would argue (often unconvincingly) that their technological contraband was crucial to their note-taking and real-time access to additional information on the topic at hand. I was waging a losing battle against what then seemed to be a ubiquitous foe.

Millennial students were the bane of my existence for a while—until I discovered, through my own research, that they were part of a contemporary demographic birthed by a culture immersed in and fascinated by portable communication devices. As I learned from Diana Oblinger's essay "Boomers, Gen-Xers, Millennials: Understanding the New Students," they "have never known life without computers and the Internet. To them, the computer is not technology—it is an assumed part of life" (40). Comments made by Richard Sweeney, a New Jersey Institute of Technology librarian, during an October 2007 EDUCAUSE conference echo this sentiment.[2] In a panel discussion entitled "Disconnects between Library Culture and Millennial Generation User Values," Sweeney described today's college-aged students as

> a huge generation of impatient, experiential learners, digital natives, multitaskers, and gamers who love the flat, networked world and expect nomadic connectivity, 24x7. More importantly, they are demanding consumers who expect more selectivity, personalization, and customization in their products and services. They are the Millennials (a.k.a. NextGen, GenY, C Generation, M Generation, and Echo Boomers), the generation born 1979 through 1994.

Curriculum 21: Essential Education for a Changing World shed additional light for me on the mind-set of the wired students that I encounter:

> Today's students have the frontal lobe of their brains stimulated by video games, television, cellular devices, and instantaneous Web-based communication for many hours each day. One of the common causes of boredom in the classroom is students' perception that the methods of how the curriculum is delivered to them are irrelevant to how they learn. (199)

Additional research led me to Neil Howe and William Strauss, historians who have studied and written extensively on generational dynamics. Their *Millennials Go to College* characterizes this age group as "the first generation in history to grow up in a digital age, "[who] expect non-stop interaction with their peer group in ways that would have been unimaginable in previous generations of youth" (121).

What these sources have in common is their certainty that any attempts to control the flow of technology into the classroom would prove to be futile for today's college-aged students. Educators therefore should adjust their approaches to learning in order to keep pace with the world that the millennials inhabit. Heidi Jacobs, a curriculum specialist, puts it this way: "As educators, our challenge is to match the needs of our learners to a world that is changing with great rapidity. To meet this challenge we need to become strategic learners ourselves by deliberately expanding our perspectives and updating our approaches" ("New Essential Curriculum").

The Need

My students' short-lived adherence to course policies, their joined-at-the-hip communication devices, and my newfound knowledge about their generation moved me to explore ways to think like a student but act like a professor. This approach proved to be especially useful in redesigning lesson plans with the millennial student in mind. My ability to connect with members of the Net generation was significantly improved by my involvement in Howard University's recent push to infuse its undergraduate curriculum with more emphasis upon interdisciplinary teaching and research and to help students discover meaningful connections among the disciplines. Standing in My Grandfather's Shoes: An Interdisciplinary Course Inspired by the Plays of August Wilson was a step in this direction.

When several workshops on interdisciplinary teaching and research were offered during June 2011—compliments of the Andrew Mellon Foundation—Howard University faculty members gathered from disciplines as varied as music, African studies, English, and law to devise effective syllabi for pilot courses grounded in this approach. At the close of these workshops, the group had conceptualized and constructed an eclectic array of shovel-ready syllabi that they believed would encourage students to generate research questions by analyzing a problem from more than one disciplinary perspective, to infer what researchers from two or more disciplines would need to know to solve a problem, and to integrate into their projects research approaches from two or more disciplines to solve difficult problems or explore complex issues in original ways. Workshop leaders were determined that the syllabi produced would enhance the undergraduate research experience.[3]

The August Wilson Society (AWS), a Howard University–based learning community composed of faculty members from the departments African Studies, History, Philosophy, Psychology, Theatre Arts, English, African American Studies, Art, and Music, took a keen interest in these Mellon-sponsored workshops.[4] From its inception in spring 2006, this eclectic gathering of Howard's faculty understood that August Wilson's plays were inherently interdisciplinary in the various intersecting disciplines represented in each play in the cycle. They also understood that a multidisciplinary group of faculty members such as this could find no better common subjects than ten plays teeming with African American cultural referents. The group's automatic embrace of interdisciplinarity and its gravitation toward the plays of Wilson therefore went hand in hand.

The AWS perceives itself as a model for cross-disciplinary collaboration. Its members see in the university's advancement of interdisciplinarity in the classroom an opportunity to breathe life into Wilson's plays for millennials while simultaneously diminishing the traditional silos that so often stifle creativity and suppress the development of community within the ivory towers of academia. Just as important, they see this push toward interdisciplinarity in the classroom as a way for each to highlight, through the prisms of their respective disciplines, Wilson's efforts to uplift African American culture—that is, to put it in the playwright's own words, "to focus on what I felt were the most important issues confronting black Americans for that decade, so ultimately they could stand as a record of black experience over the past hundred years presented in the form of dramatic literature" ("Interview" [Powers] 5). In effect, members of the AWS considered the playwright's agenda to be in sync with Howard University's historical focus upon topics of importance about Africa and the African diaspora.

The Planning

My colleagues and I were sold on the benefits of an interdisciplinary approach to teaching and learning, but the course that was our brainchild proved that a marriage between this approach and Wilson's ten-play cycle—from *Gem of the*

Ocean to *Radio Golf*—worked beautifully. Much of the credit for this outcome must be attributed to the painstaking early efforts of the society to conceptualize and design the course and, just as important, to enlist a group of knowledgeable and willing professors to bring it to life. In the planning phase, we identified five major themes that come out of the African American cultural experience and that manifest in various ways in Wilson's Pittsburgh Cycle plays: African systems of thought, the Middle Passage, the Great Migration, the psychology of slavery; and the Harlem Renaissance.

As the Mellon workshops progressed, I realized that my colleagues and I shared a distinct advantage. Even before notices of the interdisciplinary initiative reached the Howard University faculty community, the AWS had made significant headway toward designing a common syllabus to introduce students from across Howard University's curriculum to interdisciplinary learning by way of Wilson's ten-play cycle. Months earlier, we had hammered out details of lesson plans, course objectives, challenging research questions, classroom assignments, strategic reading lists, and ultimately we had a shovel-ready syllabus that was based on the principles of interdisciplinary teaching and learning.

During the several months following the Mellon workshops and leading up to the spring 2012 launch of the interdisciplinary course Standing in My Grandfather's Shoes, I worked closely with the chair of the Theatre Arts Department to identify and recruit members of the AWS to become interdisciplinary teaching and research teams. Their mission was to apply interdisciplinary lenses to five predetermined themed topics that emerge from Wilson's ten plays and that spotlight both triumphs and tragedies of African American life from 1904 to 1997: African systems of thought, the impact and implications of the Middle Passage, the Great Migration (was it a mistake or destiny?), the psychology of slavery, and cultural capital, claims, and commodification during the Harlem Renaissance. The results of this unique collaboration was the course syllabus. The course description underscores interdisciplinarity as an especially effective approach to teaching the plays of August Wilson:

> This course identifies as its starting place the ten-play cycle of one of America's greatest playwrights of the twentieth and twenty-first centuries: August Wilson. By applying an interdisciplinary lens to his so-called "Century Plays," the course will introduce new ways of illuminating the black experience in America from Emancipation and Reconstruction eras on through to more recent cultural and historical watershed moments in African American life. Most significantly, this new way of reading the black experience through drama will draw upon expertise offered by Howard University faculty from a range of disciplines, including African Studies, English, Philosophy, Art, History, and Music. This new way of reading Wilson, in particular, and African American Drama, in general, will set the stage for the discussion of potential research topics that are embedded in other important African American texts.[5]

To make sure that Standing in My Grandfather's Shoes was truly interdisciplinary and that it provided students with a window to see meaningful connections in Wilson's plays, designers of the syllabus took great care in selecting thematic units and in pairing representatives from various disciplines. As the course outline that materialized demonstrates, these five multidisciplined teams of professors were strategically paired according to their fields to explore the interdisciplinary implications of themes in two or more of Wilson's plays. Each set of instructors was tasked with collaborating in the design of a challenging learning unit based upon one of the five themes that emerge from Wilson's Pittsburgh Cycle. To ensure the interplay among disciplines, each teaching unit grappled with two or more of Wilson's plays that reflected, on some level, their respective disciplines. After a significant planning phase, these professors settled upon an approach that included detailed lecture notes, reading assignments, *YouTube* clips, in-class role-playing, in- and out-of-class research and writing projects, and an ongoing e-portfolio construction project.[6]

With the added feature of an embedded librarian, the course proved even more welcoming to millennials, many of whom suffered from familiar reservations about the research process and long hours holed up in a library. The embedded librarian, Celia Daniel, coordinator of research and instruction at Howard University's Founders Library, became an extremely valuable and integral part of the course. Much to the students' delight and benefit, she functioned very much like a teaching assistant—that is, as a troubleshooter in identifying topics on which students needed intervention, and she made herself available for conferences outside the classroom. Frequently, she brought the library to the students and to faculty members wherever they convened. While this floating librarian made her presence known in the classroom, she was also available through digital access, using *Blackboard* as a platform. Among Daniel's most lasting and most valuable contribution to the class was her meticulously researched and student-friendly Web site (http://libguides.howard.edu/augustwilsoninterdisciplinarycourse). Through a link posted on *Blackboard*, the novice student could find, for example, a plethora of biographical information on Wilson, along with key statements by and about the playwright, bibliographies containing supplemental readings, links to other relevant Web sites, posted assignments, and information in support of each of the interdisciplinary teaching units offered.

Daniel also erased quite a few lingering stereotypes and misconceptions about her profession. She insisted upon participating in the class, both as a student and as an instructor, and read the assigned works and participated in the discussions. Not only did she enhance the dynamics of the class with her deep and broad range of knowledge about digital literacy, the library's holdings, and its facilities but she also brought with her an impressive knowledge about Wilson, drama, and African and African American studies. She also urged students in her interactions with them to think more critically about the interplay among the disciplines in Wilson's work. She emphasized as well various research strategies and methodically led students through the process of discovering viable research questions for their term projects. Outside the classroom, she hosted a lab class that focused upon strategies for navigating online sources in the library's arsenal.

Throughout the course, the embedded librarian provided students with customized information. Her sustained interaction with them in class enabled her to teach critical thinking skills and, in collaboration with the lead faculty members, evaluate each student's use of information sources in class discussions, written assignments, and the culminating project or presentation. After the rhythm of the course was established, the embedded librarian delivered a short lecture on Wilson's women in honor of Women's History Month and subsequently worked with acting students in the Theatre Arts Department to present for the class and for the university at large a well-received series of scene reenactments entitled "Exceptional Women in August Wilson's Plays." As the semester progressed, students came to depend upon the library's facilities and the embedded librarian's one-on-one instruction to complete meaningful research projects. Some, no doubt, established relationships with Howard University's library that will extend beyond this class.

The Execution

Standing in My Grandfather's Shoes, put on a fast track to debut in spring 2012, helped dissolve many of my misconceptions about the Net generation students in my charge. Over the fifteen-week span, students who would have been more than likely preoccupied with their gadgets suddenly became active, attentive learners. This noticeable increase in enthusiasm for the course owed much, I believe, to the unorthodox approach to learning that was laid out before them. A factor may also have been the biweekly rotation of a succession of dynamic and well-informed instructors who stood before them—each with his or her unique teaching style and with his or her own discipline-specific reading of Wilson's plays. From the perspective of the student accustomed to changing the scenery by depressing a key on a laptop or on the face of an iPhone, this revolving, *Facebook*-like feature of the class was a welcome change from the single-teacher model to which they had become accustomed.

Despite the frequent instructor turnover, my role as teacher of record in the course was to suggest constancy while at the same time handling the required record-keeping and administrative paperwork and serving as an on-hand resource on Wilson and each of his ten plays. The students appreciated the change of instructors but also responded well to me as a unifying agent. Sitting in the audience among them allowed me to better assess their levels of engagement and understanding of interdisciplinary concepts as applied to Wilson's plays. When my thoughts were trained on colleagues who stood before the class, I could better discern the nuances of their teaching styles as well as the overall effectiveness of the teachers' approaches to interdisciplinarity. Both perspectives allowed me to tell whether my colleagues' lesson plans and their delivery of them were effective. Ultimately, the "fly on the wall" perspective I gained as teacher of record allowed me to float in and out of two roles to collect valuable feedback for improving repeat offerings of this course.

Aware of the strategic importance of requiring students to immerse themselves in Wilson's life, politics, and art before they approached the plays, I assigned them, through *Blackboard* postings, key texts to read *before* day 1 of the class. The most important text, in my estimation, is Wilson's 1996 speech turned manifesto, "The Ground on Which I Stand," which delineates his stance on a number of issues ranging from his ideas on race to financial starvation of black theater due to underfunding. Other key texts include several interviews in Jackson Bryer and Mary Hartig's *Conversations with August Wilson*; Wilson's hot-button essay "I Want a Black Director," in Alan Nadel's collection *May All Your Fences Have Gates*; and Robert Brustein's "The Lesson of *The Piano Lesson*," in the *New Republic.* Both after my lead lectures and at the close of each subsequent teaching segment, students were given assignments to assess their understanding of material covered.

Following my turn at providing a basic introduction to Wilson, students were taught strategies for discovering interdisciplinary connections in a weeklong series of in-class exercises grounded in both text and performance. To encourage them to think outside the box, Kim Bey, from the Theatre Arts Department, played samples of work songs and asked students to interpret what they heard by, first, imagining the different disciplines suggested in the lyrics and, then, translating what they heard into visual images. They were asked to draw tangible symbols of what they heard and asked to explain their choices.

As each new set of instructors introduced students to novel ways of reading Wilson's plays, all agreed to ground their lessons in one of the playwright's most fundamental beliefs: that his characters are Africans in America and therefore must be read and understood as such. That is to say, any assessment of what his African American characters say or do or believe must be made through Afrocentric rather than Eurocentric lenses. This immersion into Wilson's Africanist worldview set the stage for a uniquely revealing examination of his plays.[7]

In the hands of two professors, one from the African Studies Department and one from the African American Studies Department, Africa was given its rightful place of prominence in Standing in My Grandfather's Shoes. At the outset students were schooled in African systems of thought and given specific terminology for discussions that involved Africa's multilayered influence in select plays. Clarification of terms such as *cosmology, deities, ancestors, God almighty, community,* and *African ontology, priests, and priestesses* dominated the early class discussions and galvanized and kept student attention. Instructions for one of several culminating assignments for African systems of thought required students to "research and learn the definition of *ritual,* especially within the context of African and African American cultures. Do a close reading of *Gem of the Ocean, Joe Turner's Come and Gone,* and *The Piano Lesson,* paying special attention to various rituals that are performed throughout the daily lives of the respective casts of characters" (Zewde and Carr). To fulfill this assignment, students were provided with a chart containing examples of rituals, ritual actions as demonstrated through characters, and what these actions symbolize from an Africanist perspective. At the close of the class, the African studies instructor, Ama Oboakyew, offered very helpful feedback on what was attempted and achieved in the segment on African systems of thought:

> In weeks 3 and 4, I wanted to provide students with foundational knowledge of African systems of thought in terms of the African cosmology, worldview, epistemology, and ontology, as well as a working understanding of spiritual praxis and ritual specialists. This information is invaluable for deciphering the African metaphysical ramifications of character and action in *Gem of the Ocean*, *Joe Turner's Come and Gone*, and *The Piano Lesson*. . . . Students were enthusiastically engaged with the materials presented and found numerous correlations with their own spiritual/religious experiences. The success of the lectures depended upon keeping the discourse relevant to students' lives and meeting the students on terms that resonate in their awareness. We were also continuously bridging the gap by associating spiritual and cultural threads within the African Diaspora. It was a joy to teach within such an intellectually diverse class, and at every turn I found their questions challenging and stimulating. I believe that working in tandem with Dr. Carr, the students received a full picture of the historical and spiritual forces that formed the African-centered nucleus of Wilson's plays.

Equal emphasis was placed upon the profound importance of the Middle Passage to an understanding and appreciation of Wilson's plays. Gregory Carr of Howard University's Department of African American Studies gave students solid grounding in historic, geographic, and statistical details of the Middle Passage. For two weeks, he held students spellbound with his encyclopedic knowledge of the African slave trade, with a display of maps and fascinating discussions on the complicit involvement of African peoples in this industry. Wilson's plays targeted for discussion of the influence of the Middle Passage were *Gem of the Ocean* and *Joe Turner's Come and Gone.* Students were then given a writing assignment that required them to view the popular PBS documentary *Slavery by Another Name*. Instructions for the assignment required students to

> discover and formulate a strong thesis argument based upon significant parallels you see between the documentary's presentation of slavery and its portrayal in August Wilson's *Gem of the Ocean, Joe Turner's Come and Gone,* and *The Piano Lesson.* Write an engaging and well-crafted 3–5 page essay that discusses certain nuances in how the documentary and Wilson's play(s) convey "the peculiar institution" of slavery. You must

> reference each of the above three plays in your discussion. Essay must offer a balanced treatment of the documentary and the three plays. The PBS program "Slavery by Another Name," airs on Monday, February 13 from 9 p.m. to 10:30 p.m. After February 14, you can access the program online at PBS.org.

For more information on this program, students are referred to Courtland Milloy's *Washington Post* article "In America, Racial Oppression Is Not Ancient History."

While continuing to expose students to Wilson's African-centered agenda through an interdisciplinary lens, another set of instructors captured the essence of his aesthetic. Their unit, entitled "The Psychology of Slavery," showed students that the psychological repercussions of slavery had to be framed in terms of an African worldview. This section of the course brought together a professor of psychology and a professor of criminal justice. Both had gone through a phase of preplanning during which they conceptualized an interdisciplinary approach that would marry their two disciplines in a way that prompted a new set of challenging critical questions for students to pursue in class discussions and in their research. Six of Wilson's cycle plays—*Gem of the Ocean, Fences, Two Trains Running, Jitney, King Hedley II,* and *Radio Golf*—were selected for this work.

The psychology and criminal justice professors began their teaching unit by demonstrating the complex interrelation between the psychology of oppression and tendencies toward what society has deemed to be criminality among African American males. After students were introduced to some traditional Western perspectives on mental disorders and then given some examples of the realities of today's one-size-fits-all penal system, they were urged to look at the problem from an African perspective.[8] Their exposure to these opposing ideologies positioned them well to later grapple with a similar kind of dichotomy that emerges in most of Wilson's plays. Put simply, Wilson's characters were to be viewed as Africans in America, despite the consternation that this seemingly paradoxical label may cause. This sense of double consciousness is evident in a statement that the two professors shared with students at the beginning of their teaching segment:

> The psychological impact of racism results in a range of behaviors, some of which society may deem abnormal or deviant. However, oppressive forces, including racism and sexism, complicate the already complex problem of defining mental health and mental illness. August Wilson's characters provide us a unique window through which we can view psychological health. In the seminar this week, we will discuss approaches to mental disorders and psychological health found in mainstream psychology and psychiatry. In addition, we will review perspectives on mental health advanced in writings of African-centered behavioral scientists. We will consider definitions of psychological disorders in light of the wisdom

> and tragedy found in the words and lives of women and men in Wilson's plays. Our purpose is to show how Wilson's vivid portrayals actually help resolve some of the perplexing problems that arise in the study of mental health and wellness among African Americans.[9]

Class exercises for this unit of instruction pushed students to find African-centered correlatives to the many mental disorders that Wilson's characters suffer. To further drive this point home, the psychology instructor used a graphic to show students the stark differences between the traditional view of mental disorders and the African-centered view of them. Students were pressed to analyze these differences further in an assignment in which they were instructed to "find in the plays of August Wilson explicit or implicit treatments of mental disorders or mental health," placing characters in each of the quadrants of the "Mental Disorders Classification Table."[10]

Hands down, the most referenced scenes during this exercise were Citizen Barlow's climactic metaphysical journey to the City of Bones in *Gem of the Ocean* and Herald Loomis's convulsive collapse onto the boardinghouse floor in *Joe Turner's Come and Gone*. I witnessed how the students' reactions to and understanding of the symbolic meaning in these spectacles went from expressions of apathy and light chuckles to epiphany. From my vantage point, the instructors succeeded in getting them to see the new meaning by applying African-centered belief systems. Students, moved from the comfort zones of their thinking, were able to challenge Western logic behind the often dismissive and derisive diagnoses of these characters. Loomis's condition, for example, could easily be mislabeled schizophrenia, epilepsy, or dementia, when his recurring nightmares about bones, his thrashing about the floor, and his explosive rage are, within the context of an African belief system, symptoms of his body's rejection of Western codes of conduct and thought, on one hand, and an avowal of African ancestral memory, on the other.

The instructor of criminal justice prefaced her discipline-specific discussion of Wilson's plays with a concentrated overview of some of the principles of her field along with a sobering look at staggering statistics that tied soaring crime rates among young African American males to poverty, lack of education, racism, self-hatred, and a prevailing sense of hopelessness. She then provided students with a reading list that could prepare them for substantive discussions of Wilson's plays from the dual perspectives of psychology and criminal justice.[11]

The jointly conceived interdisciplinary lesson plans made by the professor of psychology and the professor of criminal justice demanded that attention be paid to what underlies correlations between the troubled psyches of Wilson's male characters, such as *Fences*'s Troy Maxson and *Two Trains Running*'s Sterling, and the disproportionate numbers of African American males in this country's penal system. Toward this end, students were directed, during class time, to examine pertinent statistical data as well as several case studies of black male inmates whose sentences were inappropriately harsh for the crimes (in some cases, misdemeanors) that they had been accused of committing. While the criminal justice instructor was careful not to condone any type of criminal activity, she moved students to a more complex level of understanding that was the result of contextualizing these men's violations within a judicial system that, as Wilson often noted, "keeps changing the rules" (see *Radio Golf* 78 and *Jitney* 85). The culminating writing and research assignments from this teaching segment demanded sophisticated critical analysis of any of the cycle plays that entail some form of incarceration—in other words, *Fences, Jitney, Two Trains Running, The Piano Lesson,* and *King Hedley II*.

The unit entitled "The Great Migration: Mistake or Destiny," dealing with issues that pertain to black women migrants, brought together a professor of history and a professor of African American literature and women's studies. Both found common ground in their design of multilayered lectures on women migrants as portrayed, for example, in plays such as *Joe Turner's Come and Gone*, *The Piano Lesson,* and *Fences.* The black woman as migrant is the focus of ongoing research for Elizabeth Clark-Lewis,[12] and it was her umbrella theme for discussing Wilson's plays. Early in her teaching unit, Clark-Lewis captured students' attention with clips of her award-winning documentary *Freedom Bags,* which tells the story of African American women who migrated from the rural South during the first three decades of the twentieth century:

> Hoping to escape from the racism and poverty of the post–Civil War South, these women boarded segregated trains for an uncertain future up North. Having had limited education, most could find jobs only as domestic workers. With spirit and humor, the women remember their tactics for self-preservation in the homes of their employers, where they often faced exploitation and sexual harassment. . . . These were proud women who kept their dignity and sense of worth through difficult times.

With her PBS documentary serving as context and with several scholarly studies adding still more rich material, Clark-Lewis urged students to understand the realities that faced Wilson's Black Mary, Bertha Holly, Mattie Campbell, Molly Cunningham, Martha Pentacost, Rose Maxson, Ruby, Louise, and Vera. She drew from her own book, *Living In, Living Out: African American Domestics and the Great Migration* to fuel a poignant discussion of the challenges facing *The Piano Lesson's* Berniece Charles, who leased herself to work in the homes of affluent whites. Clark-Lewis introduced students to Tera A. Hunter's *To 'Joy My Freedom: Southern Black Women's Lives and Labors after the Civil War* to make clear some of the choices and conciliations forced upon black women such as Black Mary, Bertha, and Martha. Spencer R. Crew's *Field to Factory: Afro-American Migration, 1915–1940* helped her underscore for students the cultural shift that took place when African American men and women abandoned the dead-end dirt farms of the South in favor of the impersonal and monotonous, low-waged factory labor in northern cities and towns.

A complementary angle to Clark-Lewis's interdisciplinary approach to Wilson's female characters was offered by Dana Williams, a professor of African American literature and women's studies scholar, who in her focus upon theoretical issues pertaining to their depictions melded her approach with the foundation laid by her historian predecessor and interdisciplinary teaching partner.[13] Before meeting the class, Williams e-mailed me a document for *Blackboard* posting: Lindon Barrett's "Institutions, Classrooms, Failures: African American Literature and Critical Theory in the Same Small Spaces," which addresses the use of angst as an excuse by today's students when they encounter African American texts that hark back to historical moments. Williams prefaced her discussion of Wilson's women by inviting students to examine the faulty premise in their attributing their difficulties in analyzing historically set African American literary texts to the lack of personal knowledge. In her essay in this volume, she embraces Barrett's way of dismissing this excuse:

> Barrett does rightly note that the student would not have likely made a similar comment about being unable to relate fully to an experience in a course on Renaissance or Victorian literatures, he does not contest the supposition that African American literature is more experiential than other literatures. As Morrison suggests in *Playing in the Dark: Whiteness and the Literary Imagination*, national literatures have long been used to explore emerging and/or threatened social, cultural, political, and economic histories and realities and are, thus, inherently experiential. African American literature's tendency to probe the conditions of its political body is no exception in this regard, though it is commonly characterized as being more experiential than aesthetic.

Having preempted this familiar line of defense and having laid the foundation for a close reading of Wilson's black female characters, Williams channeled the attention of these students to some of the same black female character types in Wilson's plays that were introduced by the history professor who had preceded her: Rose, Berniece, and Ma Rainey, for example. Williams then turned to critics in black women's studies as a way to further examine the lives that these black female migrants reflect.

The Payoff

From the very start, Standing in My Grandfather's Shoes took on a decidedly different tone from countless other semester openings. Instead of rolling out the usual laundry list of taboos, I spent most of the class time educating a class full of alert students on the concept of interdisciplinarity, explaining our course design, and sharing with them our plans for executing it. As these students began to grasp related concepts of interdisciplinary learning, it appeared that a window was opened for them to pursue multiple layers of meaning in Wilson's ten-play cycle. This pursuit challenged the millennials in the class in positive ways. A combination of rich and relevant African American historical and cultural material, the constantly changing scenery around them, the eclectic nature of the lessons, and the rewards of pursuing original interdisciplinary research questions stretched their critical thinking and pushed them to think outside the box.

This approach spoke to the millennial students in ways not entirely unlike the culture of communication devices that has so engulfed them. One student submitted the following assessment of the course at its close: A sampling of course evaluations revealed that the millennial learners saw great merit in our joint efforts to harness today's communications technology to innovate approaches to teaching the past. Such feedback underscores Jacobs's argument: "Students engaged in interdisciplinary learning often find the content more exciting and relevant, especially if teachers can connect the disciplines not only to each other but also to the past and present in a way that relates to students' lives" ("How Might Interdisciplinary Learning"). Interdisciplinary courses like the one described in my essay pushed Howard students as well as my teaching colleagues to engage in a higher level of critical thinking and learning and to go outside the box of conventional pedagogical practices. Instructors in this course succeeded in each of these areas, I am convinced, by thinking like students but teaching in ways that connect with millennials.

NOTES

[1] On millennials, see "Millennials."

[2] EDUCAUSE is a nonprofit association whose mission is to advance higher education through the use of information technology.

[3] The litmus test for an effective interdisciplinary syllabus was its ability to successfully encourage students to formulate appropriate research questions or hypotheses that addressed significant yet previously less-explored aspects of a topic; to synthesize and evaluate the related literature; to design a viable research study; to apply appropriate research methodologies; to interpret primary sources, data, or artifacts from the perspectives of the discipline or disciplines; to draw logical conclusions from the findings while discussing the limitations and implications; to compose a research project that fulfilled the purposes and conventions of scholarly activity; and to prepare a presentation that effectively integrated oral, written, quantitative, and visual communication skills to enhance meaning.

[4] The August Wilson Society (AWS) is composed of Howard University faculty members and student representatives from diverse disciplines who sponsor projects that use the life and legacy of Wilson to foster cultural understanding and to bridge disciplinary divides. Shortly after the October 2005 death of the two-time Pulitzer Prize–winning playwright and May 2004 honorary degree recipient, I spearheaded an effort to establish a learning community at Howard University to honor the playwright's legacy. Cofounding members of this initiative included professors from the Art, History, African Studies, Philosophy, Theatre Arts, African American Studies, English, Music, and Psychology departments. Since its inception, AWS has facilitated a series of campus-wide events

where dialogue inspired by the resounding themes in Wilson's plays dismantled the usual silos of academia and prompted cross-disciplinary conversations. The AWS has adopted the following as its chief mission: "to define, promote, and celebrate the artistic and cultural legacy of August Wilson, who dedicated his life and genius to chronicling and rendering into poetry and drama the history, decade by decade, of African Americans in the twentieth century" (*About Us*).

[5] Materials for this course cited in this essays are taken from "*Standing.*"

[6] The e-portfolio was a required feature of this interdisciplinary course. It is defined as a meaningful selection of artifacts that display evidence of students' abilities and achievements in the course. Its contents include written reflections, in which students explain the significance of those artifacts. In this course, students stored artifacts such as academic papers, group projects, exams, slide shows, syllabi, and assignments. It also included students' bibliographies or favorite research links, videotapes of their presentations or performances, photographs of their artwork or posters, and written comments by instructors or peers on their work.

[7] Suggested further readings on Wilson's Africanist dramatic agenda are Richards, "Yoruba Gods"; Harrison, "August Wilson's Blues Poetics"; and Shannon, "Audience and Africanisms."

[8] Students were asked to develop a working vocabulary of useful terminology and current trends in both disciplines. In psychology, for example, they grappled with the terms *abnormal behavior, mental illness, insanity, psychopathology, critical psychology, African-centered psychology, and neuroscience.*

[9] This language was taken directly from the course outline of Camara Jules Harrell, the psychology professor, who with Terri Adams-Fuller, the criminal justice professor, conceptualized an interdisciplinary approach based upon a collapse of the borders between their respective disciplines.

[10] This assignment was conceptualized by Harrell.

[11] The list was: "Traditional and Critical Perspectives on Corrections," chapter 8 in *Corrections: A Critical Approach* (Welch 82–122); "The Incarceration 'Experiment,'" chapter 2 in *Race to Incarcerate* (Mauer 16–39); "African Americans and the Criminal Justice System," chapter 7 in *Race to Incarcerate* (130–56); *From Victims to Victimizers: Interviews with Twenty-Five Ex-Pimps in Chicago* (Raphael and Myers-Powell); "Race and the War on Drugs: The Social Consequences of Presidential Rhetoric" (Yates and Whitford); "Keep the Paying Guests Coming: Filling Up the Prisons" (Kahn and Minnich); "Pathways to Prison: Life Histories of Former Clients of the Child Welfare and Juvenile Justice Systems" (Kapp); "The G.I. Bill of the Twenty-First Century: Mass Incarceration and How Crime Is Paying" (Day); "Re/Constructing Black Masculinity in Prison" (Nandi); "Death by a Thousand Little Cuts: Studies of the Impact of Incarceration," chapter 5 of *Imprisoning Communities: How Mass Incarceration Makes Disadvantaged Neighborhoods Worse* (Clear 93–120); "In Their Own Voices: People in High Incarceration Neighborhoods Talk about the Impact of Incarceration," chapter 6 in *Imprisoning Communities* (121–48); and "Criminal Incarceration Dividing the Ties that Bind: Black Men and Their Families" (Browning, Miller, and Spruance).

[12] Clark-Lewis is a historian of the United States. She has taught courses on African American women, women in the United States, African American history, the history of the District of Columbia, and the history of African Americans in Pennsylvania. She is director of Howard University's Public History program, where she also has offered courses on museums and archives, oral history, and historic preservation. She has taught

students at Howard University about genealogical research and family history and genealogy. She is the author of *First Freed: Emancipation in the District of Columbia* and *Living In, Living Out: African American Domestics in Washington, DC*.

[13] In her essay in this volume, Williams writes, "I use critics' efforts to grapple objectively with Wilson's limited portrayal of women to introduce students to critical ideas in black women's studies and, concurrently, to complicate African American literature's intersection with literary theory." Lindon Barrett explores the ways critical theory and African American literature appear to fail each other.

APPENDIX

The following assessment tools were designed to engage students with the information imparted during my opening session, entitled "The Ground on Which I Stand":

Research Assignment

Directions: Consult at least four sources to put together your own case study of the high-profile controversy that erupted between *New Republic* critic Robert Brustein and August Wilson in the early 1990s. Include (1) a brief history of the relationships among Brustein, Lloyd Richards, and Wilson; (2) a clear articulation of the positions held by both Brustein and Wilson in the controversy; (3) your own assessment of the larger implications of this argument and a discussion of what was and is ultimately at stake; and (4) a list of works cited, using MLA format.

Organize your case study into subheadings that correspond to those listed above.

Length is not an issue in this assignment; however, you need to provide clear and detailed information beneath each subheading.

HINT: I suggest that one of your four sources include the review of Wilson's *The Piano Lesson* by Brustein.

Essay 1

Directions: Locate and read Wilson's speech "The Ground on Which I Stand" in its entirety, paying special attention to what we referred to as nuggets or major assertions of his cultural, artistic, racial, professional, and political positions.

In a typewritten, double-spaced essay of three to five pages, focus upon one such nugget. Make your own thesis argument and provide convincing evidence in support of it.

At the top of the first page of your essay, include the excerpt from Wilson's speech that is to be the focus of your discussion.

The essay must have a strong introduction in which you frame your thesis argument and indicate an organizing principle that will help the reader to determine early the structure and direction of your argument.

Give your essay a catchy but relevant title.

Discussion Board Prompt 1

> "I am what is known, at least among the followers and supporters of the ideas of Marcus Garvey, as a race man. That is simply that I believe that race matters." ("The Ground on Which I Stand")

Do you believe that Wilson's cultural nationalist ideas on the centrality of race are out of step with the current times? Share your thoughts on this prompt in an actual discussion with your classmates. With the exception of the initial post, do not post isolated comments. You must engage your colleagues on this topic.

Assignments given for the section entitled "The Interdisciplinary Connections of August Wilson" included the following:

Essay 2

Gem of the Ocean (set in 1904), *Joe Turner's Come and Gone* (set in 1911), and *The Piano Lesson* (set in 1936)—choose one of these three plays as the basis for a study of living conditions for African Americans in the decade in which the play is set. Tell this story by using an interdisciplinary approach; that is, show how African Americans fared by discussing their circumstances through the lens of multiple disciplines. For example, consider the impact of economics, race relations, the Great Migration, music, criminal justice, dance, slavery, African belief systems, Christianity, labor relations, politics, gender issues, and entrepreneurship. Where possible, show how disciplines collide, intersect, or coexist. Cite specific examples from this play that mirror the times.

Discussion Board Prompt 2

Discovering the interdisciplinarity in the works of Wilson involves exploring issues and ideas beyond the boundaries of individual subject areas. It yields new knowledge by focusing upon fields that cross traditional boundaries between academic disciplines or schools of thought.

With this definition in mind, use an interdisciplinary approach to discuss what the lyrics to Wining Boy's song ("Arkansas," by Henry Thomas) may reveal not just about his life experiences but about black men or African Americans in general. Pay attention to how various fields or disciplines are introduced and discuss the possible meanings they convey.

Professors in African and African American studies equipped you early with a sophisticated vocabulary for the later exercises that involved identifying and discussing Africa's influence in Wilson's plays. That list includes the following:

Cosmology: how Africans structure the spiritual universe

God Almighty: the Creator of the universe and everything in it; a nongendered force that is omniscient, omnipresent, omnipotent

Deities: lesser spirits who are given power through God almighty to help human beings aided by their spiritual intermediaries in the person of priests, priestesses, and other trained and qualified practitioners. Deities can dwell in nature in the form of trees, lakes, rivers, wind, lightning, and so on.

Ancestors: those human beings who have died but are still considered a part of the family with lingering spiritual presences that must be addressed and tended to on a regular basis in order for people to live a good life and perpetuate the growth and prosperity of the family. In order to be considered an ancestor, you must have lived an exemplary life. This is part of an ongoing lineage through the living, the dead, and the yet unborn.

There are also *other-than-human beings*, which manifest themselves in the form of dwarfs, ghosts, or fearsome creatures that test the moral fiber of human beings.

African Worldview: What the West calls African traditional religion, Africans call indigenous practice or their culture—this culture is a way of life that is passed on from generation to generation and forms the foundation of problem solving in everyday life. This culture aligns the mundane world of human beings with divine power, while it maintains order and peace within the society, heals physical and spiritual diseases, prophesizes coming events or crises, and facilitates counseling and therapy to adherents and participants. In the African context, the word *religion* or thought of it is reserved for Christianity, which was introduced to Africa as the forward prong of colonialism. The culture of indigenous practice and the religion of Christianity are in some places part of a syncretic or complementary set of beliefs and practices that can be appropriated separately or together in order to get the desired outcome. Africans are looking for an antidote to infertility, poverty, accidents, natural disasters, and destructive witchcraft. While indigenous praxis serves as a talisman for winning at sports, politics, as well as professional and family life, it holds all its participants to a high moral standard in order to bring about positive results. Not following the time-honored taboos and rules could result in financial disaster, illness, insanity, or death.

The idea of good and evil is seen as a part of God almighty's creation, human beings having the ability to choose between the two. It is largely accepted that evil people can exist in the form of witches. These are people with powers that they choose to use for evil—for example, hurting other people to forward their own gains. Even in the view of evil, there is no concept of the Devil in indigenous praxis as in Christianity.

African Ontology: concept of reality: invisible spirits and beings are accepted as real and taken for granted as a part of everyday existence. They were created in the beginning by God almighty and given instructions to help humans. This idea of reality crosses religious lines and is an integral part of the culture.

A person has a part of his or her soul that is divine and came directly from God almighty when that person was born; when this godly spark is extinguished, the person dies. Also human beings have a destiny that is given to them by God. This is their life's mission or what they are sent to earth to do. This destiny is thought to be unalterable, but most cultures agree that even if you were born with a bad destiny, you can make it good through rituals and living a good life.

The *African self or concept of personhood* is seen as the various parts that come from the divine soul as well as from the blood of the mother, the personality of the father, and the astral part of the self that travels in dreams. So there are material and immaterial parts of the self.

The *community* is primary to African reality, but the individual is not made subordinate to the community. Each person is encouraged to develop fully so she or he might have more to bring to benefit the family, household, community, and state.

African Epistemology: the source, scope, and nature of African knowledge. God created order, knowledge, and death, according to African oral tradition, but people always need help with understanding why they die, why bad things happen to good people, why there is injustice, why we have catastrophes, and what the future brings. For help, people go to priests, priestesses, and other spiritual practitioners.

African Ritual Specialists, Priests, and Priestesses: these are persons from the family, from the community at large, or within many African states who have been called to be the voices and bodies of the gods who accompany a family, town, or state. Priests (used as a nongendered designation), through spiritual possession and divination, heal, enact rituals, and resolve conflicts. They are trained for no less than three years and tend to belong to a long line of priests in a particular family or lineage. When one priest dies, another is called to fill the vacancy in order to ensure that the needs of the people are met. This position is not taken lightly, and celibacy and rules of moral behavior are mandated. No priest is socially isolated; a priest is on twenty-four-hour call to help people in all manner of issues. Through dreams, prophecies, divinations, and possession, priests are constant sources of continued knowledge. They not only cure physical diseases but also serve as the first line of defense against spiritual diseases, which have no known physiological source but come from evil spiritual attack or because the patient broke a taboo or offended ancestors.

The priests also have a cadre of helpers or elders who help protect them and aid them in their work. The work is done in an organized hierarchal community, which is a reflection of the community at large. The organization includes the chief priest-leader, senior priests, junior priests, council of elders, spokespeople, and others who perform vital functions to keep the shrine of the deity running smoothly.

The following assignments served to culminate the segment on the psychology of slavery.

Essay 3

Review all the statistical data, related terminology, definitions, and so forth on both Western and African-based assessments of mental conditions that were contained in the documents distributed by Professors Harrell and Adams-Fuller on the incarceration of African Americans and both the immediate and long-term psychological impact that prolonged periods in prison have on people.

Analyze one of Wilson's particularly troubled or noticeably enigmatic male or female characters using an African-based system of thought. Consider, for example, Risa (*Two Trains Running*); King Hedley (*Seven Guitars*), Troy Maxson (*Fences*), King (*King Hedley II*), Berniece (*The Piano Lesson*), and Fielding (*Jitney*).

Consider also minor characters as topics of your discussions.

To help you identify a worthwhile thesis argument, consult references that provide a clear and useful definition of psychoanalytic literary criticism, complete with explanations and names for the various mental defenses. Focus upon one particular condition and show how it is applicable to the conditions of the Wilson character that you choose as the focus of your essay. Look for additional enlightenment on various aspects of an Afrocentric analysis that may apply to the Wilson character.

Research Question on the Psychology of Slavery

Incarceration is a reoccurring theme in Wilson's work. Unfortunately, some of the issues we see played out by formerly incarcerated characters reflect the reality of life for thousands of African American men and women.

Conduct an analysis of some of the social, political, and economic conditions that have led to the high incarceration rates for African American men and women. Include statistics, personal testimony, or references to particular cases. Ground your analysis in the circumstances of one fictional character from any of Wilson's plays who has spent time in prison. Examine closely the character's economic situation, the terms of this character's incarceration, and the crime committed, then move to an analysis of real-life circumstances for real-life African Americans.

AFRICAN ROUTES

Teaching *Joe Turner's Come and Gone*

Harry J. Elam, Jr.

Back in November 1987, I took students in my class Introduction to the Theatre at the University of Maryland, College Park, to see *Joe Turner's Come and Gone*, by August Wilson, at the Arena Stage Theatre in Washington, DC. Following the critical success of his *Ma Rainey's Black Bottom*, this new work garnered significant critical attention, as did his bold plan to write a twentieth-century history cycle documenting black history with a play for each decade of the twentieth century. *Joe Turner* would be his play for the 1910s, set in 1911 at a time when the Great Migration of African Americans from the South to the North was just beginning. As would become their custom, Wilson and his director, Lloyd Richards, were previewing the play at the Arena Stage, using the regional theater circuit to work out kinks in content and casting as it wound its way to Broadway. Richards, one of the most important influences on Wilson's early dramaturgy, was the first black director on Broadway, with *Raisin in the Sun*, by Lorraine Hansberry, back in 1959, and he was the director of the Yale Drama School and the Eugene O'Neill Playwriting Center. Richards is credited with discovering Wilson when Wilson submitted *Ma Rainey* to the O'Neill for the summer playwriting workshop competition. With the reading of this play at the O'Neill, Richards and Wilson began a collaboration that would stretch through the first six plays in the cycle, including *Joe Turner*. Powerfully, the first act of *Joe Turner* ends with the protagonist, Herald Loomis, lying prone on the stage floor possessed and obsessed as Bynum, the mystical roots worker, stands over him attempting to ease his anxiety. The two engage in a spirited call-and-response as the other characters look on. Bynum beckons Loomis to stand and walk. Loomis valiantly seeks to comply with this command but fails and crashes again to the floor. He exclaims, "My feet they won't stand up," as the lights black out on the first act (253 [1.4]). Stirred by this emotionally packed ending, my Maryland students gathered around me. "We loved it," they exclaimed. "But what did it mean?"

To be sure, *Joe Turner,* Wilson's favorite play in his cycle, poses specific challenges to those attempting to teach the play and help students negotiate Wilson's complex, multilayered meanings. As the ending of the first act testifies, *Joe Turner* pushes against conventional limitations of realism by incorporating African-based symbolism and ritual. A central concern for Wilson throughout his cycle is examining how historically Africanness becomes manifest in African American experience and identity. Purposefully, he sets *Joe Turner* in 1911, a time when, he argues, African Americans were particularly close to their African roots and thus the presence of African retentions within their cultural practices and spiritual beliefs was palpable. And yet, in order to recognize the presence of Africa in the play, it is important that one knows and can read the codes and symbols that Wilson employs. In working with this play with an undergraduate or graduate class, I believe it is critical to examine with the students how ritual operates in the play, to determine the ritual action of the play, and to analyze how Africa is ritualized and how such symbolic enactments inform Wilson's reworking of African American history during this period of the Great Migration.

Consequently, reading and teaching *Joe Turner*'s codes of Africanness necessarily involves interrogating and potentially embracing critical theories of and definitions for ritual. Jean Comaroff and John Comaroff, anthropologists, provide a useful starting point for this type of engagement with the play when they classify ritual as both a "signifying practice" and a "symbolic mediation" (xvi).[1] As a signifying practice, the Comaroffs maintain that a ritual enactment has meaning or significance for the gathered community. Bertha's repeated action of preparing breakfast biscuits and feeding them to each of the characters can be read as such a signifying act, not only because it provides the tenants of Seth's boardinghouse with tangible sustenance but also because it functions as an act of community and communion that endows these transient travelers, cut off from their past and from their families, with a connection to hearth and home. As symbolic mediation, the Comaroffs argue, ritual offers a link from the earthly community to powerful spiritual forces beyond. Accordingly, Bynum's unseen offstage pigeon dance and bloodletting incantations at the opening of the play symbolically associate him with African spiritual practices, connect him with his gods, and prepare the way for the entrance of Loomis, the troubled protagonist, and his daughter, Zonia, into Seth's boardinghouse. Within such ritual practices, historical patterns are, as Catherine Bell notes, "reproduced but also reinterpreted or transformed" (83). Context is critical to ritual, and Wilson creates circumstances that are conducive to ritual action and in which the invocation of rites—such as Bynum's incantations—becomes a practical response. The effect of Wilson's rituals in *Joe Turner* is the reaffirmation of collective faith even as the ritual actions advocate for self-definition and self-determination. As "signifying practices" and "symbolic mediations" (see Bell 80–83), these rituals operate in ways that are both situational and strategic: they seek to restructure the given reality, they construct meaning and mediate the dynamics of power, and they bring the African past and African American present into relation.

Of importance to reading ritual in *Joe Turner* is also the consideration of embodiment and embodied practice, because how characters like Bertha and Bynum embody spirituality and participate bodily in ritual processes is critical to the action of the play. Bell maintains that central to an understanding of ritual as cultural practice is the primacy of the body moving within a specially constructed space, "simultaneously defining (imposing) and experiencing (receiving) the values ordering the environment. For example, the body movements of ritually knowledgeable agents actually define the special qualities of the environment, yet the agents understand themselves as reacting or responding to this environment" (82). Bynum as ritually knowledgeable agent imposes himself upon the environment. His body moving through the space of Seth's boardinghouse or dancing around in circles in the front yard defines the special quality of the space. Bertha, near the climax of the play, moves around the kitchen, first spreading salt to the corners of the space and then convulsing in an uncontrollable burst of laughter. Wilson writes in the stage directions:

> [She moves] around the kitchen as though blessing it and chasing away the huge sadness that seems to envelope it. It is a dance and demonstration of her own magic, her own remedy that is centuries old and to which she is connected by the muscles of her heart and the blood's memory. . . . She begins to laugh. It is a near hysterical laughter that is a celebration life, both its pain and its blessing. (283 [2.5])

Bertha performs an embodied, dichotomous rite of celebration that is both spiritual and practical. At a time of liminal uncertainty in the play, she laughs to keep from crying. Her physical engagement in cultural practices—moving around, blessing the house—is a form of what Joni L. Jones terms "bodily knowing" (7), enabling Bertha to connect "by the muscles of her heart and blood's memory" to forces beyond. Bodily knowing—embodied knowledge garnered through actual experience and inculcated within the body—is operative in this blessing of laughter for Bertha and at key moments of ritual enactment in *Joe Turner.* Evidenced in Bertha's drawing on her "own magic" and a remedy that is "centuries old," such bodily knowing depends on the particular social and historical circumstances as well as the social, cultural, and historical experience of the participant. As Elyse Lamm Pinneau writes, "[O]ur bodies are differentially marked by cultural norms" (46). Bertha's laughing rite is contextual, for ritual is a matter of invention in particular circumstances. Within the ever-changing sameness of performance, it is reinvented each night—not only in the diverse interpretations of different actresses but also in the nonreproducible, ephemeral moment of the character Bertha's "near hysterical laughter." Bertha's infectious laughter becomes a participatory ritual. Those around her, Mattie, Zonia, and even Seth, become involved in this embodied, spirited laughter. Not only does Bertha transform the practical mood of the kitchen, but also the metaphysics of her laughter enables the kitchen to become a productive site for Herald Loomis's ultimate ceremony of freedom. In my experience, discussing in class Bertha's ritual of laughter can open up larger questions of how bodies function in this play. I want the students to think about how "bodily knowing" affects the characters' experience as well as our own interpretations of meaning.

What I ask of my students when we study *Joe Turner* is collaborative, participatory, interactive engagement with the text. I call for them to function collectively and to research actively the historical context. I call for them to read closely the play script, to discuss openly the ideas, and even to physicalize the action. While potentially a productive strategy in teaching any dramatic text, such collaborative and participatory engagement is all the more important with a work such as *Joe Turner* because of the play's emphasis on ritual, spirituality, and the politics of race. In *Joe Turner,* the personal and the political, the spiritual and the historical all intersect, and as consequence their collisions are prime subjects for class exploration. Students enter the classroom with various racial investments, religious beliefs, and cultural baggage. Black students who have firsthand experience with racism, students who have grown up in the South or in Pittsburgh, and religious studies majors who have studied the Bible may have a particular insight into moments of *Joe Turner.* Yet experience must not be an end in itself but must be processed, tested, and then marshaled in the service of critical analysis—racialized experience or religious advocacy may enlighten a reading of the play but can also lead one astray. Chandra Talpede Mohanty points out that experience within the classroom needs to be critically engaged and understood as "historical, contingent and the result of interpretation" (52). Thus while I would encourage and accept such experiential insights, my objective in teaching the play is not to privilege one set of experiences over another but rather to work toward what Henry Giroux terms a "critical pedagogy," where diverse opinions are encouraged but students must negotiate and substantiate their arguments in terms of how it informs the play. My hope is to create the classroom as a space of open exchange where experience-based assertions are subject to democratic investigation and where the central point of emphasis is the text. Our goal is to understand what race means, how blackness signifies specifically in terms of *Joe Turner.*

Focusing on the text helps prevent students from asserting authority through experience or race and facilitates the formulation of what Amie A. Macdonald and Susan Sánchez-Casal call "communities of meaning," in which students and teacher struggle collectively for knowledge (10–14). Within the classroom, communities of meaning are diverse and ever shifting; they allow for association and coalitions across cultural, racial, and gender borders as students work together in collaborative negotiations of meaning. Such communities, formed and reformulated around issues within the text, serve to preclude the students as well as me from making racialized assumptions about how a black student or white student or Asian student might respond at a given moment. Such thinking is too reductive a way of understanding the class or its reaction to a text such as *Joe Turner.*

Concentrating on textual interpretation through a community of meaning checks assertions of racial territorialism, which is invariably important when I ask students to participate by reading aloud. Reading aloud helps them appreciate not only the play as a performance piece but also Wilson's rich use of language, vernacular humor, and imagery. Wilson finds music and poetry in the everyday speech of African Americans. Through culturally specific references, his dialogue speaks to a particular constituency but at the same time reaches across racial and ethnic borders through messages that are accessible to a wider audience. In so doing, he counters the pejorative claims that black English is a subordinate, inarticulate form rather than one capable of what James Baldwin describes in *The Fire This Time* as "this passion, this skill . . . this incredible music" (qtd. in Rickford and Rickford 3). Wilson validates the vernacular, a vernacular that is inherently musical. Given his engagement with the musicality of black speech, reading aloud helps students recognize that meaning in performance is located not simply in the connotations and contexts of the dialogue but also in the sounds, inflections, and accent of the lines.

Equally significant when students read *Joe Turner* aloud is that they must inevitably engage the word *nigger*. In all his plays, Wilson makes particular and particularized usage of this word. In this day and age, when the NAACP has held a symbolic burial of the N word, when its use by white comics such as Michael Richards has gained national attention in the United States, students may feel uncomfortable or anxious when encountering it and when expected to voice the word aloud in class. Regardless of whether the reading of the dialogue calls for a black student to utter the N word in a class full of other black students or a white student to utter it in a class where the ethnicities are decidedly diverse, the N word always and already carries with it a history and thus becomes a possible point of contention or unease. My immediate response is to diffuse and avert such conflagration by stating up front that students who do not wish to say the word, even though it is written in the text, need not do so. I want them to understand not what the word means in the light of their surrounding social and cultural contexts but in terms of Wilson's employment of it in the text. One example is that in *Joe Turner,* Wilson has Seth, the boardinghouse owner, the northern-born son of a free man, use this epithet to differentiate himself from other blacks, those ex-slaves and children of slaves migrating up from the South and, most particularly, to differentiate himself from the troubled protagonist. When Bertha asks Seth why he does not tell Loomis what he knows about the whereabouts of Loomis's wife, Martha, Seth responds, "I ain't gonna tell this old wild-eyed mean-looking nigger nothing" (236 [1.2]). In this employment, "nigger" functions as the site of both difference and denial. Through class discussion of such moments, we can explore how such word usage enables Seth to imagine himself as distinct from and even superior to his black migratory boarders. And yet Wilson's play points to the inevitable ironies present in such a self-perception. Early in the play, Seth presents what he perceives as a foolproof, lucrative business plan but finds that the white bankers will not loan him the money to start his own business, despite his certainty that his skills at making pots and pans would produce a profit: "They can't see that. Neither one of them can see that. Now, how much sense it take to see that? All you got to do is be able to count. One man making ten pots is five men making fifty pots. But they can't see that" (242 [1.3]). The white bankers, in their prejudiced socioeconomic perspective, can see Seth only as a black other, as no different from Loomis. Consequently, Seth must resign himself to working the late shift for a white man, Mr. Olowski.

While in-class reading provides a forum for provocative communal discussion, it is outside group research that offers foundational insight into the historical roots and ritualistic meanings at the center of *Joe Turner*. A logical place to start this process is with an examination of the title. Who was Joe Turner? I ask. The students, when they do research, will discover that in African American cultural history Joe Turner took on several incarnations: a blues singer in the 1930s, for example. They may also encounter Joe Turney, a sheriff hired by his brother, Peter Turney (the twenty-seventh governor of the state of Tennessee from 1893 to 1897), to transport black convicts. Turney became a figure of mythical proportion known for his midnight runs in which he captured young black men, to convey them in chain gangs from Memphis to the state penitentiary in Nashville and to prison farms along the Mississippi. In the process of folk recreation, the name became Joe Turner rather than Turney, and "Joe Turner's Come and Gone" signified, according to W. C. Handy, the father of the blues, a lament sung by the women left behind to grieve their husbands, sons, and brothers who had been snatched up and carried away. "Joe Turner Blues" is perhaps the earliest recorded blues song. Another version of the story, the version that Wilson transfigures in the play, has Joe Turner luring unsuspecting black men into crap games on Memphis streets and then carrying them away and keeping them in servitude on his plantation for a period of seven years. In the figure of Joe Turner, culture and history, myth and reality all collide. His image is at once functional and symbolic. The singing of the song "Joe Turner," for the black women who lost their loved ones in Memphis of the 1890s as well as for Bynum and Loomis in the play, operates a signifying practice with profound impact for those gathered.

The history, myth, and legend of the song and of Joe Turner and how they figure within the title and the play itself are fertile issues for class discussion. Students can appreciate how Wilson shapes history to his own end. His account of Loomis's encounter with Joe Turner conflates myth and history, the fictitious and the real. Wilson sets the play in 1911, and Loomis informs us that he has been on the road in search of his wife for four years, after being kept in servitude by Turner for seven, which would put the time of his capture in the year 1900. But by then Pete Turney was no longer governor and Joe Turney no longer sheriff. Hence students, by investigating the historical details that inform the play, come to understand that Wilson consciously shapes an alternative history to serve his purposes. The question in the play is not whether Joe Turner or Turney was real but how Loomis can overcome the psychic scars of his harrowing servitude. His suffering under Joe Turner, and his ability to endure and overcome symbolically, resonate with the collective trauma and internalized oppressions endured by black Americans.

Another important site for the students' historical excavation and symbolic revelation is the work of the visual artist Romare Bearden. Wilson discovered the art of Bearden, a fellow Pittsburgh native, in 1977, when his friend Charles Purdy purchased a copy of Bearden's collages *The Prevalence of Ritual* (1964; see Washington). Viewing this artwork had a profound effect on Wilson: "My response was visceral. I was looking at myself in ways I hadn't thought of before and have never ceased to think of since. In Bearden I found my artistic mentor and sought, and still aspire, to make my plays the equal of his canvases" (qtd. in Fishman 134). I find the title *The Prevalence of Ritual* extremely significant, for, like Wilson's *Joe Turner,* Bearden's work functions ritualistically, returning to the originating moments of rupture within African American history—the Middle Passage, slavery, the Depression—refiguring the past, the losses of history and the history of loss. Bearden's formula for collage, his use of found objects, and his blending of past and present parallel Wilson's pastiche style of playwriting and his interest in the impact of history upon the present. In the artistry of both men, the metaphoric and ritualistic coexist with the everyday experiences of African Americans. Unfortunately Wilson and Bearden never met in Bearden's lifetime.

Bearden's collage *Mill Hand's Lunch Bucket* (1978) directly inspired Wilson's *Joe Turner* (fig. 1). In fact, Wilson had thought at one point to call the play "Mill Hand's Lunch Bucket." Accordingly, once the students research Bearden and locate his *Mill Hand's Lunch Bucket* and bring this image to class, they can use it as a critical site for close reading in relation to the play. Like Seth and Bertha's boardinghouse in the play, the setting for this classic Bearden work is a Pittsburgh boardinghouse, constructed from Bearden's memories of his childhood. In 1920, when Bearden was in the fourth grade, he lived with his maternal grandmother, Carrie, and her husband, George Banks, in their boardinghouse in the Lawrenceville section of Pittsburgh, not far from a steel mill. At the center of the collage is a dining table and kitchen area. Seated at the table is a man dressed in black and wearing a wide brimmed black hat with his head bowed. This brooding figure became the source for Wilson's Loomis. To the right in the collage is a proportionately larger open window presenting a view of the steel mills with smoke rising in the distance. From his grandparent's actual boardinghouse on Pennsylvania Avenue, Bearden could see the factory's steeples and flames and hear the whistle signaling the end of each shift. Students can discuss the significance of this window and its placement. They can consider how the threatening presence of the mill, constructed with Bearden's careful, conscious use of color and shading, intersects the domestic reality of the boardinghouse. Correspondingly in Wilson's play, the mill also lurks in the background, as an unseen presence, the place where Seth must work evening shifts, his desire to open up his own business making pots, pans, and other utensils from steel unrealized.

History and memory are as critical to Bearden's collage as they are to Wilson's play. The collage is part of Bearden's series *Profile / Part I: The Twenties*, where Bearden reflects on his Pittsburgh memories. In the center of the back wall of *Mill Hand's Lunch Bucket* is a framed painting of an elderly dark-skinned black woman in a long blue working dress and matching head scarf; the woman has unusually large hands. The painting in its centrality signals to the past, to perhaps a lost relative remembered through this portrait. The representation within a representation provides this imagined boardinghouse with its own imagined history. The portrait archives the past. In *Joe Turner,* Wilson foregrounds the presence of the past as he appropriates this image within an image. Reuben, the young next-door neighbor, explains to Loomis's daughter that Seth has a picture of his mother, Miss Mabel, hanging in the boardinghouse:

> ZONIA: Who Miss Mabel?
> REUBEN: Mr. Seth's mother. He got a picture of her hanging up in the house. She been dead. (276 [2.4])

The fact that Miss Mabel "been dead" is very important, as Reuben reports that her ghost has returned to set right the past. As Reuben explains, Miss Mabel confronted him, interceding for his recently deceased young friend Eugene. Reuben had promised the critically ill Eugene that upon his death he would release his pigeons, but thus far he has failed to do so, holding on to them as remembrance. Miss Mabel, as Reuben tells Zonia, scolds him, "'Didn't you promise Eugene something?' Then she hit me with her cane. She say, 'Let them pigeons go.' Then she hit me again. That's what made them marks. . . . She had this light coming out of her and then she just melt away" (276 [2.4]). Miss Mabel appears because Reuben must release the pigeons in order to free Eugene. Literally marked by death, Reuben comes to a new understanding not only of what he must do but also of how he must honor the dead. Wilson's use of the names Reuben and Eugene references actual history and pays tribute to Bearden, for Reuben is, as Joan Fishman notes, "a representation of Bearden himself as a boy" (136) and Eugene is the name of Bearden's dear friend, a talented young artist, lost in childhood. Thus, examining *Mill Hand's Lunch Bucket* and its creator, Bearden, further enables students to consider the ways in which Wilson merges real history with the fictive in service of ritual ends.

An image from Bearden's *Mill Hand's Lunch Bucket* also figures in Bynum's story of the shiny man. Early in the first act, Bynum relates to Selig (the white peddler), Bertha, and Seth the metaphysical adventure that led to his discovery of the meaning of his life. Bynum describes being led by a "shiny man" to a mystical place where he encountered his father, whose "hands . . . were as big

Fig. 1. Romare Bearden, *Mill Hand's Lunch Bucket.* 1978. From the Profiles / Part I: The Twenties series. Collage on board. © Romare Bearden Foundation. Licensed by VAGA, New York, NY.

as hams" (212 [1.1]). The image of large hands references the collage, where a man with an enormous hand crosses down the stairs.

Bynum's story of the shining man is all the more significant in terms of how it relates to the overall plot and what it suggests about his spiritual powers. As Bynum details, his father led him to the edge of an ocean where "my daddy taught me the meaning of this thing that I had seen and showed me how to find my song" (213 [1.4]). Bynum is born again, filled with the spirit, and endowed with the power of his song. The song he receives gives the ability to bind people's souls, to "take the power of his song and binds them together" (213). His description of his song underscores the power of identity and the need for self-definition.

Yet students also need to appreciate that the concept of song is critical not just to Bynum but also to Loomis's journey and Wilson's concept of African American identity. As such, the notion of song operates both functionally and symbolically. Wilson argues that African Americans generally, and Loomis specifically, need to rediscover their song. This song, as Wilson writes in the introduction to *Joe Turner's Come and Gone,* "is both a wail and a whelp of joy" (203). This multilayered notion of song evokes the pleasure and pain, the struggle and survival, the complexities and contradictions inherent in African American experience.

Bynum's vision of the shiny man and discovery of his own song connects Bynum psychically and symbolically with Loomis. Joan Herrington's excellent book on Wilson's playwriting process, *I Ain't Sorry for Nothin' I Done,* is particularly good at delineating how Wilson revised *Joe Turner* through several drafts to articulate more effectively the linkages between Bynum and Loomis and is worth assigning to students as supplementary reading (see 79–93). As the play now reads, the two men are profoundly joined by their words and actions. In his "shiny man" monologue, Bynum describes how, taken to the water's edge, he sees "something I ain't got words to tell you" (213 [1.1]). These words foreshadow Loomis's later revelation at the end of the first act. Loomis recounts his own traumatic reverie of water "that was bigger than the whole world." Echoing Bynum, he reports, "Herald Loomis done seen some things he ain't got words to tell you" (250 [1.4]). Their parallel expression purposefully suggests that they have seen a similar vision. For both men it is a symbolic reference to the Middle Passage, the perilous journey of slaves across the ocean from Africa to America. Their shared vision of water foregrounds the Middle Passage as an African American collective cultural memory as well as a bond that these two men share. Accordingly, when Bynum helps Loomis give voice to his vision, he is also finding the words to express his own memory. Witnessing Loomis knocked to the floor by a powerful force, Bynum stands over him and encourages him to stand. "What you done seen, Herald Loomis?" Bynum asks. "I seen these bones rise up out of the water. Rise up and walk on top of it," Loomis, transformed into a visionary, replies (250). Tellingly, Loomis's powerful image of bones walking on top of the water captures the dichotomy of, at once, mourning souls lost on those terrifying voyages aboard slave ships bound for America and a celebration of the resilience of a people that survived this ordeal. The image of bones walking on the top of the water equally references the valley of dry bones from the Bible (Ezek. 37.1–28). Ezekiel relates a vision of a valley full of disconnected bones. When God breathes on them, they come to life again. Loomis too seeks new spiritual life. Under Bynum's coaxing, Loomis discloses that he fervently desires to stand and join the legion of marching bones as they become flesh and walk onto the land. When he first starts to walk, he fails. Through our discussion enriched by historical research, students come to understand his inability to stand as the physical manifestation of the psychological trauma enacted upon him by forced servitude under Joe Turner. Loomis's particular psychic objective in the play, with assistance from Bynum, is to be able finally to stand and walk with the others. In class, we chart and analyze both the actual events and ritual acts that constitute and condition this odyssey.

Significantly, this analysis involves close reading, through which we discover that Bynum's desire to assist Loomis is not simply altruistic. For Bynum, Loomis represents a man whom Bynum can help, but Loomis also has the power to assist him. Careful examination of Bynum's shiny man speech establishes that Bynum must locate another "shiny man" like the one who showed him the way to his song. He relates, "I asked him [Bynum's father] about the shiny man and he told me he was the One Who Goes Before and Shows the Way. Said there was lots of shiny men and if I ever saw one again before I died then I would know that my song had been accepted and worked its full power and I could lay down and die a happy man" (213 [1.1]). Loomis represents and eventually becomes the shiny man Bynum seeks.

A close exploration of critical events in this play reveals that Bynum purposefully helps Loomis discover how to shine. In act 2, Bynum knowingly sings the song "They Tell Me Joe Turner's Come and Gone" and causes Loomis to explode, "Stop singing that song!" Bynum's singing functions ritualistically as a signifying practice and represents another example of the functional, social power of song. His singing of this song compels Loomis to remember his imprisonment on Joe Turner's plantation, a period of incarceration that left him isolated, alienated, and confused. "What I got he want?" Loomis asks (269 [2.2]). Bynum explains, "What he wanted was your song. He wanted to have your song be his. Every nigger he catch he's looking for the one he can learn that song from. . . . But you still got it. You just forgot how to sing it" (270). Hence, examining how Loomis, with Bynum's assistance, moves to a point of rediscovering his song and its larger ramifications is critical to the overall meaning of the play and central to its ritual movement.

Moreover, Loomis's ultimate act of self-empowerment constitutes the fruition of Bynum's own desires. In the climactic final scene of the play, Loomis cuts his own chest and covers his face with his blood. This act repeats and revises Bynum's earlier encounter with the shiny man, who rubbed his hands together and produced blood, and then "[t]old me to take and rub it all over me . . . say that was a way of cleaning myself" (212 [1.1]). What Loomis does is similarly a cleansing as well as a bold, symbolic act of self-determination, after which he feels spiritually liberated and historically reconnected. Proudly he exclaims, "I'm standing! I'm standing!" To which Bynum replies, "Herald Loomis, you shining! You shine like new money!" (289 [2.5]). Rather than singular achievement, then, the play's end celebrates mutuality and communion. It is both an act of symbolic mediation and signifying practice. Standing enables Loomis to shine for Bynum, fulfilling Bynum's life mission and, in so doing, blessing the greater gathered community.

In teaching *Joe Turner*, a major matter for debate and discussion must be how much of all this action is controlled or orchestrated by Bynum. He is always behind the scenes, potentially dictating future events. After the arrival of Martha, we, along with Loomis, discover that Martha had asked Bynum to bind her daughter to her. Even before the arrival of Loomis and Zonia, Bynum performs rituals in the yard, and, immediately following these rituals, Loomis and Zonia actually arrive at the boardinghouse door. Bertha informs Seth that Bynum was out in the yard all morning: "I don't know what he's doing. He had three of them pigeons lined up out there. He dance around till he get tired. He sit down awhile then get up and dance some more" (234 [1.2]). Bynum knows of or induces Loomis's coming and must prepare.

Notably, the offstage rituals that Bynum performs can be read as African-based spirit practices. To give students a greater understanding of these practices, working with Robert Farris Thompson's landmark book, *A Flash of the Spirit,* is particularly useful. Farris Thompson examines the ancient African civilizations of the Yoruba, Kongo, Ejagham, Mande, and Cross River. His descriptions of Yoruba spiritual practices can directly inform a student's appreciation of Bynum's ritual actions. Later in the play, on the night directly preceding the day that Loomis and Zonia are scheduled to move on, Bynum again engages in unseen ceremonies, and they prefigure Martha's return. Reuben, Zonia's playmate, tells Zonia, "Something spooky going on around here. Last night Mr. Bynum was out in the yard singing and talking to the wind . . . and the wind just be talking back to him" (275 [2.4]). Bynum continually summons the spirits, repeating and revising African ritualistic traditions to support him.

In fact, Bynum produces the eventual appearance of Martha and affects the final climactic confrontation between her and Loomis. At the opening of the second scene of act 1, Seth informs Bertha that he knows that Martha, whose name is now Pentecost, has moved with her church to Rankin, to a building that used to be a shoe store. Seth, however, refuses to tell Loomis her whereabouts: "I ain't gonna tell this old wild-eyed mean-looking nigger nothing!" Although Bynum is not present in this scene, he somehow manages to deduce her location from Seth, because later, just before Selig leaves on his traveling salesman rounds and in search of Martha, Bynum delivers to him this indirect message: "You going upriver huh? You going up around my way. . . . Used to go up into Rankin and take that first right hand road. I wore out many pair of shoes walking around that way. You'd have thought I was a missionary spreading the gospel the way I wandered all around them parts" (240 [1.2]). Bynum loads Selig with clues that direct him to find Martha. When Selig does return with Martha, he explains, "She was right out there in Rankin. You take that first right hand road . . . right there at that church on Wooster Street. I started to go right past it and something told me to stop at the church and see if they needed any dustpans" (284 [2.5]). One could ask why Bynum didn't simply tell Selig where Martha was living. However, Bynum's methodology, like that of many Yoruba religious parables or teachings, is to enable to come to decisions on their own.

Still, Bynum's spiritual practices, much like Loomis's vision of bones walking on water, are not simply African; they are tinged with references to Christianity as well. Teaching *Joe Turner* means engaging in readings from the Bible as well as in scholarship on African-based religious practices. Bynum's story of his shiny man contains strong allusions to the Bible in addition to Yoruba spirituality. Kim Pereira relates Bynum's spiritual reformation to that of Saint Paul (Acts 9.10–19): "Both took place on a road, both were accompanied by a shining light . . . and both resulted in missions of healing." Pereira also notes that Christ gave Saint Peter the binding power just as Bynum receives that power from his father ("*Joe Turner's Come*" 72). Yet this reference to Saint Peter is equally African, for in Haitian vodun, a New World descendant of Yoruba spiritual observances, Saint Peter becomes associated with Eshu, the spirit of the crossroads, the messenger of the gods in worship practices. "In the course of supposed Westernization," Farris Thompson writes, "Haitians actually transformed the meaning of the Catholic icons by observing their similarities to African spirits" (169, 172). Bynum's spiritual acts throughout the play link him, then, to both Saint Peter and Eshu, who Farris Thompson terms "the ultimate master of potentiality" (19). What happens in Wilson's dramaturgy is a profound syncretism, as African practices conjoin with Christian rites in a distinctly African American cosmology.

Wilson scholars—Paul Carter Harrison, in "August Wilson's Blues Poetics" (312), and Pereira, in "*Joe Turner's Come and Gone:* Seek and You Shall Find" (66)—have associated Loomis with the Yoruba deity Eshu or Esu Elegba. Eshu is the messenger and guide of the Orisha, a companion on the road, and the guardian of the crossroads. Certainly Loomis's act of self-sacrifice—his slashing his chest with his knife and cleansing himself with his own blood—which ends the play and symbolically creates a path for others to follow, can be associated with the spirit of Eshu. For Loomis finds life through this act, and Eshu, as Farris Thompson notes, is "the principle of life and individuality" (19). Eshu, however, is also a trickster figure, a mischievous spirit that plays jokes on both gods and human beings. The sense of the trickster, I would argue, is not present in the dispossessed and desperate figure of Loomis. Thus the associations with Eshu seem incomplete and of service neither to Yoruba connections nor to Wilson's play. I would not represent Loomis as an African American descendant of Eshu but would instead associate him with the Yoruba god Ogun, the god of the roads and of iron and the first tragic practitioner. The critical text that I would use to make this association and assign in class is the essay "The Fourth Stage," by the Nobel Prize–winner Wole Soyinka. "The Fourth Stage" is not an easy read for students, but it is an important one. In this text, Soyinka describes the journey of Ogun, the first tragic actor. According to Soyinka, Yoruba tragedy replicates the initiating act of Ogun, one of the central spirits in the Yoruba pantheon and the patron god of Yoruba theater. In Yoruba culture, the worlds of the living, the dead, and the unborn represent the first three stages. The transitional space among them is the fourth stage. Soyinka refers to this stage as the "chthonic realm," the transitional yet "inchoate matrix" of death and becoming (28). He describes Ogun's entrance into and transcendence of the fourth stage. Ogun, as the first actor, entered into this abyss and was disintegrated, but he escaped complete annihilation and was able to reassemble through the power and determination of his will. Will, according to Soyinka, is the "truth of destructiveness and creativity in acting man." Ogun performed a symbolic act that reaffirmed the power of the human will to overcome. In Yoruba tragedy, the protagonist enters the chthonic realm and "within the mystic summons of the chasm, the protagonist actor . . . resists, like Ogun before him, the final step toward complete annihilation" (28). Loomis, I would argue, is the tragic protagonist replicating the path of Ogun, desiring spiritual transcendence and facing the great chasm, the gulf of transition. Soyinka maintains, "On the arena of the living, when man is stripped of excrescencies, when disasters and conflicts (the material of drama) have crushed and robbed him of self-consciousness and pretensions, he stands in present reality at the spiritual edge of this gulf" (32).

Loomis stands in such a position. Through his seven-year incarceration and his subsequent trauma of dislocation, he has experienced "the mystic summons of the chasm" and, because of his psychological alienation, he is now threatened with "complete annihilation." Separated from his identity and in danger of dissolution, he enters Seth's Pittsburgh boardinghouse in need of a spiritual and cultural foundation that he can call his own.

Soyinka's "Fourth Stage" provides a basis for how to read Loomis's reunion with his wife. In this climactic meeting, Loomis faces spiritual and psychological dissolution and must survive through an act of will. This final scene also juxtaposes Christian ritual and African symbolism as it creates a powerful synthesis of the two. Martha and Loomis engage in another moment of call-and-response. She represents the forces of Christianity and asks him to return to the calling of the Bible to be saved. He refutes her theology and questions her reliance on Christian faith. Martha's new name, Pentecost, reflects her being born again in Christianity. Pentecost in the Bible is the seventh Sunday after Easter, the day in which the Holy Ghost descended upon the disciples, possessing them and causing them to speak in tongues: "And they were all filled with the Holy Ghost, and began to speak with other tongues, as the Spirit gave them utterance" (Acts 2.4 [King James Vers.]). Pentecost represents for the disciples a new beginning in faith, a new life marked by the celebration of the Holy Spirit. In addition to the symbolism of Pentecost, Martha's first name explicitly invokes biblical images of the Martha who greeted Jesus at the sepulcher after he was resurrected on the third day.

Yet for Loomis Christianity has become a bankrupt religion—he was, after all, picked up by Joe Turner while he was proselytizing for Jesus. In his spirited exchange with Martha, Loomis makes a profound and poignant denunciation of Jesus Christ: "Great big old white man . . . your Mr. Jesus Christ. Standing there with a whip in one hand and tote board in another, and them niggers swimming in a sea of cotton" (287 [2.5]). This is a critical moment for class consideration and discussion of evocative communities of meaning as it comments so pointedly on the spiritual politics of the play. Loomis imagines Jesus Christ as a white overseer exploiting and oppressing his black labor force. What, then, does this image say about black faith in Christianity? What, then, does the play advocate in terms of an alternative practice? The subsequent action of the play and Wilson's own words are particularly useful in addressing these questions. In a conversation with Samuel Freedman, Wilson relates:

> I think it was Amiri Baraka who said that when you look in the mirror you should see your God. All over the world, nobody has a God who doesn't resemble them. Except Black Americans. They can't even see they're worshipping someone else's God, because they want so badly to assimilate, to get the fruits of society. The message of America is "Leave your Africanness outside the door." My message is "Claim what is yours."
> (qtd. in Freedman)

Wilson clearly opposes the concept of blacks' worshipping a white god and argues that such faith in "someone else's God" can have a deleterious effect on African American agency, identity, and self-empowerment. He rejects not Christianity but rather the tenets of it and the imagery in it that promotes whiteness. His message "Claim what is yours" is symbolically underscored by Loomis's slashing of his own chest and covering his face with blood. This act recalls Bynum's unseen African-based spirit practices with pigeons. It repeats and revises Bynum's earlier encounter with the shiny man, where the man rubbed his hands together and produced blood, and then "Told me to take and rub it all over me . . . say that was a way of cleaning myself" (212 [1.1]). Loomis's act is also a cleansing. It is equally unmediated, self-initiated, and self-defining. He "claims what is his" through a ritual that is symbolically African.

At the same time, the Christian resonance of this moment is significant. Wilson replaces the Communion ritual of Christ bleeding as a surrogate for the sins of the multitudes with Loomis's cutting his own chest and bleeding for himself: "I don't need anybody to bleed for me! I can bleed for myself." Just before Loomis slashes his chest, Martha asks him to accept Christ and understand that Jesus bled for him and to prepare himself to be "washed clean with the blood of the lamb" (288 [2.5]). In Christian doctrine, those metaphorically washed clean in the blood of Christ could be born anew, could enter heaven and receive eternal life. Yet in *Joe Turner* Wilson's protagonist seeks practical, not eternal, salvation. Signifying on the processes of transubstantiation, his bleeding makes literal what is symbolic in the Christian Communion service. Loomis, as Christ-like agent in his own image, with this ritualized act of bloodletting signals to other African Americans the need for similar agency and self-determination. "I'm standing now!" he exclaims to Bynum (289). Through this act he is born anew: Herald is heralding a new day for himself and for African Americans.

The entrance of Martha into this final scene is also a good place to raise questions around the constructions of gender in the play. Martha is one of four women in *Joe Turner,* the largest number of women in any play of the Wilson cycle. At issue with Martha, and with the other three women, is how they are drawn in relation to the male figures. How do they comment on and contribute to the play's critical issues? One of the major criticisms levied against Wilson and his cycle has been his depiction of women who seem not to possess any agency. The world of his cycle is largely one of black men. Martha enters and clearly her response to the despondent Loomis precipitates his self-determined action. The boarders Molly and Mattie are each in their own way women intent on discovering their song. Both are romanced by the itinerant worker Jeremy. He tells each woman that she needs a man, and they are both persuaded by this argument. The students should learn that the need for male protection, male companionship, and legitimacy was considered a social and economic reality at this time. Molly and Mattie have both taken the unusual step of traveling up to Pittsburgh from the South by themselves, and as women alone they are vulnerable. Accordingly, research into the migration of blacks from south to north during this period can be useful, as can a discussion of gender roles and their historical construction (see Wilkerson). The singular black female migrant was the exception rather than the rule. According to Hazel Carby, "The movement of black women between rural and urban areas and between southern and northern cities generated a series of moral panics. One serious consequence was that the behavior of black female migrants was characterized as sexually degenerate and thereby socially dangerous" (23).

Given this historical context, what the class can and should discuss is how the women of *Joe Turner* express their own will and determine their own destiny in relation to the men. Molly sets Jeremy straight: while she will accept his offer and accompany him, "Molly ain't going South" (263 [2.1]). Similarly, Mattie on her own determines to follow after Loomis in the final moment of the play. In each case, the women demonstrate a complex agency that reflects their relationship to men as well as their own desire. Perhaps the most interesting woman in this regard is Bertha, Seth's wife and the proprietress of the boardinghouse. Her domain is the kitchen, and within it she constantly feeds the other characters biscuits. Accordingly, students might mistakenly assume that she is subservient or even stereotypical in this role. Yet, when one reads more deeply, the domestic space is more complex, as it is a place where Bertha asserts control and agency. In the kitchen, she finds ways to stand up to her husband. While working in the kitchen, she speaks her mind as to the real truth about the white peddler, Selig, the so-called people finder. Bertha knows that the only people Selig finds are ones he led away in the first place. Her nurturing of the others functions as her method of literally and figuratively fortifying them against the forces beyond. For Bertha, the domestic is a powerful social space and even a site of ritual force. Her kitchen ritual of laughter symbolically cleanses the kitchen and prepares it for Martha's entrance and the final transformative scene.

With the introduction of Martha, Wilson breaks a purportedly cardinal rule of American realistic playwriting, by introducing a pivotal character in the last scene of the play. To be sure, throughout the play, we have anticipated her arrival. Still, adding such a figure into the final climactic scene goes against conventions. This departure enables us to discuss and understand that Wilson's playwriting in *Joe Turner* does not conform to the customary tenets of domestic realism. Instead of being driven just by plot, *Joe Turner* is propelled by the psychological and spiritual development of the characters. The metaphysical and metaphoric journey of Loomis and his desire to stand and join the legion of bones people are perhaps outside the normal trajectory for and development of realism, but they reflect the concepts of ritual and rite. In my estimation, *Joe Turner* is Wilson's most nonrealistic play, conveying the power of history, ritual, and the infusion of spirit and spirituality.

I try to foreground these ideas by ending the class with a discussion of—and then a participatory enactment of—the final scene of the first act of the play. At this moment, the boardinghouse members, save for Loomis, participate in a possessed juba dance, reminiscent of the slave ring shout. Lynne Fauley Emery points out in *Black Dance* that "[u]nder the guise of Protestantism, the Ring-Shout retained the characteristics of African sacred dance. The purpose of the Shout was possession, as it was in Voodoo, Shango, and Nanigo. Possession in the Shout, however, was by the spirit of the Lord, not Damballa or Shango" (120). Possession in the African American ring shout, as Emery relates, established a relationship with the divine that was experiential and personal. The embodied act of dancing connected the celebrant with spiritual forces beyond. To a certain degree, each of the characters in the juba scene from *Joe Turner* is possessed. The African diasporic experience of possession is not simply about harnessing the spirit of the gods, it is also about expressing a subversive freedom, a jouissance away from social, cultural, and especially gendered constraints. The black slave, a being possessed in real life, found in the experience of spiritual possession a liberation from the normal constraints of his or her everyday plantation existence. Wilson implicitly and explicitly connects the juba moment in *Joe Turner* to such African traditions of spiritual and social empowerment by granting the actors the license to improvise. Thus, for actors undertaking Wilson's juba scene, the dance is often more than simply an acting experience; it is potentially a moment of ritual embodiment. The performance of possession requires a real commitment to the context, circumstances, and meanings of the enactment. Wilson, in his stage directions, allows, "*It should be as African as possible, with the performers working themselves up into a near frenzy. The words can be improvised . . .*" (249 [1.4]). In this improvisation, the performer concentrates not only on being a particular character but also on doing the dance, experiencing and expressing the free flow of energy and spirit among fellow performers. The dance, not simply staged by the director, becomes real and immediate in its execution. Because of the nature of improvisation, the fervor of the juba scene in *Joe Turner* is different and new with each performance. The stage moment is both captivating, capable of sweeping the audience up in its energy, and dangerous.

To illustrate this idea, I involve the class as a whole in enacting the juba scene. I select one or two class members to function as Bynum and Jeremy, who keep the beat and call out the rhythm and words and lead the rest of the group in the juba. We create a call-and-response as the rest of the class moves around in the circle clapping their hands and repeating the words and echoing the rhythms that the callers cry out. My own participation in the ritual—I am there not just watching but fully committed and involved—is critical to helping the class feel safe, free, and engaged with the activity. To be sure, some students feel self-conscious and even silly. Sometimes they laugh. There have also been times when the words and the singing of the callers were so moving that they helped create a powerful communal experience. In any case, after about five minutes of the juba, I ask the students to return to their seats, and we talk about what they experienced. I ask them to describe their responses to participating in the juba. They generally discuss their awkwardness and even discomfort but come around to express and to understand how critical active involvement is to this scene. Through their own encounter with doing, they recognize how much Wilson leaves open to actors and directors and how this scene depends on what the actors feel, sense, and do in the moment. Within this staged religious ritual, there is the possibility of active and actual spiritual interaction and even transformation, which is not scripted but rather reliant on the embodied commitment of the actors.

This active participation and discussion around the juba returns us to the moment that began my discussion in this essay, the reaction to my class many years ago to viewing Herald Loomis's impotence at the end of act 1. Juxtaposing the uncertain response of students watching that scene in 1987 to anxious laughter of the students involved with the classroom performance foregrounds the power of embodied knowledge and experiential learning. The students witnessing the play without context lacked a place and space of reference. The enactment of the juba, on the other hand, can provide students with an embodied, epistemic understanding of the significance of spirituality in this moment and in the play. Loomis's ability to stand and walk is, of course, not literal. Rather, he is spiritually blocked and dependent on his own embodied recognition of his singular abilities to define himself, to discover his song, to connect to his past, and in so doing to determine his future. The implications of his ensuing journey in the play are at once individual and communal. Loomis's odyssey symbolizes the need of African Americans to reconnect with their past and with one another, to renegotiate their perceptions of and relations to history. Similarly, my students must negotiate new understandings of the power of history and even become coproducers of meaning through their own investment in and active engagement with the play. Perhaps they might even find their own song.

NOTES

The edition of *Joe Turner's Come and Gone* used in this essay is from Wilson's *Three Plays*.

[1] For a fuller discussion of ritual in social protest drama, see Elam, *Taking* 11–17.

African Codes and the Satiric Impulses in Wilson

Femi Euba

Instructors in search of new teaching and directorial approaches to some of August Wilson's more challenging plays would do well to study the implications of ritual and satire. Heavily ritualized plays, such as *Joe Turner's Come and Gone*, *Gem of the Ocean*, and *The Piano Lesson*, contain African codes that reveal attempts by the playwright to recall and connect his African past with his American present. In *Joe Turner*, for instance, the playwright, while presenting the reader with the African American juba dance, gives the following instruction: the dance "*is reminiscent of the Ring Shouts of African slaves* [and it] *should be as African as possible*" (52). Also, Bynum is a character who appears to be loaded with these codes. Described as "a conjur man, or rootworker" (n. pag. [dramatis personae]), he is the one who raises the song and dance of the juba. With the rituals he performs in the backyard of the Hollys, he seems to hold secret knowledge of African traditions, whether physical or mental. Decoding the African codes in the play would therefore be an asset to instructors and directors and offer insights that are valuable to students and actors.

This approach to teaching *Joe Turner* takes into account the identity of the codes through the rituals of Yoruba culture, a tradition that is probably the most influential in the African diaspora in the New World, given its resonance in such places as Brazil, the Caribbean, and the American South. It is from the South that the play demands we begin charting Loomis's objective and need in Pittsburgh. The focus on the Yoruba tradition inevitably reveals important cultural gods such as Obatala, the god of creation; Ogun, the god of iron and metallurgy, the creative principle; Sango, the god of thunder and lightning; and Esu, the trickster god of fate, who develops the impulses of satire. All these gods are significantly present in the New World.

As the god of fate, Esu would seem to implicate the fate of all the characters in *Joe Turner*. They all are searching for something that is meaningful to their lives, especially Loomis, on whom the playwright focuses the most—Loomis is looking not only for the wife who deserted him eleven years ago but also for self-definition. The challenge for the instructor or director is therefore to relate to the god as a satiric potential, to see how this potential affects the needs and objective of Loomis, and consequently to see the play in the light of satiric impulses. Cracking the puzzle of these concepts elicits a new approach that makes the instructor and the director see the play with a new vision and therefore brings the students and the audience to a new level of understanding the play. More important, the approach helps decode Wilson's implicit African codes as well as evaluate the play's ritual and satiric dimensions.

To be able to access the concepts of ritual and satire needed to interpret *Joe Turner,* one should take into consideration several factors:

a background of African culture needed to inform the play—that is, the Yoruba culture and its relation to African American culture
concepts of ritual and satire and their particular application to drama
African codes in *Joe Turner* and how they inform the ritual and satiric dimensions in the play
which character or characters describe and manifest these ritual and satiric dimensions
seeing *Joe Turner* as a ritual and satiric construct

A valuable way to introduce the class to Africa in general is to show them a map of the continent, one that gives all the divisions of the various countries that constitute it and the dates in which these countries achieved independence from their respective European colonizing power (*African National Independence*). Such a map enables a discussion on colonization, the impact of colonization on the African continent, and the conditions and influences of European rule in some of the African countries, especially the West African countries, including Nigeria, which was under British rule from the mid–nineteenth century to 1960, when the country received independence. *Wikipedia* is a quick and good resource for students to do preliminary research on the effects of colonization and subsequent decolonization. A focus on Nigeria helps situate and distinguish the Yoruba community in the western part of the country, the culture that informs the ritual and satiric concepts to be used to decode the African codes located in *Joe Turner.* Furthermore, a focus on the Yoruba community can lead to a discussion of transatlantic slavery on the West African coast, particularly the effects of slavery among the Yoruba and subsequent transportation of their culture to the New World.

A good way to introduce students to some of the cultural imperatives of Yoruba culture is the video *The World Began at Ile-Ife: Meaning and Function in Yoruba Art.* It could be shown alongside another video that gives some background of theatrical developments on the African American stage, some of which may have influenced Wilson: Woodie King's *Black Theatre: The Making of a Movement.* Providing these videos also enables the instructor and the students to discuss slavery in relation to retentions of African cultures in the New World and what made these retentions possible in certain places and not in others. Students will be better able to connect vision with thought when looking at the video on Yoruba culture if they are given guide questions relating to these topics:

the Yoruba creation myth, which puts the town of Ile-Ife at the center of the world and makes it the heart of creativity
the two worlds constituting the Yoruba worldview, which distinguishes physical space from the metaphysical

the symbolism of the river, which suggests the adaptability of the culture
the system of divination, which introduces the Yoruba diviner
Àse—power of the spoken word that manifests creativity
the gods identified—particularly Esu, the god of fate
the crown of the king and its symbols of power and control
the role of women and their power in the community
Gelede—the cult of men in honor of women

Every culture across the world has its own idea of how the world began, and the Yoruba community is no exception. The video begins with the Yoruba creation myth. It goes on to explore other facets of the Yoruba worldview: a culture in which men and women perform different roles—roles, however, that are of equal importance for the cohesion of the community. It discusses the power of the spoken word, fate of the individual, and the prominent gods and goddesses, especially Esu—all of which will be important to the concepts of ritual and satire in our approach to Wilson's plays.

Before deliberating on ritual and satire, the class discusses the concept of god in the Yoruba worldview. This discussion dispels formerly misconceived notions that Africans are either idol worshippers or surrounded by many pagan gods. Most American students do not know that there is a supreme being in Yoruba belief (i.e., Olódùmarè). Comparison can be made with the Greek Zeus and the Olympian gods, but a better comparison, and one more familiar to the students, is the Christian God and the saints. The African slaves in fact employed that plurality of subordinate but holy beings to justify and affirm the continuity of the gods they brought to the New World. Consequently, these African gods, especially the Yoruba gods, as aligned with the Catholic saints, are present still in the New World, in places such as Brazil, Haiti, Cuba, and even the United States—for example, in Louisiana (New Orleans), South Carolina, and New York. The gods exist in the various so-called cults of orishas, such as Candomblé, Macumba, Santeria, and Voodoo. It is necessary for students to pair some of these gods with Catholic saints. For instance, Exu, Elegua, or Papa Legba (various names of the Yoruba Esu) is identified with Saint Peter, Saint Anthony, or the devil, depending on the location (Bastide 260–84). While the class notes that Esu is sometimes identified with the Christian devil both in Africa and in the New World, it should know that there are radical differences between the two identifications (Euba, *Archetypes* 3; Bastide 277). Furthermore, it should note that the choice of comparison of Esu with Saint Peter has to do with the fact that both god and saint are guardians of the gate (Euba, *Archetypes* 5; Bastide 263).

The fusion of attributes leads to a discussion about syncretism. The class should note that the manifestation of Yoruba gods in the New World is a result of the syncretism that occurred between the gods and the Christian saints, which created conceptual differences. The saints tended to become transcendental essences as opposed to the Yoruba gods, who were terrestrial, humanlike beings and usually not above being punished for crimes committed (Soyinka, "Morality" 11–25). In this regard, noteworthy are Esu's affinities with the Greek god Hermes and the marked differences between them: Hermes's tricks are devised with impunity and as magical, comical artifices, whereas Esu's more functional tricks are levied to make his-her victims aware of their wrongdoing or crime (Euba, *Archetypes* 56).

Next in the discussion is the concept of ritual, which can be somewhat problematic for students at first, due to the misconceptions brought about by the loose use of the word *ritual*. While relating to it in its common usage as a repetitive action or gesture, the class should come to agree that it is more productive to see the concept as more than just that. First, the instructor frames a ritual action in the context of commemorative festivals in traditional cultures, such as the Yoruba—for example, the annual celebration of deities or ancestors, in which devotees or celebrants reconsecrate themselves. Then, in contrast, the instructor describes a ritual action in a context that is modern and more familiar to students—the repetitive action of, say, a news show on television to bring a point home to viewers. In either example, the action is not just repeated but performs a social or political function. These kinds of ritual do not just present a repetitive action but also define a structure, have an objective, desire an outcome.

However, the outcome of a ritual usually demands some form of sacrifice, specific or general. Ritual therefore conceives a structure that fulfills a need or accomplishes a goal (Euba, *Poetics* 1 and *Archetypes* 6–7). Ready examples abound. There may be the need for rain because of a drought, so by tradition animal sacrifices are offered to a particular deity. In a modern-day hostage crisis, a team of rescuers may be sent to the scene, and their action may result in the death of some of the rescuers or of some of the hostages, and those deaths are considered a sacrifice to the cause. Students are encouraged to give more examples of how human beings have been involved in some form of ritual since the beginning of time. The characters of *Joe Turner's Come and Gone,* especially the central character, are all searching for something they need and therefore offer themselves, consciously or not, as sacrifices—in other words, they do whatever it takes to achieve their objective.

With this concept of ritual in mind, the class considers the concept of satire. For students to be able to make the connection more easily, they need to see ritual as a dramatic structure upon which satire is eventually built. An action is dramatic if it confronts an obstacle to its objective. Examples of ritual are used to suggest that most dramas that we read or see onstage have a similar structure, a structure that the central characters often describe. There is a need, and the characters offer themselves as sacrifices in order to meet that need, either for themselves or for the community. Therefore any ritual could be called a drama (*Archetypes* 6). As Wole Soyinka puts it simply, ritual is the "drama of the gods" ("Morality" 1–2). In this regard, it is easy to see the stage, or the location where a play is set, as a ritual arena—the space designed for a dramatic action to take place. The instructor can then immediately connect this idea to the set of *Joe Turner*—a representation of the boardinghouse of the Hollys, which is the arena for the central character to experience his ritual action and process.

Once the processes of ritual and drama are firmly established, discussion on the satiric implications in *Joe Turner* can begin. First, the instructor should recall the satiric interventions of Esu, who levies actions on his victims to make them aware of their wrongdoings or crimes. There is a play, a ritual drama, that dramatizes a Yoruba myth of one of the principal gods, which should be of help. In *The Imprisonment of Obatala,* by Obotunde Ijimere, Obatala, the god assigned to create perfect human beings, got drunk one day on palm wine, an African alcoholic beverage, and consequently molded deformities, thus committing a cosmic crime. Since Yoruba gods, like human beings, must suffer for their crimes, Obatala must be brought to an awareness of his misdeed through sacrifice. This is what the play dramatizes—on three occasions he is confronted by Esu, who makes a mockery of him and draws him to anger. Obatala, remembering his crime, is able to surmount the impositions of Esu through patience and endurance. The myth and its reenactment at annual festivals of Obatala serve the god's devotees as a moral lesson in patience and endurance. The devotees, along with their god, internally or mentally suffer the punishment and thereby reconsecrate themselves to their god.

The drama fulfills a ritual process in terms of the need of Obatala and, by extension, the need of his devotees, who offer themselves as sacrifices in order to expiate their wrongdoings and consequently maintain their attributes of patience and endurance. But the drama also fulfills a satiric process: Obatala is made aware of his cosmic crime through ridicule and suffering.

Before going further, the instructor should clarify the difference between the Western concept of satire and the kind of ritual satire operative in the *The Imprisonment*. Robert C. Elliott, in his *The Power of Satire,* has successfully linked ritual satire to the work of Greek, Roman, and Irish playwrights, suggesting that the curse, a power of the word, is an implement of satire. The Western concept of satire, familiar to students, and ritual satire, unfamiliar to them, actually have much in common. For satire, in general, is a double-edged sword, conveying both ridicule and seriousness. Both derive from the grotesquerie it pronounces upon its victims through its attack using the power of the word. For example, a night-show host paints a grotesque image of a politician. This ridicule of the politician makes us laugh, but it also makes the politician and the viewers think, become aware of the quality, wrongdoing, or crime being ridiculed, with the result that the politician may make amends and the viewers may think twice before emulating the politician. Esu's ridiculing of Obatala by presenting a grotesque image of him furthers the moral improvement of his devotees. (For further development of this concept of satire, see Euba, *Archetypes*, ch. 3.)

Turning to *Joe Turner,* the class is asked to identify the central character, the one who establishes the dramatic process of the play. Although this identification is almost a given, it is not so easy for some students, who might prefer Bynum to Loomis. Part of the difficulty is the fact that everybody in the play appears to be searching, to have a need, and Bynum seems to be very influential in meeting, or not meeting, these needs. However, it is worth the effort to identify the character whose search is the most important in the play, strengthening the power or increasing the relevance of the other searches: Loomis. The ritual arena upon which he describes and undergoes this ritual-dramatic action is Seth and Bertha's boardinghouse, and the class can begin to assess the satiric implications of that action.

The trope that helps illuminate the satiric process is discussed more formally in my book *Archetypes.* It can be very useful for the instructor to point to the illustration of Obatala in *The Imprisonment.* In the introduction and chapters 1–3 of my book, arguments are presented that Esu, the Yoruba god of fate and trickster figure, is not only the focal point of ritual but also an ironist, a master of peripeteia, and a satirist. A story about his metaphysical identity and an explanation of his fateful-fatal potential in two or three of his praise chants should establish these qualities.

Esu is responsible for the fate of every person. He is Onibode, the keeper at heaven's gate who chooses the fate of each individual before he or she enters the physical world (*Archetypes* 5, 34). Each body goes to a central location in the metaphysical world to be given a head, the physical representation of the body's fate; thereafter Olodumare, the supreme being, gives the body breath. The chosen fate is forgotten when the individual enters the physical world, and the individual continually aspires to remember his or her fate as he or she journeys through life.

The Yoruba believe that fate has to do with one's character and will; metaphorically it is worn like "an emblem, a halo, or a habit." It is also "an elusive shadow" that often appears to play tricks on one—which is in keeping with the elusive and slippery nature of Esu. In anticipation of such tricks, which can lead to confusion or delirium, the individual must constantly acknowledge Esu, praying mentally or verbally for a clear direction (35–36). Hence the supplication and inducement suggested in one of his praise chants:

> Elfin deity, come home and eat mashed yam
> Come quickly and eat the festive mashed yam
> Eat, (that) of money
> Eat (that) of children
> Eat (that) of immortality, Master of wealth
> (Eat that) of abundance, of good health and long life,
> That our lives may be peaceful and calm. (37)

Esu, at the crossroads of every action, reaction, or decision, possesses the power of the word (*ase*); consequently he needs to be consulted or coerced. He is the embodiment of the good and evil in every individual, forces that the individual constantly seeks to keep in balance in order to be a perfect person. But such balance is difficult and keeps eluding human beings—as many praise chants suggest (58–59).

Trickery, elusiveness, and difficult balance manifest Esu's satiric potential. The praise name Odara, often attached as a suffix to Esu, on the surface means "one who tricks." But this attribute or characteristic implies an ironic function: "throw(ing)," that is, tricking, confusing, or deceiving, "his victim for attempting to 'throw' him—in other words, for attempting to cheat fate" (59). Many of his praise chants tell of individuals who are satirically thrown, deflated, chastised, or whipped for going against their chosen fates. And there are those individuals who use Esu to accuse, vilify, or curse the fate of people who have wronged them—in other words, they use their individual fate's power of the word to curse or satirize the fate of their victim (59–60).

It is important for instructors to note that the desired effect brought on the victim of a ritual satire satisfies the objective of satire in general, which is to ridicule and punish through sardonic grotesquerie in order to improve the thinking or behavior of the victim or community. This improvement is not necessarily achieved, given the flawed nature of human beings.

The instructor should also remind the class that this use of a curse, the satiric power of the word, is not foreign to Western experience. The classical Greek poet Archilochus, described as the earliest recorded ritual satirist in iambic meter, possessed a power that "vibrated for centuries after, (and) felt by later satirists who use the archetype as a warning to offending, vice-ridden men" (Elliot 3–15). More important to the study of *Joe Turner,* this satiric power is not unknown in African American culture, especially through that culture's diasporic connection to African culture. The class should begin to see the attempt by the playwright to dramatize the close, and yet somewhat distant, relation between the African and the African American. The distance requires a struggle to recall, but the closeness makes *Joe Turner* particularly accessible as an example of a ritual-satiric process.

It should become evident that Bynum is the most African character in the play, by the fact of the binding rituals he performs as a root worker and "conjur man" (Wilson, *Joe Turner's Come* 4). He is an equivalent of an African divination priest. If any one of the characters understood the dynamics of Esu and the satiric power he manifests on victims, it would be Bynum. When Loomis enters the scene, Bynum recognizes him as a "marked" man, in other words, as one who has been cursed by fate—in the hands of Joe Turner (70–71). Therefore it is through Bynum that Loomis describes and realizes his ritual-satiric process. It should be understood by the reader or audience that Bynum is not an Esu in the play, since he is not Loomis's fate. He is only an agent, guide, or diviner who helps Loomis understand his fate and what he must do to fulfill it. Every individual has his or her own Esu or fate, and no individual has immunity against its satiric power. Rather, the individual needs a guide to make him or her understand the cause of the affliction and what it takes to surmount it. The instructor should make comparisons with the situation of Obatala in the *Imprisonment of Obatala,* how Obatala has to undergo his ritual-satiric process because of his cosmic crime and how he understands this need through a diviner.

To further clarify the fact that Bynum is a guide, albeit a questing one, in Loomis's satiric process, the instructor should also make comparisons with Bynum's own process, the mystical experience he once had (9–10 [1.1]). Describing that experience, Bynum states that everything was grotesquely (satirically) larger than life. His father, as his guide, explained to him the circumstances of his "song," that is, his chosen fate in the metaphysical world, one that describes his identity and establishes his vocation in the physical world. As Bynum relates, it grieved his father that Bynum in the living world was "carrying other people's songs and not having one of [his] own." In other words, he had strayed from his fate and had been left, like Loomis, "dissatisfied," empty, and confused (71). The class should be reminded of the purpose behind Esu's satiric indictment, which is the purpose of satire in general—to make people aware of their failings so that they can change. Understanding the full implications of his religious experience, which informs his binding song, Bynum has set out to help others bind themselves to their song or true identity.

In the play, Loomis becomes Bynum's most important encounter. The instructor or director should note that the playwright is very emphatic about Loomis's already satirized appearance and his need: *"He is at times possessed. A man driven not by hellhounds that seemingly bay at his heels, but by his search for a world that speaks to something about himself. He is unable to harmonize the forces that swirl around him, and seeks to recreate the world into one that contains his image"* (13–14). This appearance will be used to track Loomis's satiric process, which is aligned with the dramatic process, as Loomis seeks to reclaim his identity. His need to find his wife has to do with his song, which is the fate that constitutes his character, will, identity, and vocation.

The next stage of the ritual-dramatic-satiric process, sacrifice, can be understood from the stories Loomis relates. Through these stories the class realizes that this stage began before the curtain opened. First was the circumstances of his victimhood, when Joe Turner drafted him into the chain gang, a form of slavery. Loomis was a church deacon, doing the work of God (admonishing gamblers) when he was taken and drafted along with the gamblers, an action that must have raised in him questions about God and His elusive design.

Loomis's assumed vocation in the physical world as a church deacon was not consistent with his inborn African religious imperatives, which include his chosen fate in the metaphysical world. In terms of the concept of Esu as satirist, Loomis was a victim of his fate, suffering in the hands of Joe Turner to the point of confusion and delirium, hence his grotesque appearance. He therefore needs to be brought into full awareness of what caused his suffering, his enslavement. The sacrificial condition has resulted in a mental paralysis, which the play begins to establish for us in physical terms, through the guidance of Bynum, whose ritual roots are in Africa.

Bynum has been interested in Loomis since Loomis made his entrance. That interest has increased and is at its highest level at the end of act 1, when Bynum calls the juba, the household's after-dinner Sunday ritual. Both characters, as well as others as audience, are present in the ritual arena.

The class is asked to consider the possible etymology of *juba* from various interpretations by scholars. For instance, Beverly Robinson discusses the origin of the word from the Bantu *diuba,* meaning "to pat, beat time, the sun, the hour" to its minstrelsy derivations and influences (215). The word's origins in Africa should be of particular interest to any director or instructor who wishes to consider this satiric approach to teaching *Joe Turner,* especially if the origin were to be located in Yoruba culture.

The Yoruba word *ijuba,* (literally, "a salute") not only identifies a ritualistic praise acknowledgement of and pledge to the divine but also recalls the opening glee or thanksgiving chanted and danced in early Yoruba music dramas. Although its call-and-response style is similar to the one Bynum called, a significant difference exists between the two renderings. Wilson implies this difference in his description of the dance, which the class should now read in full: *"The Juba is reminiscent of the Ring Shouts of the African slaves. It is a call and response dance. Bynum sits at the table and drums. He calls the dance as others clap hands, shuffle and stomp around the table. It should be as African as possible, with the performers working themselves up into a near frenzy."* The playwright goes on to suggest the song components of the dance: *"The words can be improvised, but should include some mention of the Holy Ghost"* (52).

The difference is in the syncretic nature of the ritual expression, a mixture of Christian and African religious precepts. It is also implied and reacted to by Loomis with the term "Holy Ghost." The instructor should discuss the syncretic influences that occurred over time as African slaves were acculturated to American Christianity. The class should keep in mind that Bynum, ritual diviner and guide and the most African character in the play, understands this and therefore is tolerant. When Loomis charges in, calls a halt on the dance, and "*starts to unzip his pants,*" Bynum just watches while others object with horror (52). Taking Bynum's African point of view, the class needs to consider his gesture not in the obvious Christian terms of sacrilege or desecration, especially because of what happens afterward.

To link the past with the present and show that Loomis's dramatic and satiric process in the present is consistent with the past, the instructor and the class may recall his preaching against gambling and his subsequent capture and redraft into slavery (the chain gang). His capture and enslavement for seven years is a satiric indictment of him for having strayed from his chosen fate. Thus the class realizes that the indictment was the beginning of his mental paralysis that took him through the chain gang and the separation from his family and his delirious search for his wife, a mental condition whose satiric implications Loomis needs to become fully aware of, in physical terms, before it can be resolved. The instructor should point out that this process is what the center of the play, the juba scene, dramatizes.

As soon as Loomis charges into the Hollys' dining room (the ritual arena of his self-awareness) and is confronted with the juba, he challenges its African authenticity by halting its process and desecrating it. But the desecration is done not in Christian but in African terms. It is the beginning of his self-realization. What happens after is the next stage of the process—possession. The instructor should pursue this stage also in African terms. The class, on the basis of its knowledge of Esu as the satiric leveler, should conclude that the god is the African presence in control here. To use a voodoo term, Esu (or Papa Legba, as he is known in the New World orisha cults) is the possessing god that rides his victim, causing him to speak in tongues, to the point of crippling him, a satiric, physical expression of his mental paralysis. A distinction should be made between the Christian and African ideas of possession. The first can be seen from the point of view of Pentecostal experience, the second from the point of view of African religious experience. Loomis's speaking in tongues should not be conceived as Pentecostal utterance but as a god's expression through his or her victim.

Finally, the class considers the third stage of the ritual-dramatic-satiric structure, the outcome in which everything should fall into place. To make a connection with this stage, the instructor should call attention to the full implications of Loomis's vision of bones, through which Bynum guides him (53–56). The class should read aloud the dialogue between Loomis and Bynum to understand and feel this experience.

The vision is a result of Loomis's possession, and, consistent with the African perspective, it is the climax of his sacrifice, which culminates in the moment of his self-awareness, the moment to which Esu, the possessing satiric god, has been leading him. This vision not only affects him with paralysis (bones "like you and me," "walking across the water" and then "sunk down" and "washed over land" unable to walk) but also shows him what he must do (the bones, standing and "saying goodbye to each other and walking every whichaway down the road"). The vision leaves Loomis crippled and makes him aware that he has "got to stand up" (55–56).

The satiric picture at the end of act 1, along with Loomis's awareness, allows the class to investigate and interpret the final picture at the end of act 2. The instructor and the director should note that the second picture is an extension of Loomis's ritual-satiric awareness at the end of act 1. This final image should be conceived as the realization of his objective of finding his song—the ritual-satiric outcome. The outcome is achieved by his finding his wife, Martha Pentecost, from whom he must now free himself in order to find himself. The class should note the opposite positions Loomis and Martha take: Her firm religious faith through the indoctrination of Western and Christian values; his exposure to the African sensibilities that constitute his African American personality. His self-determining African values defiantly challenge Martha's Christian precepts, and insisting on redefining his satirized identity and on assuming his fateful-fatal responsibilities leads to his salvation. The class should note the final symbolic image: *LOOMIS slashes himself across the chest. He rubs the blood over his face and comes to a realization* (93).

The satiric approach, based on Yoruba cultural imperatives, offers new insights to teaching not only *Joe Turner's Come and Gone* but also some of Wilson's other plays that share ritual constructs with *Joe Turner.* For instance, the ritual-satiric strategy could be used to consider Troy's fate process in *Fences,* Levee's in *Ma Rainey's Black Bottom,* or Citizen Barlow's in *Gem of the Ocean,* a play in which Aunt Ester's character equals Bynum's in Africanness. The satiric perspective also extends to the consideration of other central characters in other plays by African Americans, such as Clay and Walker Vessels in LeRoi Jones's *Dutchman* and *The Slave,* as suggested in my *Archetypes* (ch. 4). In the referenced plays by Wilson there seems to exist a struggle to investigate, break up, and reconnect the African component of African American. It is a struggle that ultimately suggests Wilson's satiric strategy, which indicts as well as brings awareness to what it means to be an African American in white America.

NOTE

This essay uses the 1988 New American Library edition of *Joe Turner's Come and Gone.*

"You on an Adventure": Teaching August Wilson's *Gem of the Ocean*

Sandra L. Richards

> You on an adventure, Mr. Citizen. I bet you didn't know that. It's all adventure. You signed up for it and didn't even know it.
>
> —Wilson, *Gem of the Ocean*

Having sung Citizen Barlow a lullaby that promises a mother's protection against a hostile world, Aunt Ester counsels the sleeping man with words linking adventure to life itself (24). Given Barlow's resonant first name as well as the title of the play, an abbreviated title of a song that unofficially competed for nearly a century with "The Star Spangled Banner" as the American national anthem (*Columbia*), questions about citizenship, personhood, and freedom are at the forefront of this August Wilson drama. Citizen Barlow has come to Aunt Ester's house in the Hill District of Pittsburgh in 1904 for advice as to how to live in ethical relationship to others. In teaching the play, instructors and students embark upon a similar adventure in order to examine, from the perspective of dispossessed black citizens, constructs of community and nation and their applicability to students' contemporary moment.

Briefly stated, *Gem of the Ocean* revolves around Citizen Barlow, who has come seeking absolution for having stolen a bucket of nails and failed to confess his crime, thereby allowing the amazingly resolute Garret Brown to drown rather than stand falsely accused of theft. Brown's refusal to come out of the river and be punished has, reportedly, instigated a community crisis in which black people, fed up with poor living and work conditions, decide to resist. An industrial strike, stoked by mounting violence in Pittsburgh along with reports of hard times in the South at the hands of "crazy" white folks (15), forms the sociopolitical context for this quest for meaning and community. Barlow is a recent migrant from Alabama. He has heard that Aunt Ester, whose age corresponds to the numbers of years people of African descent have been in the United States, can aid troubled individuals. In her house he encounters Black Mary, a twentyish young woman who is learning Aunt Ester's conjuring skills and who is the sister of Caesar, the constable policing black people. Also present are longtime friends Eli and Solly Two Kings, who protect Aunt Ester and aid members of the black community. Rounding out the cast is Rutherford Selig, a white itinerant salesman and friend.

Though I regularly teach at least one Wilson drama in my courses on African American theater and have offered a ten-week seminar on his work, I have not yet taught *Gem of the Ocean*. My remarks, therefore, are akin to a scenario that I would further adapt. In teaching this play to a class of primarily upper-level undergraduates, drawn from the African American Studies and Theatre Departments, in both of which I am housed, I would allot at least three class sessions (or one week out of a ten-week quarter) to the text. Like other Wilson plays, *Gem of the Ocean* is rich in its intricate layering of characters and issues. Thus, the first session would concentrate on more obvious elements in order to ensure that students possess a basic understanding of the plot and its significance. Subsequent sessions would scrutinize some of the ways in which Wilson, like a jazz musician, complicates and amplifies the base line. Not only would students be expected to come to class prepared to discuss questions related to plot and character, but they would also be assigned to small research groups in order to share with classmates references that may be inaccessible to those not solidly grounded in American and African American history and culture.

Just as I would use different pedagogical strategies in the classroom, I have written this essay in a style that is divergent in its manner of address. That is, those sections covering the first two class meetings are discursive, offering my analysis of events and positions within the American mainstream. The last section of the play, devoted to a fantastical journey to the depths of the Atlantic Ocean, requires greater cultural literacy and theatrical imagination from the reader. Accordingly I have deployed a style that is both more bibliographic and speculative: I suspect instructors will welcome additional resources in assigning research topics to students, and given the textual density of this portion of the play, I identify likely questions and responses that may emerge from students' research.

A Bottom-Up History and the Meaning of Freedom

Structuring the first class discussion are two interrelated questions. First, given Wilson's project of writing a play about the African American experience for each decade of the twentieth century (Elam, *Past* xii–xv; Shannon, *Dramatic Vision* 3–5), what history does *Gem of the Ocean* project? Second, to what extent does this bottom-up history conform to the official or normative histories students have learned in school or through popular culture?[1] In considering the second question, we as a class are in fact analyzing the play's relevance to our present circumstances—that is, we are asking questions about how our current assumptions and knowledge impede or aid in an understanding of these characters and how Wilson, through his construction of this fictional world, is commenting upon a contemporary moment.

Starting with basic facts, students see that Wilson's characters are less than fifty years removed from slavery. Some of the characters, like Eli and Solly Two Kings, have memories of enslavement, escape, and participation in the Underground Railroad. Though born "after freedom came" (26), Citizen Barlow carries the legacy of his slave heritage, for his mother has given him a name expressing her hopes for his future status, and he has come north seeking better job opportunities. But unlike what students may have learned in school, freedom is not something given or a fixed end point. As Eli tells Citizen, and Solly concurs, "Freedom is what you make it," and, "You got to fight to make it mean something. All it mean is you got a long row to hoe and ain't got no plow. Ain't got no seed. Ain't got no mule. What good is freedom if you can't do nothing with it?" (28). The idea of agency and struggle toward the interrelated goals of freedom, citizenship, and personhood is repeated several times. For example, Reverend Tolliver is quoted as advising his congregation on the feasibility of a strike with the observation "the hand of justice was at the gate but the people still had to open it" (24); Solly tells his sister, who writes for help in fleeing the racial terror of the South, "The best faith is in yourself even though God do have a hand in it"(26); and even Aunt Ester confides that though she gives advice to those who are spiritually or emotionally troubled, "If you tell them they still don't know. You got to show them how to find it for themselves" (64). While the struggle for black empowerment is often represented in popular culture as spearheaded by whites—one need only think of John Adams, who must prompt the captured Cinque to speak up for his liberty in the movie *Amistad*, or of William Wilberforce (rather than the former slave and popular speaker Olaudah Equiano) as the primary figure inspiring the British public to support the abolition of the slave trade in the film *Amazing Grace*–Wilson's play insists upon ordinary black people's conceptualizing and fighting for their freedom.

Not only is an emphasis on agency uttered repeatedly but also it is apparent that the constitution of freedom changes depending on the historical context. For the older generation, *freedom* at one point meant emancipation from slavery; for Solly's sister in the post-Reconstruction South, *freedom* would entail the absence of racial violence and exploitation; for the newly arrived Citizen, *freedom* means nondiscriminatory, well-paid employment and psychic equilibrium.

Further, these different concepts of freedom are not structured around predominant American discourses celebrating the rugged individual as the exemplary citizen. Having made his way to freedom in Canada, Solly has returned to the slaveholding United States because"[i]t didn't feel right being in freedom and my mama and all the other people still in bondage" (57). For Solly, freedom is collective rather than individually articulated; it is rooted in an ethical relationship to others, whereby the well-being of the individual and society are coconstitutive. Indeed, historians, like Elsa Barkley Brown, Thomas C. Holt, and Jacqueline Jones, contend that once freed, African Americans organized social institutions around concepts of interdependence. Says Brown:

> The vision of social relations that [many southern African Americans] articulated was not the traditional nineteenth-century notion of possessive individualism whereby society is merely an aggregation of individuals, each of whom is ultimately responsible for her/himself. In this individual autonomy, "whether one eats or starves depends solely on one's individual will and capacities.". . . Such a notion of freedom and social responsibility

> was diametrically opposed to the one that undergirded [southern] black institutional developments . . . in the post–Civil War period, where the community and each individual in the community were ultimately responsible for every other person. ("Labor" 75)[2]

Much to the chagrin and frustration of white Freedmen's Bureau officials who "consistently sought to reeducate and assimilate freedpeople . . . by introducing a different . . . economic and political world view as well," blacks, no matter how poor they were, persisted in "thoughtless[ly]" helping others to the detriment of their own economic advantage (76 [Brown citing Jones]).

Note that this commitment to the health of the community can even override biological kinship, for Black Mary ultimately renounces her ties to Caesar because he has opted to support a system of governance built on oppressive discrimination. And the white salesman Selig, though his motives go unarticulated, subscribes to this communal ethic by helping Solly and Citizen evade Caesar's clutches.

Two events point to the operation of another temporality in this play: Solly repeats his struggle for freedom by attempting to free the Pittsburgh strikers from jail, and by play's end Citizen Barlow dons Solly's clothes and heads to the South, fully becoming his surrogate. Official history declares that slavery ended and black freedom began with Emancipation. The American nation-state has abrogated for itself a linear, progressive conception of time in which the nation's future is divinely guaranteed to be better than its past. Under such a definition, slavery is not understood as central to and constitutive of American democracy; instead, it is considered a regrettable moment in the progress of democracy.

These black folk know the difference between the legal document and actual practice—hence their sense that in the United States "[i]t's a war and you always on the battlefield" (58), or Aunt Ester's rejection of a paper that certifies her freedom (78). These black "citizens"[3] have experienced and subscribe to what James Clifford, building upon Ralph Ellison's observations about jazz, characterizes as a "discrepant temporality" in which time is syncopated, sometimes stopping, repeating in a different manner, or leaping toward a new beginning (263–64). From their position of what Ellison would term invisibility, they have a different sense of time that contests and recalibrates mainstream national narratives.

Thus in summary, for August Wilson's characters freedom is an ongoing process whose objective changes with changed historical circumstances. The citizen—and by implication the nation—understands identity as constituted relationally and therefore acts continually to enhance the life chances of those most in need, even when that choice defies the socially imposed boundaries of race, gender, class, or biological family. Speaking through the early twentieth century to contemporary audiences, Wilson insinuates that everyone in the theater, or in the class, is obligated to choose, again and again, to act as an individual and citizen positioned in relation to others; neither an inheritance of a history of oppression or of privilege exempts a student (or faculty member) from this challenge.

Moreover, introduced to the phenomenon of discrepant temporalities, students can be challenged to consider whether or how their contemporary moment may repeat an earlier period in the same or a different way. Have freedom and citizenship been achieved in the United States? By whom? What constructions of citizenship are enacted, for example, in present practices of incarceration? When Eli repeatedly greets visitors with the assertion that 1839 Wylie Avenue is "a peaceful house" (7, 30, 77) and Black Mary says it is a "sanctuary" where the desperate may find refuge and over which government has no jurisdiction (79), how might these claims be instances in which time leaps forward to the present? How does the concept of sanctuary operate in the contemporary moment? What does the play's definition of *citizen* imply about our responsibilities for current INS practices of rounding up immigrants who have illegally entered the country?[4]

Storytelling and the Enactment of Community

Assuming that I had at least three class sessions to devote to *Gem of the Ocean*, I would focus the second session on Wilson's deployment of the black vernacular practice of storytelling in order to underline the pedagogical and social functions of this mode of orature.[5] This session would also serve as preparation for analyzing the most fantastical segment of the play, namely, Citizen Barlow's journey to the City of Bones. I would start with a brief lecture concerning the various venues in which storytelling most often occurs within African American, African, and black Caribbean cultures: in both history and the present, it can occur in intimate family settings; in commercial places like barbershops, beauty parlors, and bars; and in sacred settings—as part of a preacher's sermon, for example. Very often, storytelling is only one element in a larger universe of performance practices that include hide-and-seek games for children, reflections on the day's activities by grownups, riddling, proverb swapping, and singing. The narrator may intend not only to entertain listeners and reinforce the sentimental bonds of all those assembled but also to project desirable modes of behavior and offer commentary in a manner that does not exacerbate existing social tensions. The narrator may devote considerable detail to a number of loosely related episodes, and listeners can amplify the story with interjections or take over the telling entirely if they feel that the first speaker is lacking in imagery or performance impact (Abrahams 1–20; Bascom; Richards, "Spreading" 93–94). Given the dialogic, polyvocal quality of storytelling sessions, the assembled community of speakers-listeners constructs a public sphere, in which issues of pressing social concern are debated.

Wilson takes these everyday practices and transposes them to the formal stage in ways that intrigue, puzzle, and teach. For example, when Citizen Barlow finally shares his problem with Aunt Ester, she responds with a dizzying series of seemingly unrelated stories about a man who loved pigs, Peter's denying Christ, and a man who attempted to fix a wheel that turned backward rather than forward. This storyteller-conjurer proceeds in an indirect fashion, offering representations of the known in order to encourage her listener to extend himself toward the unknown or unrecognized. Into a story about the familiar world of farm animals, she inserts what is undoubtedly a lie about the man's seeing pigs in the sky, but the lie is couched in such graphic terms as to render a memorable truth about this farmer's emotional imbalance. Stating the moral of her story, Aunt Ester says, "He lost everything he had. He lost the center of his life 'cause it wasn't inside him. It wasn't something nobody could take away." Lest Barlow resist connecting the pigs to his own plight, she continues, "See, Mr. Citizen, right now that bucket of nails is at the center of your life. You only have one life, Mr. Citizen. It's your life. Can't nobody else claim it" (44). But resist Barlow does, claiming in response to her next story about Peter and Christ that he does not "know much about the Bible" (45).

Aunt Ester's stories about fixations on pigs, the biblical Peter, and wheels turning in the wrong direction operate as metacommentary on theater itself, for a good story with vivid descriptions and ambiguous significance keeps a spectator invested in a process of meaning making shared with the actors, design and production staff members, and other people in the audience. Further, as Geneva Smitherman, a linguist, observes about African American speech, "[t]o testify is to tell the truth through 'story,'" whether in a sacred or secular space. Noting the nonlinear way in which a good storyteller will proceed, she also posits:

> The retelling of these occurrences in lifelike fashion recreates the spiritual reality for others who at that moment vicariously experience what the testifier has gone through. The content of testifying, then, is not plain and simple commentary but a dramatic narration and a communal reenactment of one's feelings and experiences. Thus one's humanity is reaffirmed by the group and his or her sense of isolation diminished. (*Talkin and Testifyin* 150)

But because Barlow—and presumably Wilson's twenty-first-century audience—has not fully grasped the implications of the conjurer's stories for the conduct of his life, he (and we as spectators or readers) must be sent on a quest that will engage the body and imagination in profound ways. He must go back and relive the moment of historic violence and psychic rupture that converted him from human being into black commodity, for in that abyss he may find himself as person and citizen. He must journey to the City of Bones.

The Marvelous City of Bones

In preparation for the journey, Aunt Ester spreads a quilt, which she terms a map,[6] and gives Barlow a boat made from the paper on which her slave bill of sale was written. As the journey proceeds, interrupted by the older men's reminiscences of their adventures as conductors on the Underground Railroad, by poetic recitations,[7] blues moans,[8] meditations on the difference between freedom and emancipation, and news of the ongoing industrial strife in Pittsburgh, this boat is eventually identified as the *Gem of the Ocean*, whose captain abandoned both crew and enslaved cargo to a watery death. Understandably, at the outset Barlow objects to her misrepresentation of these material objects, but the old woman replies that their magic or power lies in his belief. Similarly, the persuasiveness of Wilson's representation of the Middle Passage specifically and of a twentieth-century black American world more generally lies in audiences' willing suspension of disbelief or investment in the fictional lie of art in order to apprehend an essential truth. Here, students will need what VeVe Clark termed a "diaspora literacy" or knowledge of black cultures, for Aunt Ester and her helpers draw upon discourses drawn from the Bible, seventeenth-century Puritan ideology, nineteenth-century American literature, West African cultures transposed to the Sea Islands of Georgia and South Carolina, as well as twentieth-century blues cultures in order to facilitate for Barlow a conversion experience that takes him far beyond the purview of a Christian god.[9]

Obviously, the journey to the City of Bones deserves its own essay or essays, and class time is limited. Before this class discussion, I would assign groups of students to research specific topics. Their findings, shared with the class, could construct an interpretation of this segment of the play. Though I assume that students can provide the most basic definition of the term *Middle Passage*, I would nonetheless assign one group to do further research concerning not only the historical facts (tight vs. loose packing on slave ships, for example) but also the traumatic legacies of that passage. The PBS program *Africans in America* in both its DVD and print formats brings together invaluable commentary by slave ship captains, surgeons, and captives, while Genevieve Fabre's essay on dance offers brilliant analysis concerning the identities that were being forged through performance.[10] Another group would be assigned to identify biblical references, such as tongues of fire, tongues and words, and the new Jerusalem with its twelve gates. A subset of this group would be asked to trace links between the new Jerusalem of the book of Revelations, descriptions of "the city set on a hill" found in the book of Matthew, and the political reinterpretations of the city as exceptional American identity ordained by God. Another group would read a section of Albert Raboteau's *Slave Religion: The "Invisible Institution" in the Antebellum South* in order to learn more about enslaved people's indoctrination into Christianity. Another group would be assigned readings of John Michael Vlach and of Margaret Washington Creel concerning African American funeral practices (see esp. Vlach, ch. 9 [sec. "African Antecedents"]). Other students could be assigned sections of my essay on Yoruba-inflected dramaturgical structure, "Yoruba Gods on the American Stage: August Wilson's *Joe Turner's Come and Gone.*" With these resources as supplements to Wilson's text, we would be prepared to chart our own map of Barlow's journey to the City of Bones.

Hopefully, the Middle Passage research group would impress upon the class the utter dehumanization and trauma suffered by the captives on those transatlantic voyages. Violently transformed from human into chattel, the enslaved labored in myriad ways—including dance on the slave ships themselves—to reestablish their humanity in their own minds as well as in that of their captors. "Why return to that site of complete helplessness?" someone in the class might ask. The groups assigned readings concerning religious belief and practices might begin with the simple observation that the Atlantic Ocean is the place where millions of enslaved people or ancestors are buried, and in various African belief systems, as well as in those developed in the Americas, ancestors are viewed as powerful intermediaries, concerned with the spiritual and physical well-being of their descendants. Like the Yoruba god Ogun who ventured through the abyss in order to reestablish contact between the divine and the human (Soyinka, "Morality" 27–31), Citizen Barlow must take Ogun's symbol of iron on his journey through the diasporic aporia of lost lineage, hence nonhumanness, to restore his contact with the ancestors and possibly bring a meaningful message back to those assembled as witnesses to the journey (Richards, "Yoruba Gods" 95–99).

The BaKongo peoples of the Congo believed that "the deceased ancestors become white creatures called *bakulu*, who inhabit villages of the dead located under river beds or lake bottoms; they may return from this underworld to mingle with the living without being seen and can direct the course of the living" (Vlach 143). Like Vlach, Creel documents how those African beliefs continued in African American practices of decorating graves with seashells or mirrors, which, in addition to paying homage, write black history, for as Creel quotes an elderly Gullah informant, "The shells stand for the sea. The sea brought us, the sea shall take us back" (90). From the group of students who have read Raboteau, the class would learn that in some Christian practices enslaved peoples recognized parallels with their African belief systems. More specifically, Christian discourses concerning baptism echoed preexisting beliefs that an uninitiated person endured frightening travels or dreams in which his or her individuality was tested and died (sometimes symbolized by immersion in water) in order for a new person to be born, one connected to the spirit world and the material community of believers (Creel 79–81; Sobel 90–91, 108–20). Thus Barlow's travel to the ocean depths replicates the terror-filled experience of confronting one's human vulnerability in the hope of finding divine salvation.

The group researching specific biblical references would, presumably, observe that Aunt Ester and Solly speak of this City of Bones in terms conventionally associated with descriptions of heaven. The city is where their deceased relatives live, and it is their desired place of eternal rest. An astute student may also note that both Ester and Solly speak of returning to this marine heaven (52, 56), an idea that diverges from normative Christian understandings. Indeed, these elders gesture instead toward a hybrid, Afro-Christian belief in which the living retrace the trajectories of utter abnegation and resurrection experienced by the gods, who may be named Ogun or Jesus Christ. Aunt Ester insists more than once that the inhabitants of the City of Bones have a "burning tongue" (53, 68) whose song cannot be extinguished. As the class would learn, this phrasing may refer to passages in the book of Isaiah in which an association is made between fire that burns dry grass and the destruction that awaits those who have rejected God's holy word (5.24). Linking the words *tongue* and *fire,* they may find Isaiah's report that Jerusalem and Judah have fallen because its people, through their speech and actions, rebelled against God (3.8).

A student may ask why, after Barlow has survived the cramped slave ship and arrived at the gates of heaven, do its residents, who are presumably enjoying salvation, have "their tongue on fire" prophesying destruction (68)? An answer may begin to emerge from research concerning biblical references to the twelve gates that mark the perimeters of heaven (Revelations 21.12, 21.18), also called the new Jerusalem (21.2). As Black Mary observes, twelve gates also surround this marine city. But whereas the biblical heaven is said to shine from the splendor of gold, clear glass, and divine light that permeates the space, the streets of Barlow's City of Bones "look like silver," and the people "glitter . . . dressed in their splendors. It's a sight like you ain't never seen" (68). In order to enter this city, Barlow, like his biblical predecessors, must be free of sin (Revelations 22.14) and therefore must confess his crime and offer penance, as symbolized by his giving the two pennies that he labored to find before embarking on this perilous journey.

Considering that early English settlers saw themselves establishing a new Jerusalem on the North American continent (Bercovitch 7–9), research on links between biblical teachings and political ideology becomes relevant to class discussion. Having read Matthew 5.14–16, where Jesus exhorts the early Christian community to conduct its civic life like a lamp or "city set on a hill," whose light cannot be hidden and whose actions function as a model for others,[11] students would also report that this formulation has served as a core American ideal since 1630, when John Winthrop urged his fellow Puritans to transform a land of wild beasts and men into a community that would be envied by the rest of the world and testify to their inheritance of the covenant between god and Israel. This idea of the United States as a beacon of light (and democracy) to be emulated by the rest of the world has been sustained through time and mobilized by modern presidents such as John F. Kennedy, Ronald Reagan, George Herbert Walker Bush, and his son, George W. Bush, as well as the 2008 presidential contenders. In fact, David Howard-Pitney, a historian, contends, "No belief has been more central to American civil religion than the idea that Americans are, in some important sense, a chosen people with a historic mission to save and remake the world" (5). That Wilson's residents in the City of Bones have tongues of fire that prophesy the destruction of those who have rejected God's teachings, departs from the normative conception of the United States as a promised land or new Jerusalem. Created from the trauma of transatlantic slave crossings, like that of the ship *Gem of the Ocean,* and redeemed by their residence in a new, oceanic heaven, these citizens testify against American claims of providential exceptionalism.

Their testimony conforms, in part, to the tradition of jeremiad practiced by both white and black American orators. Yet Barlow's final journey departs from that tradition. The American jeremiad discursive tradition utilized a tripartite structure in which God's selection of Americans as the new, chosen people was reiterated; criticism was voiced concerning the ways in which the citizenry had failed to live up to divine expectations; and finally the populace was exhorted to resume its responsibilities so that society could be redeemed and the covenant with God realized on earth (Bercovitch cited in Howard-Pitney 6–7). In testifying to slavery, the marine ancestors in Wilson's play identify the sin that invalidates the American democratic project. But whereas the jeremiad, particularly as practiced by white orators, exuded "unshakeable optimism" that the United States would inevitably fulfill its divinely appointed role (6), Wilson's *Gem of the Ocean* does not conclude with such a guarantee. Barlow learns that redemption is possible only through his relationships to others—hence his decision to accompany Solly south on a postslavery Underground Railroad mission. But as they try to leave Pittsburgh, Solly is killed. He has laid down his life attempting to help others. His death is consistent with many African beliefs concerning sacrifice and with the Christian story of the crucifixion, in that blood is shed so that the lives of the living community can be enhanced. Choosing to take up the older man's mantle and toasted with the line "So live" from William Cullen Bryant's nineteenth-century poem (85), Barlow departs for an unknown future. "So live" is in fact the last line of the play. Perhaps his mission will end with the sister's liberation, or perhaps it will end in his own death. That the future is ambiguous is signaled by the rest of the cast's preparing Solly's body for interment and singing, "Let's go to the burying ground" (84). The graveyard is a space of both mourning and joyful contact with the spirit world, and each individual must decide the particular significance of that contact, depending upon his or her own psychic resources as shaped by a community of witnesses. Having come to 1839 Wylie Avenue, Citizen Barlow has embarked upon an adventure that has profoundly changed his life. Hopefully by play's end, the class too has had an unexpected adventure. Hopefully, their visit to 1904 black Pittsburgh has helped them understand themselves, citizenship, and nation in the early twenty-first century.

NOTES

I would like to thank Rashida Shaw, Sandra Shannon, and Jennifer Simpson for helpful feedback and Martha Biondi for bibliographic suggestions concerning American exceptionalism.

[1] Note, however, that it is important to emphasize for students that Wilson takes liberty with historical data, producing what Lene Brondum terms a "composite history" in which "historical 'facts' are selected for representation according to whether they effec-

tively reveal something about the 'essence' of a culture or historical period. . . . As such, composite history functions as a revision of the traditional Western definition of history" (155).

[2] Brown's "The Labor of Politics" is an excerpt of her essay "To Catch the Vision of Freedom: Reconstructing Southern Black Women's Political History, 1865–1880."

[3] I flag the word *citizen* in the spirit of Houston A. Baker, Jr., who argues, "There is no such thing as second-class citizenship. . . . Either one is a citizen, or one is not. Exclusion is a flagrant denial of citizenship"(*Betrayal* 3).

[4] Instructors could certainly introduce considerations about historical continuity into the present. They could suggest that students research movements to abolish the prison-industrial complex, spearheaded by people such as Angela Davis, Ruth Wilson Gilmore, and Joy James. In addition to publications by these scholars, students may want to consult the Web site for the grassroots organization Critical Resistance (http://criticalresistance.org/). On the subject of sanctuary, instructors could cite medieval religious traditions of sanctuary from government, the tradition of sanctuary associated with the Fugitive Slave Law of 1850, the sanctuary movement of the 1980s–1990s that sheltered Central American refugees, or the contemporary movement that supports the human rights of illegal workers. See, for example, Engber; the New Sanctuary Movement Web site (www. newsanctuarynyc.org).

[5] For a definition and discussion of orature, see Okpewho; Ngũgĩ wa Thiong'o 105–13.

[6] One may want to read Katherine McKittrick and Stephanie M. H. Camp concerning the alternative geography that enslaved people continually traced in defiance of a geography of containment as represented by the map, an official document produced by a hegemonic class. For a more theoretical analysis of black geographies, see McKittrick. A complementary but more historically oriented account is available in Camp.

[7] Solly's recitation that begins, "So live, that when thy summons comes . . . ," is part of William Cullen Bryant's meditation on death entitled "Thanatopsis," written between 1811 and 1813. Time permitting, one might want to challenge students to speculate about how Solly and Eli learned that poem. Were they literate? Did they learn it through oral transmission? How did white Americans learn this poem? My objective in pursuing this line of discussion would be to impress upon students the extent to which enslaved people actively participated in aspects of dominant culture, appropriating that culture for their own, subversive ends.

[8] Solly's intoning of "Dark was the night and cold was the ground" (56) to describe the slave experience is a quotation of the title of a wordless blues song moaned by the guitarist Blind Willie Johnson (1897–1945) and recorded in the late 1920s. Because Johnson spent his life preaching and singing on the streets of Beaumont, Texas, this song is thought to refer to the crucifixion of Christ, but here Wilson uses it anachronistically, constructing a composite history to insinuate a basic truth about the humanity and divinity of a people treated as a commodity. Students can hear Johnson on *YouTube* (www.youtube.com/watch?v=BNj2BXW852g).

[9] I am using the term *diaspora* to signal that enslaved Africans entered the Americas as multiply diverse culture bearers, synthesized and adapted their knowledges, and appropriated aspects of Native American and European epistemologies in order to confront the changed environmental and sociopolitical ecologies they encountered.

[10] For *Africans in America,* see "The Slave Coast" and "The Middle Passage." This material is supported by *African Slave Trade and the Middle Passage*. One may also want to suggest that students note the a cappella group Sweet Honey in the Rock's dirge-like

adaptation from Du Bois's *The Souls of Black Folk* that plays over the menu section of the CD. Their treatment of his challenge, "Your country? How came it yours? Before the Pilgrims landed we were here," prompts questions such as: What claims to land does the song assert? What is the significance of the claim? Does that claim exclude others from the nation, even while arguing for inclusion of blacks? An instructor may want students to read more about Olaudah Equiano than what is provided in the PBS materials; if so, chapter 2 of *The Interesting Life of Olaudah Equiano; or, Gustavus Vassa the African Written by Himself* recounts his African parentage, capture, and slave ship experiences (Equiano). For a more self-consciously interpretive account of what black writers, up until the last half of the twentieth century, have treated as a virtually unrepresentable experience, students may also view *The Middle Passage* film, whose script was written by Claude Chonville and Patrick Chamoiseau.

[11] Verses 14–16 read, in the New International Version, "You are the light of the world. A city on a hill cannot be hidden. Neither do people light a lamp and put it under a bowl. Instead they put it on its stand, and it gives light to everyone in the house. In the same way, let your light shine before men, that they may see your good deeds and praise your Father in heaven."

Teaching the Cycle: Understanding August Wilson's Fractal Dramaturgy

Faedra Chatard Carpenter

Much has been made—and rightly so—about the fact that August Wilson penned a ten-play cycle, writing a play for every decade in the twentieth century. Such a feat is momentous in itself, unmatched by any other American playwright. What is also of interest is that we refer to this particular collection of plays as a *cycle* rather than using more linear-minded terms, such as a "dramatic sequence," "chronology," or "series."[1] *Cycle* implies a sense of interrelatedness, yet it can also suggest—as some of my students have tried to assert—a circuitous redundancy. It is the latter assessment, that Wilson's decade cycle suffers from unwarranted or simplistic repetition, that this essay addresses. As one who has taught semester-long courses focused solely on the works of Wilson, I recognize the need to frame the nature of his self-referential plays in a matter that grants students a deeper appreciation of his artistic style and cultural sensibility. In doing so, I teach his decade cycle through the lens of what I call fractal dramaturgy, a creative strategy that encourages an Afrocentric interpretation of Wilson's intertextual playwriting.[2]

The Afrocentric Sensibility in Fractal Dramaturgy

In relating the notion of Afrocentricity to Wilson's playwriting, I heedfully conjure the formative work of scholars such as Maulana Karenga, who asserted that Afrocentricity is "essentially a quality of perspective or approach rooted in the cultural image and human interest of African people" (404).[3] While Afrocentric perspectives and practices are expressed in a number of ways, what interests me most about this particular perspective in relation to Wilson's dramatic ethos is the way an Afrocentric outlook champions the merging of art and life and Afrocentricity's imagistic, metaphoric, and sociological emphasis on circularities. In regard to the former, an Afrocentric approach to art making is one that seeks to create a complementary balance between form and content, aesthetics and functionality. In regard to the latter, as Nilgun Anadolu Okur has noted, "One of the basic arguments in Afrocentric criticism rests on the prevalence of circular rather than linear qualities in terms of form, shape, and structure in African art," a recurring motif that complements and supports Afrocentric aspirations toward "unity" and "wholeness" (102–03). Grounding my analysis on these fundamental considerations, I contend that Wilson's dramas powerfully stage an Afrocentric aesthetic through their dramatic structure as well as their subject matter.

One of the most memorable (and self-evident) expressions of Wilson's African sensibility is found in the electrifying juba scene in *Joe Turner's Come and*

Gone. Wilson writes in his stage directions that "the Juba is reminiscent of the Ring Shouts of the African slaves," and this literary and embodied reference highlights the ways in which Africanisms have persisted among African Americans ([New Amer. Lib.] 52). Not only does his reference to the ring shout infer the cultural significance of this counterclockwise dance ceremony in African American society but also, as noted by Sterling Stuckey, a historian, the circular configuration of the ring shout itself is emblematic of the religious symbolism of many West Africans:

> There is, in fact, substantial evidence for the importance of the ancestral function of the circle in West Africa, but the circle ritual imported by Africans from the Congo region was so powerful in its elaboration of a religious vision that it contributed disproportionately to the centrality of the circle in slavery. The use of the circle for religious purposes in slavery was so consistent and profound that one could argue that it was what gave form and meaning to black religion and art. (11)

Thus, if we recognize the centrality of circle imagery in West African cultures, it should not surprise us that such imagery can be traced throughout the visual and literary arts of contemporary African Americans.

An example is found in the work of the acclaimed novelist and educator Toni Morrison. Writing of the persistent use of circle imagery in her *Beloved,* Philip Page convincingly demonstrates how "circles and circle metaphors dominate" her work, arguing that "[a]n examination of these explicit and implicit circles and their implications reveals the subtle relationships between the novel's content and its form" (32). Similarly inspired by the way Morrison's stories employ cyclical elements, Nina Mikkelsen has observed what she describes as the "fractal aesthetic" in Morrison's oeuvre. Citing the prize-winning author's frequent use of contrapuntal narratives (a literary framework in which various aspects of a story line are told among many characters), Mikkelsen asserts, "The story structure that emerges in Morrison's novels is not unlike the mathematical 'fractal' visual pattern seen in African architecture and in decentered *kente* cloth patterns as a scaling, infinitely repeating design, which corresponds to the social structure prevalent in pre-colonial African culture." According to Mikkelsen, this fractal design "reflects the need members of oral cultures have of initiating new generations into the culture through storytelling, the endlessly repeated stream of stories keeping heritage and ancestral properties intact" (97). Her observations regarding Morrison's writing could easily apply to the writing style and intentions of Wilson: "No one view is the 'right' one; no one version is the only one; each is a part of the whole fabric of black folklore that [he] is embedding, and recasting, in the [plays] to produce new insights on black history, culture, and folklore" (98). Drawing from the work of both Page and Mikkelsen, I believe that the plays of Wilson reveal a fractal dramaturgy that not only informs the content and form of his decade cycle but also offers insight into black history and culture in multiple and profound ways.

Fractals, as in fractal geometry, are "characterized by the repetition of similar patterns at ever-diminishing scales," and their study and application has traditionally been limited to the fields of mathematics and computer science (Eglash 4). However, as the observations of Mikkelsen illustrate, fractal concepts are increasingly applied to work in the humanities and social sciences. To that end, the work of Ron Eglash has been particularly helpful to me in clarifying my understanding of Wilson's dramaturgy. In his book *African Fractals,* Eglash merges the studies of science and anthropology to demonstrate how the patterns found in fractal geometry "are surprisingly common to traditional African designs, and some of its basic concepts are fundamental to African knowledge systems" (3). Noting how the recursive nature of fractals are marked by "a sort of feedback loop, with the end result of one stage brought back as the starting point for the next" (8), Eglash studies the self-referential configurations that are frequently found in traditional African architecture, textiles, painting, sculpture, metalwork and woodwork, household goods, recreational exercises, religious doctrine, and hairstyles. Just as the recursive construction of fractals produces a feedback loop, I would argue that each play in Wilson's decade cycle sets the stage for the next.[4] This is true not only in terms of the obvious chronological progression of the texts but also in terms of how the task of divining each consecutive play affected the writer's dramaturgical process.

While Eglash wisely cautions his readers to recognize that fractal designs are not limited to, nor intrinsically characteristic of, African culture, the links he makes between African cultural expressions and fractal theories open the possibility for us to consider how aesthetic tendencies and cultural patterns persist despite diasporic dispersal. Eglash's scholarship provides a new way for us to reflect on the perseverance of Africanisms within contemporary African American life, including dramatic literature. Moreover, by reading Wilson's writing through the lens of fractal dramaturgy, we can also more readily identify the ways his work reflects both his personal and professional investment in an Afrocentric sensibility.

Throughout his career, Wilson fervently expressed his belief that there is a direct link between the social and cultural behaviors of African Americans and those of their African ancestors, as he unequivocally (and repeatedly) stated that "black Americans *are* Africans" ("Ground" [*Callaloo*] 494). For him, the enduring existence of Africanisms in the lives and expressions of black Americans was a matter of natural inheritance, the passing down of a particular worldview from generation to generation:

> Growing up in my mother's house at 1727 Bedford Avenue in Pittsburgh, Pennsylvania, I learned the language, the eating habits, the religious beliefs, the gestures, the notions of common sense, attitudes towards sex, concepts of beauty and justice, and the responses to pleasure and pain

> that my mother had learned from her mother and which you could trace back to the first African who set foot on the continent. (494–95)

Many scholars—Sandra G. Shannon, Harry J. Elam, Jr., and Sandra L. Richards among them—have offered in-depth analyses of the Afrocentric cosmology found in the individual texts of Wilson's plays, but we must also recognize that the cycle, as an intertextual, holistic unit, reflects an Afrocentric sensibility.[5] I contend that this sensibility is expressed through the fractal nature of Wilson's decade cycle, that is, through its intentionally repetitive, self-referential, and expansive dramaturgical style.

Fractal Currents in Wilson's Decade Cycle

One of the most apparent aspects of the decade cycle's fractal nature is the manner in which themes and motifs are repeated and revised throughout the ten plays. Themes such as slavery and imprisonment, religion and spirituality, music and creative expression, rebirth and rejuvenation, love and loss, and allegiance and betrayal are filtered throughout the texts and addressed in myriad ways. This repetition is guided by both aesthetics and utility, revealing a fractal network that, similar to the African fractals studied by Eglash, disclose an intentionality in design. With African fractals this intentionality is evidenced by the progressively smaller dwellings that emanate from the center of an African settlement or the ever-shrinking braids in a cornrow hairstyle, all of which are defined by "similar patterns of different scales *within the range under consideration*" (18; emphasis mine). Likewise, the major thematic threads in Wilson's decade cycle weave themselves throughout the ten-play collection to create patterns of similarity that are at once recognizable and familiar yet distinctly shaped and bound by considerations of historical moment or social circumstance. Reminiscent of the scaling shapes in fractal configurations, the recurring elements in Wilson's canon are expressed in varying ways, depending upon the sociohistorical context of each decade, and, from play to play, they carry differing degrees of significance in terms of theme and plot. The issue of American slavery, for example, is particularly palpable in the first play of Wilson's cycle, *Gem of the Ocean.* Set in 1904, the play not only features characters that were formerly enslaved but also takes us on a journey across the Middle Passage (a journey that is viscerally revisited in *Joe Turner's Come and Gone,* set in 1911). As the cycle proceeds, the specter of American slavery never fully leaves the consciousness of the plays' characters or spectators; rather, it takes on different forms and meanings throughout the various plays.

The self-conscious repetition found throughout the decade cycle also supports Wilson's claim that the Argentine writer Jorge Luis Borges is among the playwright's greatest influences. Addressing Borges's tendency to recycle images and ideas and put them in new dress, Mary Lusky Friedman observes that "Borges structures many of his essays by examining one by one several manifestations of an image or idea as it recurs in the course of history, its meaning subtly skewed by changing cultural circumstance" (2). Just as the dramatic dimension or scale of Borges's images and ideas are modified because of "changing cultural circumstance," the forces of history also influence the representations and readings of Wilson's thematic repertoire. Friedman seems uncertain as to why Borges tends to recycle elements from his stories (she concedes that "Borges stories reuse, more than any interpretation of them has yet explained, not only the same larger themes but the same minutiae" [5]), the reasoning behind Wilson's repetition feels far more motivated and determined. Clearly crafted with intention, the recalling of core themes and images purposefully reveals how much has changed—and how much has not—from decade to decade. Accordingly, Wilson's canon offers us the opportunity to reflect on our progress as well as seriously consider what issues still demand our critical attention.

Certainly, the recurring motifs within Wilson's decade cycle could be read as animating the African American rhetorical trope of "signifyin(g)" or utilized to illustrate the notion of "the changing same." As explicated by Henry Louis Gates, Jr., *signifyin(g)* can be understood as an African American rhetorical strategy expressed by "repetition and revision, or repetition with a signal difference" (*Signifying Monkey* xxiv), while Amiri Baraka coined the term "the changing same" to describe how black music retains African elements and patterns despite various evolutionary turns (L. Jones, "Changing Same"). Although one could rightly argue that Wilson's work "signifies" on itself or models the notion of the changing same, I find that the proliferation of self-referential elements that arise out of his single authorship makes the fractal concept a particularly befitting lens through which to read his ten-play cycle.

Wilson's dramaturgy also shares compelling similarities with the work of fractal artists in the fields of visual and studio art. In writing about these artists, Susan Condé describes work that is invested in "exploring complex forms, themes of self-similarity, scaling, order and disorder, and the relationship of the microcosmos to the macrocosmos" (3). Wilson's oeuvre clearly exhibits the exploration of self-similarity and scaling that Condé ascribes to fractal artists. However, it is important to note that his plays also boast a complexity in form, dramatize notions of order and disorder, and illustrate the relation between the microcosmos and macrocosmos.

In terms of form, Wilson's work synthesizes music, particularly the blues; visual art, often honoring the images of Romare Bearden; history; literature; and folklore with elements of realism *and* surrealism to create his living, breathing collages. Appropriately, it is within these layered creations that Wilson offers charged explorations of both order and disorder. Inspired by the sociopolitical injustices and triumphs experienced by African Americans throughout the twentieth century, the decade cycle stages moments of regressive disorder and turbulence within an ultimately progressive chronicle. The dramatization of this back-and-forth movement is also portrayed through the various worldviews and disparities that distinguish Wilson's characters from one another. By creating characters with differing philosophies and perspectives, Wilson often proposes two distinct ways of thinking, both of which disclose compelling vantage points. Although we can usually deduce which way the playwright leans, his narrative is never cut-and-dried, thereby encouraging audience members to come to their own conclusions.

Addressing this dramaturgical strategy in his analysis of *Piano Lesson,* Elam, a theater scholar, describes the protagonists' argumentative exchanges as "dialectical," noting that Wilson designs his characters' debates in such a way that audience members are compelled to construct their own synthesis ("Dialectics" 362). I would add that the dialectical style of these disputes also suggests a type of order out of disorder, a narrative style reminiscent of the signifyin(g) strategy of creating a sense of "direction through indirection."[6] In both *Fences* and *Jitney,* for example, death prevents the painful rifts between a father and son to be fully resolved; their earlier disputes do not see closure. Nevertheless, despite the fact that the fathers and sons never have a chance to formally reconcile, the death of each father engenders in his son a new understanding of their relationship. Moreover, in the closing moments of both plays there is a metaphoric reincarnation of each father figure: Corey sings his father's beloved blues song with Raynell in *Fences,* and Booster answers the station's phone in *Jitney* just as his father once did. There is also uncertainty in the future of many of Wilson's characters. Herald Loomis in *Joe Turner's Come and Gone,* Solly Two Kings in *Gem of the Ocean,* and Harmond Wilks in *Radio Golf* are among the many who begin a new journey as their play comes to an end. Thus, regardless of the optimistic or tragic notes suggested when the curtain falls, Wilson's dramas abound with inconclusive exchanges and open endings, thereby avoiding the disclosure of any straightforward, irrefutable resolutions.

When considering the open-ended and roundabout trajectories of Wilson's narratives, I am again reminded of Page's observations regarding Morrison's *Beloved*: "The principal narrative strategy of the novel is to drop an unexplained fact on the reader, veer away into other matters, then circle back with more information about the initial fact, then veer away again, circle back again, and so on" (35). This same strategy of indirection can be traced throughout Wilson's plays and is exemplified by the cycle's mounting revelations regarding Aunt Ester. The audience is first introduced to this character in *Two Trains Running* (1990), but it is not until *Gem of the Ocean* (2003) that we fully understand the nature of her existence, that she is both real and phantasmal: her name, material possessions, sense of spirituality, and legendary status are passed down from generation to generation, reincarnated through the form and will of each succeeding apprentice. The truth about Aunt Ester is illustrative of how knowledge regarding characters, relationships, or past events gradually unfolds in a roundabout way instead of being presented directly to Wilson's audience. Wilson, like Borges, was interested in the process of storytelling more than in just simple plot development. The work of both writers reveals a literary practice that revels in the detailing of minutiae, one that emphasizes how a story is told instead of focusing on the story's facts, climax, or resolution.[7]

The story of Aunt Ester also illustrates Wilson's exploration of the relation between the microcosmos and macrocosmos. Each play in his cycle represents a part of a greater whole. The macroworld of the cycle is incomplete without all ten plays, and, as the revelations surrounding Aunt Ester reveal, there are nuances within each play that cannot be fully realized unless one has knowledge of its dramatic companions. The whole of Wilson's ten-play cycle is also significant in how it represents a microcosm within the macrocosm of American theater and American history. To understand American history, one needs to understand the voices and experiences of all Americans. Thus, as Elam asserts, Wilson's dramas stage matters of cultural specificity for a wide and diverse audience in order to "(w)right" history (*Past* 3). In doing so, Wilson not only offers additions and correctives to traditional, Eurocentric accounts of American history but also uses his art to fill the gaps and offer portrayals of African American life, in this way satisfying the Afrocentric aspirations toward unity and wholeness.

Circling Back to the Why of Fractals: A Conclusion

By encouraging our students to read the decade cycle through a fractal lens, we facilitate their ability to understand Wilson's artistic inspirations while equipping them with the impulse and means to identify the sociocultural issues Wilson undoubtedly deemed to be of greatest importance. Moreover, by supporting the study of his intertextual dramaturgy, we also encourage our students to consider how the continual iteration of his plays offers a unique opportunity for community building: those who are able to recognize these artistic articulations (actors, directors, scholars, and Wilson aficionados) also create a unique sense of community based on a shared knowledge system.[8]

In suggesting that Wilson's decade cycle has the potential to create and perpetuate a community circle, it seems befitting that I close this essay as I began, by referencing the imagery—and the communal power—of the ring shout:

> [T]he ring shout was the main context in which Africans recognized values common to them—the values of ancestor worship and contact, communication and teaching through storytelling and trickster expressions, and of various other symbolic devises. Those values were remarkable because, while of ancient African provenance, they were fertile seed for the bloom of new forms. (Stuckey qtd. in Floyd 266)

Wilson's conscious creation of his decade cycle—plays that speak directly to the experiences of African Americans in the twentieth century—is a noteworthy example of how African sensibilities have blossomed into new forms. Just as the ring shout animated "the values of ancestor worship and contact, communication and teaching," the Afrocentric quality of Wilson's iterative and recursive storytelling represents a powerful mode of communal and artistic expression. The task at hand for those of us who teach Wilson is to recognize the complexity behind Wilson's perceived redundancy and respond by passing on a better understanding and fuller appreciation of his fractal dramaturgy.

NOTES

[1] Notably, although the collection of Wilson's decade plays is consistently referred to as a cycle, the other titular phrases used to describe it varies. It has been referred to as the Decade Cycle, the Twentieth-Century Cycle, the Century Cycle, and the Pittsburgh Cycle (the last term used despite the fact that one of Wilson's plays, *Ma Rainey's Black Bottom,* is actually set in Chicago rather than his hometown of Pittsburgh).

[2] I would like to extend my deep gratitude to Falone Carey for introducing me to the notion of fractal art and the work of Ron Eglash.

[3] For more on Afrocentricity, see Asante, *Afrocentricity* and *Afrocentric Idea.*

[4] Of course, while the final play in Wilson's decade cycle, *Radio Golf,* makes reference to the earlier cycle plays, including the first, *Gem of the Ocean,* it also marks an end to a series of works that I am claiming is recursive. Nevertheless, the finality proposed by *Radio Golf* is not contrary to the concept of fractals. As Eglash notes, "Although we can create a mathematical abstraction in which the recursion continues forever, there are also cases where the recursion will 'bottom out' . . . any physically existing object will only be fractal within a particular range of scales" (17). Wilson's dramatic texts may represent the physical proliferation of his fractal dramaturgy, but the plays' more abstract elements—their themes, symbols, and motifs—are perpetually self-referential and iterative by design, in that they constantly reference and set the stage for one another in a cyclical, intertextual web.

[5] For a focused and insightful reading of Africanisms in Wilson's plays, see Shannon, "Audience." For more on the African cosmology in Wilson's work, see Richards, "Yoruba Gods"; Elam, *Past*, ch. 5 ["Ogun in Pittsburgh"]).

[6] Quoting from a list provided by Roger D. Abrahams, Gates writes that *signifyin(g)* can refer to many things, as it is a "'*technique* of indirect argument or persuasion,' 'a language of implication,' . . . 'the language of trickery, that set of words or gestures achieving . . . direction through indirection'" (*Signifying Monkey* 54). For further speculation on signifyin(g) elements in Wilson's dramaturgy, see Rocha, "American History."

[7] Wilson says that in Borges "it's not what happens, but *how*" (Rocha, "August Wilson" 13). This is an important element of theater—the theatricality of the story.

[8] This assertion about community building comes from a personal experience I had when I attended the production of *Radio Golf* at Center Stage in Baltimore, Maryland, in 2006. In honor of Wilson's legacy and Center Stage's long-term relation with the playwright, the playbill for *Radio Golf* contained a full-length treatise highlighting the numerous decade cycle plays that had been produced at Center Stage. Before the start of the show, a number of conversations began across and between aisles as patrons began to share their experiences with the cycle and, even more strikingly, began to reference and recall the intertextual relations among the various plays.

APPENDIX
SUGGESTED ASSIGNMENTS AND EXERCISES

Heeding the self-referential and iterative spirit of fractals, I suggest assignments that I have designed to guide students and instructors in thinking about and teaching August Wilson's fractal dramaturgy.

Historical Reflection Presentations

Each student will offer historical reflections pertaining to the decade in which his or her assigned play is situated. This will result in a concise account of the significant events, happenings, and dynamics related to the decade (or year) in which the play is to have taken place, but students should also be encouraged to consider how this specific era speaks to the play (or vice versa). What important concerns or issues do Wilson's plays underscore or elide and why? How are these events or concerns revisited in other plays within the Wilson cycle? These reflections will be dispersed among your classmates so that, at the end of the course, each student has concrete information about each play and about how the plays connect to one another.

Call-and-Response: Creative Projects

Taking their cue from Wilson and his four Bs, students will creatively "respond" to an artistic "call." In other words, they will explore the potential of a variety of sources to inspire their creative imaginings. Using a piece of visual art or a piece of music as their inspiration, students will produce a creative writing project (a creative essay, a ten-minute play, a song, a short story, or collection of poems) and will be responsible for sharing a brief (no more than ten-minute) explication of this project and its derivation to the entire class. Make sure you are able to bring a copy of the work of art that inspired your creation.

Book Review Presentations

Students will choose, from the suggested reading list, a book-length study of Wilson to review and analyze. In doing so, they should consider the author's vantage point and perspective, breadth or focus of research, innovation in thought or analysis, how the manuscript is organized or arranged, et cetera. Students will then prepare formal book reviews or presentations for the class, an exercise that will allow them to determine the similarities as well as the dissimilarities that arise when the books are compared and contrasted.

Teaching Wilson

Students will come to class prepared to share their own ideas about how one may teach Wilson—to undergraduates or to graduate students. What assignments, readings, exercises, or projects would be particularly effective in teaching Wilson? The goal is to think of new and creative ways to expand our pedagogical exchanges regarding Wilson and elements associated with his work. Inspired by their work on Wilson, students can then be encouraged to design their own seminar or course on another artist, writer, or designer of their choice. Students will share with the class their ideas for this original course.

Teaching Students How to Examine the Role of Women in August Wilson's Plays

Dana A. Williams

August Wilson's ten-play cycle is an English or theater arts professor's dream—the plays can be taught at nearly any level. Because of Wilson's ability to dramatize everyday situations so effectively, teachers can use the plays to introduce students unfamiliar with the particulars of drama as a literary genre to the art form. Teachers using his plays in lower-level courses for English and theater arts majors and minors can introduce students to literary criticism to help them enhance their interpretations of the plays. And in a more specialized course, where the plays are considered primary texts, teachers might use them to help students learn to read literature through a more nuanced lens, conducting an analysis of the plays' varied discourses that is informed by critical theory. Whatever the level, students will undoubtedly notice that men dominate the stage in all but one of the plays. Teachers should encourage students to consider the implications of Wilson's choice to foreground male characters throughout his oeuvre.

Ma Rainey's Black Bottom, which dramatizes the life of Gertrude "Ma" Rainey, has a woman as its lead character, but Ma's onstage appearances are in no way comparable with that of her male peers. *Fences* examines discrimination in sport culture and blue-collar employment and that discrimination's effect on family, and Rose is essential to the development of Troy as a character. But, like Ma, Rose does not appear on the stage as often as either of the play's two main male characters. There are five women in the cast of *Joe Turner's Come and Gone,* and they participate in much of the dialogue—especially Bertha, who runs the boardinghouse in which the play is set. But *Joe Turner* is indisputably Herald Loomis's play, with male characters Seth and Bynum providing a significant amount of its crucial dialogue. *The Piano Lesson* explores a brother-sister relationship to root out the broad swath of history's relation to life, death, and ancestry, and Berniece holds her ground among a cast of men. But *The Piano Lesson* is as much Boy Willie's play as *Joe Turner's Come and Gone* is Loomis's. Risa, the lone woman in *Two Trains Running,* cuts herself in an outright rejection of men's obsession with her body, thereby calling attention to the role of gender in the lives of Wilson's characters. But her character does not emerge fully to be anything more than a foil that facilitates the play's larger themes. Three of the seven characters in *Seven Guitars* are women, though none seem to be particularly memorable. *Jitney* explores the lives of eight black men of different generations and different opinions to help explain how each interprets the idea of family and responsibility, engaging only one female character, Rena, sparingly throughout the play. *King Hedley II,* like *Seven Guitars,* which foreshadows *King Hedley II,* has female characters who create no signature in the memory. As King represents the common man and the common man's struggle to find his place in an ever-changing world that continues to deny his worth, the women—his wife, Tonya, and his mother, Ruby—like Risa, are foils at best. *Radio Golf* tackles the issue of contemporary gentrification, a trope that appears in a number of the plays in Wilson's beloved Hill District and troubles the black middle class's complicit role in this somewhat cavalier dismissal of the past. Mame, the one female character in the play, embodies its theme in no small measure. *Gem of the Ocean,* Wilson's only play with a female lead character, fully reveals Aunt Ester, who first appears in *Two Trains Running,* as she helps others understand the present moment by looking to the past.

Each of Wilson's plays can be taught at various levels (and across different disciplines), and in each instance the woman question will surely arise. This essay, however, focuses on three approaches to teaching the plays and women's roles in them: teaching the plays to a general education population to introduce students to the genre, teaching the plays in lower-level literature and theater courses to introduce students to literary criticism, and teaching the plays in specialized courses to help students use literary theory as a lens through which to interpret or evaluate texts.

Wilson's ten-play cycle gives a variety of options to faculty members teaching courses to a general education population. In an African American literature survey course from 1940 to the present, for example, I have used the plays to introduce students to drama as genre. Because general education courses are typically populated by students from a wide range of majors, many of whom will not take another literature course but who are expected to be well-rounded enough in the humanities to understand the features of various genres, one of the course objectives is to introduce students to the defining characteristics of at least three genres. I like to include one or two of Wilson's plays to introduce students to drama—to its mimetic impulse or its attempt to have performance imitate life: to present this imitation realistically and to use realistic dialogue to make an immediate impact on the audience.

Because reading the plays tends to be a less vivid experience than viewing their performance, I have students read crucial scenes out loud in class. When I teach *Fences,* students quickly designate as the scene they want to hear the exchange between Rose and Troy after Troy's admission of having fathered Alberta's child. Without introducing the question of gender but prompting students to take great care to examine the techniques Wilson uses to enliven the play's mimetic impulse, I am often struck by their attempt to explain the scene without giving any weight or attention to gender. They argue convincingly that Wilson develops Rose's character throughout the play so that Troy's violation of their relationship with adultery provides the conflict needed to drive plot forward. No student sees Rose's character as weak or her role as limited; rather, they claim that she is a very strong, fully developed character who wonderfully imitates life and who is essential to the plot. The dialogue between her and Troy is a realistic imitation and adds tension as the play builds to its climax. Rose is so integral to the play's development that students are untroubled by the fact that she and Raynell, who has a limited role in the play, are the only two women who appear onstage. As Tara T. Green argues, Rose "disrupt[s] the confines of a male-dominated space" (151–52) and participates fully in the storytelling ritual that facilitates the play's mimetic impulse. So it is hard for students to begin to critique the limited role of women based on the strength of Rose's character. Because *Fences* is not the only Wilson play I teach in this course, I allow the woman question to emerge naturally by pairing *Fences* with *Two Trains Running*, where gender emerges, even if tangentially, as one of the play's themes.

To meet the specific objective of having students readily identify the genre's defining characteristics, I prompt them to identify common elements of dramatic structure—like the exposition of the plot (Is it climactic or episodic?), the rising action (Where is the point of attack or inciting incident?), the crisis or climax, and then the resolution. When reading *Two Trains Running*, then, students understand the role Hambone plays in developing the play's rising action. His repeated demand for his ham foreshadows the other characters' determination to get what is due them as members of the community in which they live. Students can also recognize the play's crisis point and, later, the resolution. The element of dramatic structure that requires them to do the most critical thinking and to make important connections typically involves pinpointing crucial elements of the exposition. I remind them that the exposition entails what unfolds both onstage and off. They quickly note that the play's title—"Two Trains Running"—is our first clue that at least two plotlines are running parallel. Then they offer Risa's self-mutilation as an example of relevant exposition that happens offstage. Because the published script actually tells the reader that Risa, "in an attempt to define herself in terms other than her genitalia, has scarred her legs with a razor" ([1993] 3), I ask them to consider the relation of her role as a woman specifically to the play's exposition. Why do we need to know that she has scarred her legs in order to grasp the plot with more depth? Then I ask students to cite specific moments in the play's development where this awareness enhances the play's mimetic impulse. Her determination to be viewed and accepted on her own terms is not terribly unlike Hambone's insistence that Lutz give him his ham as promised, nor is it unlike Sterling's resolve to find meaning in his own life by taking the ham from Lutz to place it in Hambone's casket. What the analysis of Risa's gendered act reveals is that the desire for self-definition animates every story line of the plot. So they see how paying attention to the way women function in the text is as revealing about major themes of the plot and about genre as it is about Wilson's choices in the characters he develops to dramatize black culture.

The plays are equally useful for introducing majors and minors to literary criticism. My comments here are limited to sketches of critical approaches that help students explore the role of women in Wilson's plays, but the plays contain a wide range of themes and tropes amenable to showing how criticism augments both the reading and performing of the plays. Because Wilson spoke so openly about his aesthetic and dramatic vision, I like to use his prose (as articulated in essays and interviews) to contextualize his work. Doing so allows me to introduce students to biographical criticism. Reading certain aspects of the plays through the lens of authorial intention offers students valuable insight to very specific scenes—consider, for example, Herald Loomis's rejection of Christianity as evidenced by his slashing his chest at the end of *Joe Turner* and its reflection of Wilson's celebration of African spiritual retentions. Instructors can find ample evidence of Wilson's authorial intention. Commenting on his (then in-process but now complete) ten-play cycle that chronicles the four-hundred-year history of Africans in America—a history he calls "the story of myself and my ancestors"—he tells Sandra G. Shannon, "'[Y]ou know I've got a 400-year autobiography. That's what I'm writing from. There's a whole bunch of material.' I claim all 400 years of it. And I claim the right to tell it in any way I choose because it's, in essence, my autobiography" (Shannon, "Blues" 540). In that same interview, when Shannon inquires whether or not he is concerned that women had not, so far, been the focus of his plays, he remarks that he is not concerned because his perspective of the world is that of a man (550).[1] But he tells her later that while he was working on a play that was to be all male, a woman showed up on the stage (as he imagined it) insisting that she have her own scene. She asks him, "'You gonna write a play about blacks in America in the 1940s and ain't going to have no women in it? How ridiculous can you get?'" (553).[2] His point, it seems, is that he is compelled foremost to represent through dramatic art a glimpse of history through culture, and he uses whatever characters and traditions available to him to develop the ideas the particular play seeks to explore. That the characters are more often male than they are female, he intimates, is more a consequence of his own gender than a deliberate or even unconscious attempt to have more male characters than female. Students, when made aware of these statements by Wilson, are better prepared to develop and sustain arguments related to the role of women in the plays and to determine the value of this line of questioning.

One way to get students to think seriously about the role of women in Wilson's plays and, concurrently, to offer them models for producing literary criticism about the plays is to assign critical essays that explore this topic. Critics frequently concern themselves with the women in Wilson's works—their absence and then their presence, their silence and then their finding a voice, their feminism and then their seeming subordination, so there is sufficient variety from which students and instructors can chose.[3] Of significance is the fact that critics, by and large, see Wilson's conversation with gender as complex. Having students read essays that grapple with this complexity allows me to show them how literary criticism can enliven interpretations of a text and how students can participate in this discourse.

When I assign Shannon's "'The Ground on Which I Stand': August Wilson's Perspective on African American Women," the goal is to have students engage the argument that Wilson's feminine portrayals allow Wilson to come to grips with the diversity and depths of black women's experiences. If I assign her "'Ain't I a Woman?': Sojourner Truth's Question Revisited in August Wilson's Female Characters," the goal is to have them contextualize his depiction of women as he imagines their roles throughout history among the larger question of the role of black women in American society. If the objective is to help them see the way a play like *Ma Rainey's Black Bottom* challenges and confronts the limitations that gender places on women, I might have them read "August Wilson's Women," by Harry J. Elam, Jr., or his chapter on women in *The Past as Present in the Drama of August Wilson,* where he argues convincingly that Wilson's women "negotiate interlocking systems of racial and gender oppression" (89). Like Elam's essay, Missy Dehn Kubitschek's "August Wilson's Gender Lesson" provides students with a good model for complicating a gender analysis by combining that analysis with another theme or trope. Kubitschek's essay examines how the plays' historical examinations of the black community require readers to pay attention to gendered interactions, especially the spiritual dimensions of those interactions. This essay helps students think of ways to write about *Gem of the Ocean,* a play that requires the audience (and readers) to suspend belief in a stable, here-and-now reality. Students, with these essays and others to complement their own interpretations and with class discussion, learn how complicated Wilson's development of women is. Stereotypical gender roles are sometimes reversed: Rose, not Troy, is in charge of the finances in *Fences*; Herald Loomis is Zonia's primary caregiver for years in *Joe Turner's Come and Gone*; Bynum and not one of the play's women is the spiritual worker willing to give of himself freely and fully to bind others; and Ma is fiercely independent and unencumbered by her sexuality in *Ma Rainey's Black Bottom.* Students are charged with finding ways to articulate their critique of Wilson's seeming imbalanced portrayal of women. Accepting this charge helps them begin to see themselves as credible participants in the scholarly discourse on literary texts.

In more specialized courses for seniors in the major (English or Theatre Arts) or for graduate seminars on Wilson or on drama or contemporary African American literature, more generally, I use critics' efforts to grapple objectively with Wilson's limited portrayal of women to introduce students to critical ideas in black women's studies and, concurrently, to complicate African American literature's intersection with literary theory. In "Institutions, Classrooms, Failures: African American Literature and Critical Theory in the Same Small Spaces," Lindon Barrett explores the ways critical theory and African American literature appear to fail each other.[4] No doubt aware of the well-rehearsed tension between African American literature and critical theory,[5] Barrett writes:

> Theory, on the one hand, is marked by a reluctance to acknowledge itself as a political body of works with *material* determinants and consequences; African American literature, on the other, is characterized by the difficulty of acknowledging itself as anything more than the oversimple redaction of the conditions of a *material* and (by negation) political body. (219)

Many of us would dispute such a characterization of African American literature, but the challenge of helping students understand the relation of critical theory to African American literature is a real one. As Barrett observes, theory is an inherently laden political act, and, since traditional theory is marked by an "unremarked politics of reading" (219) that African American literature, in its concern with contexts and in its commitment to grappling with invisible normative assumptions, requires students to remark upon and to challenge, the tension is inevitable.[6] Recent scholarship in black women's studies, instead of working within this tension, rejects, perhaps more aggressively than any other variety of African American critical theory, contemporary traditional theory as a viable lens through which to read black culture in general and black women's culture in particular.[7] The irony that I am asking students to use the critical methodologies of black women's studies (its most progressive ones especially) to meet the challenge of examining women's limited roles in Wilson's distinctly cultural productions is not lost on them. Yet, black women's studies, in ways that are not characteristic of traditional academic disciplinary spaces, requires a respect for the cultural inimitability that informs Wilson's aesthetic. The discipline thus lends itself to fruitful readings of the plays in general and of the absent presence of women in them in particular.

As Barbara Christian notes in one of the earliest articulations of contemporary black women's studies critical methodologies, "Theory is precisely the problem upon which a black feminist scholar stumbles. Having been excluded so many times from so many camps, we are . . . particularly attuned to the dangers of the abstract generalization[s]" about "culture, language, literature, and gender" and toward the "philosophical and abstract logic" that characterize theory (227). Similarly skeptical about adopting mainstream theory to read black culture, Beverly Guy-Sheftall, Christian's contemporary, argues that black women's studies scholars must arrive "at theoretical [framework] which will enable one to understand the complexity and diversity of the black female experience throughout the world" (139). Noting the challenges these scholars still face, she writes, "Much more is needed in the area of reconceptualizing Black Studies and Women's Studies so that the history, experiences, and cultures of black women will be more effectively taught and studied, thereby enabling both disciplines to reflect more accurately the diversity and complexity of experiences of blacks and women throughout the world" (141–42).

Undeniably, Wilson's plays are best understood when read through critical lenses that emerge from within and with full awareness of African and African American culture. His insistence on a black director for the movie adaptation of *Fences,* for example, makes this point explicitly: "We are an African people who have been here since the early seventeenth century. We have a different way of responding to the world. We have different ideas about religion, different manners of social intercourse. We have different ideas about style, about language. We have different aesthetics" ("I Want" 201–02). My objective, then, is to have students observe how the commitment of black women's studies to grappling with and obviating the dangers that theory poses to readings of culture, literature, and gender shows how theory that emerges from within and that is driven by the culture can actually complement African American literature.[8]

This objective helps students achieve two interrelated goals: one, to understand how culturally specific theory can make visible the often invisible politics of reading and, two, to rethink traditional gender assumptions to give primacy to the politics of culture, which often requires a different line of inquiry and which subsequently yields more meaningful responses. In an attempt to reconceptualize the interfaces among African American studies, women's studies, and black women's studies (and to highlight the limitations of women's studies especially as a lens through which to read black peoples' experiences), Valethia Watkins argues that black women's studies, especially within the context of African American studies, must

> rethink all of the gender assumptions that we now take for granted, before gender can be incorporated as a viable category of analysis within African American Studies. . . . Much of Women's Studies scholarship on Black women has been preoccupied with describing and measuring how much Black women's lives and experiences conform to or deviate from white gender norms. ("New Directions" 229)

I encourage students to consider their own and critics' interpretation of Wilson's portrayal of women on the basis of this rethinking.

Central to Watkins's argument is the position that black women's studies, especially as a mode of inquiry in African American studies, must involve the design of methodological and theoretical assumptions that are committed foremost to providing the groundwork "for the development of more complete, and integrated narratives of Black history and culture that will yield a more comprehensive, in-depth, and holistic interpretation and body of information about our past, representing both genders without prejudice" (238). Students notice that Watkins's objective is similar to Wilson's—to move beyond norms and pathologies to complicate representations and understandings of black life and culture. Her commentary about the unfortunate segregation of black history along gender lines, too, is revealing in the light of Wilson's unwillingness to participate in this segregation in his cycle, and her caution that black women's studies must reject assumptions about gender that are not culturally specific gives voice to critics' tendency to excuse Wilson for this unwillingness. It would seem that critics understand, at least to some extent, that gender is constructed by cultural groups; thus any representation of gender that is not culturally specific is problematic, especially when driven by theoretical abstractions that seem to be universalizing but in fact disguise a Euro-American cultural hegemony.

I ask students to consider Risa's rejection of the men's objectification of her in *Two Trains Running* and Rena's disapproval of Youngblood's plan to surprise her with a house as examples of the failure of a universalized approach to gender. Why does either woman make the choices she makes? Both characters' behaviors at different points in the plays, I contend, illustrate the cultural dynamics of their varied experiences and help us appreciate male-female relationships as Wilson develops them in these plays. So I prompt students to find evidence of the cultural specificity of the actions they identify as gendered. One such example involves the discussion between the men about Risa. When Memphis remarks to Holloway and Wolf that something must be wrong with Risa, first for cutting her legs and then for not wanting to be with a man or a woman, he complains that he "can't figure out where to put her." Holloway responds insightfully, "That's what the problem is . . . you trying to figure out where to put her" (*Two Trains* 32). As Holloway observes, Risa rejects any interpretation of her self that is not informed by the fullness of her experiences. In *Jitney*, students are apt to recognize that Youngblood is too committed to his desire to be a traditional breadwinner to notice that Rena rejects traditional designations and wishes, instead, to be an equal partner in breadwinning and decision making. She tells him, "You supposed to know what's important to me like I'm supposed to know what's important to you. I'm not asking you to do it by yourself. I'm here with you. We in this together" (*Jitney* [2003] 75). Neither woman accepts the universal assumption that men define women's identities, and all Wilson's women reject outright the characteristics associated with traditional, domesticated white women—docility, unconditional faithfulness, simplemindedness, hyperemotionality.

At first students have difficulty understanding and perhaps accepting that a monolithic construction of Western culture—which disguises the fact that Western culture is in fact hybrid, formed of its peoples' contact with diverse global cultures—has been universalized as the standard and that other cultures possess their own traditional ways of understanding gender or give to it no meaning or value at all. Inviting students to use Wilson's oeuvre to reimagine gender from this position consistently proves revealing. It prompts them to recognize the ways that *Ma Rainey's Black Bottom* troubles gender categories, most obviously with the allusions to Ma's unrestricted sexuality and her dominance over the men in the play, or the ways that *Gem of the Ocean* troubles gender categories more subtly, with Aunt Ester's almost gender-neutral characterizations. Aunt Ester has had four husbands, and Solly is her most recent suitor, but their relationship clearly finds conventional social roles meaningless. They accept the role bestowed upon each by culture and calling—Solly as a cultural conductor and Aunt Ester as a prophetic healer.

Critical examinations that explore Wilson's engagement with African traditions[9] tend to be most successful at enhancing this line of inquiry since such scholarship, attempting to read the plays through the lens of traditional African cultures, helps students understand that all reading is informed by theory—explicit and applied or inherent and circumstantial. Students, when they begin to see the ways that culture can and must interface with deliberate theoretical discourses, will become willing to push aside traditional assumptions about gender (and the invisible politics that attend those assumptions), to recover fully holistic narrative interpretations about African experiences in America, to ask new questions, and then to look for clues in the text and the culture to generate meaningful responses.

To help students enter this discourse, I offer these questions as initial lines of inquiry that require culturally grounded responses. What do we need to know to understand Berniece's self-assigned role as the keeper of culture in *The Piano Lesson*? What inspires Bertha to provide shelter and nourishment to the transients who visit the boardinghouse in *Joe Turner's Come and Gone*? What causes at least one of the men in each play to remark upon a man's incompleteness without a woman, and what exactly does the man mean by this? Wilson's faithfulness to a historiography that seeks to answer these seemingly simple questions with complexity is incontrovertible, as is his awareness that reading black culture requires a different critical lens. He rejects outright the idea that anyone can interpret black culture authentically, and he contextualizes the error of this assumption historically. The assumption "has to do with how Africans were first viewed in this country, the residuals of which still affect and infest our society" ("I Want" 202). He reminds us:

> The early plantation owners, unfamiliar and uninterested in African culture, viewed their slaves as slow, dull-witted, childlike, and otherwise incapable of grasping complex ideas. . . . African culture, its style and content, was so incongruent with European sensibilities and beliefs that Africans *seemed* primitive and slow and dull-witted. Elsewhere there were whites who bore a different witness and testimony . . . [seeing] Africans as black-skinned humans of a different culture capable of all the diversity of human conduct and endeavor.
>
> The shortsightedness of the plantation owners must be thought of as willful. . . . [A]n examination of the people or their culture . . . would have led to a cultural exchange of ideas, postures, worldviews, language concepts . . . and a myriad of other cultural identities.
>
> I suspect that to pursue a cross-cultural exchange would have done a violent damage to the plantation owners' idea of the correctness of their being and their manner . . . [which] became part of the society's consciousness and part of its truth. (202–03)

I quote at length here not simply to emphasize the thought and sensibility Wilson expresses but also to suggest ways to have students understand that the development of theory across literary traditions and cultures must be driven by primary sources rather than developed in the abstract. Theory will inevitably fail when limited by its characteristic reluctance to acknowledge itself as both a marked and unmarked political act. It has much to gain, then, by identifying with diasporic literatures in general and diasporic critical methodologies in particular since, at their core, both understand and grapple with the reality of theory as a political act and seek to reverse and to avoid reinscriptions of the particular as universal.

Whether teaching Wilson's plays to students in general education literature classes, to majors and minors in English or theater arts, or to students in more specialized undergraduate courses or in graduate seminars, teachers will find that careful consideration of his portrayal of women helps students meet important objectives. Introducing students to the genre of drama has the potential to enhance their critical thinking skills as they explore the ways that Wilson uses characters, scenes, themes, and settings to define and dramatize a hundred years of African American life and culture. Exposing students to critical thought about a text similarly helps them develop their own critical voices. Helping them see how theory interfaces with culture challenges them to understand the ways that culture must inform theory in general and conversations about gender in particular; it prompts them to understand and to reject the universalizing impulse, which might otherwise remain invisible but would be no less influential; and, ideally, it quickens their commitment to extending Wilson's project of recovering and then developing a useful contemporary African historiography that is concerned above all with cultural specificity.

NOTES

[1] Wilson does, of course, eventually write a play where the main character is a woman—*Gem of the Ocean,* which features Aunt Ester, who first appears offstage in *Two Trains Running,* as the main character.

[2] *Seven Guitars* is the 1940s play in the cycle.

[3] I limit my comments here to Shannon's, Elam's, and Kubitschek's essays. But consider also essays or chapters by critics like Kim Marra, Doris Davis, and Tara T. Green for excellent critical readings of the role of women in Wilson's plays.

[4] Barrett begins the essay with an anecdote about an undergraduate student who commented that she or he was unsure how to write a paper for the African American literature course Barrett was teaching, because the student had "never been a slave and [couldn't] fully relate to this experience" (218). The student apparently associated the importance of personal experience to African American literature, an association that is not intrinsic to the study of other literatures. The anecdote illustrates that African American literature, as uniquely experientially based, "reinscribes the governing dualism" between the intellectual and the experiential (219). Barrett rightly notes that the student would not have likely made a similar comment in a course on Renaissance or Victorian literature, but he does not contest the supposition that African American literature is more experiential than other literatures. As Morrison suggests in *Playing in the Dark: Whiteness and the Literary Imagination,* national literatures have long been used to explore emerging or threatened social, cultural, political, and economic histories and realities and are thus inherently experiential. African American literature's tendency to probe the conditions of its political body is no exception in this regard, though it is commonly characterized as being more experiential than aesthetic.

[5] Consider, for example, Baker, *Betrayal* and *Blues*; Gates, *Figures* and *Signifying Monkey*; Fabre and O'Meally; and Tate.

[6] The "unremarked politics of reading" to which Barrett refers alludes to the politics of race (and class), among other things. Morrison's observation in *Playing in the Dark* that "until very recently, and regardless of the race of the author, the readers of virtually all of American fiction have been positioned as white" (xii) is a good example of the racially specific politics of reading that go unremarked more often than not.

[7] I use *black women's studies* here in keeping with the nomenclature of the discipline. Generally, scholars who focus specifically on women of color designate their work in this way to reflect their interest in and commitment to black women's issues globally rather than nationally. Hence you seldom see references to African American women's studies. I use the term *African American* elsewhere purposefully, in general, to represent issues that are more national in orientation than global. However, my use of *African American studies* instead of *Africana studies*, for example, is for practical reasons (to be consistent with the scholars I engage), though Valethia Watkins especially tends to see Africana studies as representative of a discipline that is certainly concerned with black people globally rather than simply nationally ("New Directions"). I should note, too, that there is a distinction to be made between black women's studies and gender studies, which is as interested in biology as it is in culture, and feminist studies, which historically has been associated more with white women than with black women. Watkins navigates this minefield meticulously in "Womanism and Black Feminism."

[8] Scholarship on intersections of black women's studies and black studies persists after Christian's and Guy-Sheftall's well-known rehearsals of issues that come into view almost simultaneously with the emergence of black studies as a discipline. The scholarship specific to the two disciplines and their relation to each other remains largely unchanged thereafter. Watkins offers one of the most convincing interventions to these challenges. But the subsequent introduction of the legal and sociopolitical implications into the broader conversation about the intersection of race and gender by scholars like Kimberlé Crenshaw ("Demarginalizing" and "Mapping") and Patricia Hill Collins does advance the general discourse on the intersections of race, class, and gender.

[9] Consider, for example, Bogumil, "'Tomorrow'" and *Understanding*; Elam, *Past*; Euell; Fishman; Richards, "Yoruba Gods"; Bissiri; and Tyndall.

NOTES ON CONTRIBUTORS

Paul K. Bryant-Jackson is professor and director of graduate studies at Miami University, Oxford, Ohio. He is coeditor, with Lois Overbeck, of *Intersecting Boundaries: The Theatre of Adrienne Kennedy* and a cofounder of *Continuum*, a scholarly journal hosted by the Black Theatre Network. His teaching, directing, and research interests rest at the intersections of race, class, gender, and sexuality.

Faedra Chatard Carpenter is a freelance dramaturg and associate professor in the School of Theatre, Dance, and Performance Studies at the University of Maryland, College Park. She is the author of *Coloring Whiteness: Acts of Critique in Black Performance* and has served as a dramaturg for over forty plays and productions.

Keith Clark is professor of English and African and African American studies at George Mason University. He is the author of *The Radical Fiction of Ann Petry* (2013) and *Black Manhood in James Baldwin, Ernest J. Gaines, and August Wilson* (2002) and the editor of *Contemporary Black Men's Fiction and Drama* (2001).

Soyiça Diggs Colbert is associate professor of African American studies and theater and performance studies at Georgetown University. She is the author of *The African American Theatrical Body: Reception, Performance, and the Stage*, "'When I Die, I Won't Stay Dead': the Future of the Human in Suzan-Lori Parks' *The Death of the Last Black Man in the Whole Entire World*," and "'If We Must Die': Violence as History Lesson in *Seven Guitars* and *King Hedley II*."

Harry J. Elam, Jr., is Olive H. Palmer Professor in the Humanities and Freeman-Thornton Vice Provost for Undergraduate Education at Stanford University. He is author of *Taking It to the Streets: The Social Protest Theater of Luis Valdez and Amiri Baraka* and *The Past as Present in the Drama of August Wilson*and the coeditor of *African American Performance and Theater History: A Critical Reader*, *Colored Contradictions: An Anthology of Contemporary African American Drama*, *The Fire This Time: African American Plays for the New Millenium*, and *Black Cultural Traffic: Crossroads in Performance and Popular Culture.*

James Engstrom is professor of geography at Georgia Perimeter College. He is the author of "Industry and Immigration in Dalton, Georgia" (2001). His research and teaching interests include urban theory, comparative urbanization, and the interplay among race, urban space, and performance.

Femi Euba is Louise and Kenneth Kinney Professor of Theatre at Louisiana State University. He is the author of *Poetics of the Creative Process: Organic Practicum to Playwriting* (2005); *Archetypes, Imprecators and Victims of Fate: Origins and Developments of Satire in Black Drama* (1989); a novel, *Camwood at Crossroads* (2007); and plays, among them *The Gulf* (1991) and *The Eye of Gabriel* (2002).

Joan Herrington is chair and professor of theater at Western Michigan University. Her research is focused on the pedagogy and practice of theater in the last twenty years. She is the author of *I Ain't Sorry for Nothin' I Done: August Wilson's Process of Playwriting*, *August Wilson in an Hour*, *The Playwrights Muse*, and *Playwright's Teach Playwriting*. She is also the author of over a dozen book chapters and journal articles.

Douglas A. Jones, Jr., is assistant professor of English at Rutgers University, New Brunswick. He is the author of *The Captive Stage: Performance and the Proslavery Imagination of the Antebellum North* (2014).

Alan Nadel is William T. Bryan Chair in American Literature and Culture at the University of Kentucky. His books include *Invisible Criticism: Ralph Ellison and the American Canon, Television in Black-and-White America: Race and National Identity,* and *Containment Culture: American Narratives, Postmodernism, and the Atomic Age.* He is also the editor of *May All Your Fences Have Gates: Essays on the Drama of August Wilson* and *August Wilson: Completing the Twentieth-Century Cycle.*

Sandra L. Richards is professor in residence and director of the liberal arts program at Northwestern University, Qatar. She is also professor of African American studies, theater, and performance studies at Northwestern University, Evanston. She is the author of *Ancient Songs Set Ablaze: The Theatre of Femi Osofisan;* "Black Women Playwrights in American Theatre," with Kathy A. Perkins; and "Yoruba Gods on the American Stage: August Wilson's *Joe Turner's Come and Gone* (1999).

Andrew Scheiber is professor of English at the University of St. Thomas, St. Paul. He is the author of "Blues as [Agri]Culture: A Polemical Reflection," "The Origin of Texts: 'The Art of Fiction' as Evolutionary Manifesto," and "Blues Narratology and the African American Novel." He is currently working on a book manuscript, titled "Downbound Train: Blues in African American Literature since the Black Arts Movement."

Sandra G. Shannon, professor of African American literature at Howard University, is the author of *The Dramatic Vision of August Wilson* and *August Wilson's* Fences*: A Reference Guide,* editor of *August Wilson's Pittsburgh Cycle: Critical Perspectives on the Plays,* and coeditor of *August Wilson and Black Aesthetic*. She is the current editor of the *College Language Association Journal* and worked on the PBS American Masters documentary *August Wilson: The Ground on Which I Stand.*

Ayanna Thompson is professor of English at George Washington University. She is the author of *Passing Strange: Shakespeare, Race, and Contemporary America* (2011), *Weyward Macbeth: Intersections of Race and Performance* (2010), *Performing Race and Torture on the Early Modern Stage* (2008), and *Colorblind Shakespeare: New Perspectives on Race and Performance* (2006). She is a trustee of the Shakespeare Association of America.

Von Washington, a member of the performing arts unions SAG, AFTRA, and AEA, has worked as a professor, director, actor, and theatrical consultant at universities and theater across the United States. He has written plays that have been produced around the world. He is the author of *The Journey Begins* and *Views from My Window*.

Dana A. Williams is professor of African American literature and chair of the Department of English at Howard University. She is the author of *"In the Light of Likeness—Transformed": The Literary Art of Leon Forrest* (2005), the editor of *Contemporary African American Fiction: New Critical Essays* (2009) and *African American Humor, Irony, and Satire: Ishmael Reed, Satirically Speaking* (2007), and the coeditor of *August Wilson and Black Aesthetics* (2004).

SURVEY PARTICIPANTS

Jack Balcer, *Shenandoah University*
Chris Bell, *Georgia Military College*
Marcia Berry, *Indiana University, Bloomington*
Faedra Chatard Carpenter, *University of Maryland, College Park*
Keith Clark, *George Mason University*
Dean Cooledge, *University of Maryland, Eastern Shore*
Clinton Turner Davis, *Colorado College*
Harry J. Elam, Jr., *Stanford University*
Marilyn Elkins, *California State University, Los Angeles*
Kimberly Ellis, *independent scholar and consultant*
Femi Euba, *Louisiana State University*
Ann Marie Fallon, *Portland State University*
Fred M. Fretrow, *United States Naval Academy*
Patricia M. Gantt, *Utah State University*
Jerrilyn McGregory, *Florida State University*
Ladrica Mensen-Furr, *Memphis State University*
Caleen Sinnette Jennings, *American University*
Monifa Love, *Morgan State University*
Richard Noggle, *University of Kansas*
Sandra L. Richards, *Northwestern University*
Andrew Scheiber, *University of Saint Thomas, St. Paul*
Yvonne Shafer, *Saint Johns University*
Eric Sterling, *Auburn University, Montgomery*
C. Patrick Tyndall, *Pennsylvania State University*
Karen J. Weyant, *Jamestown Community College, NY*
Michael Young, *La Roche College*

WORKS CITED

About Us. August Wilson Society. Howard U, n.d. Web. 15 Apr. 2015.

Abrahams, Roger D. *African Folktales: Traditional Stories of the Black World.* New York: Pantheon, 1983. Print.

African National Independence. Empathos Natl. Consulate, 23 Mar. 2006. Web. 24 Mar. 2015. <http://www.empathosnationenterprises.com/Consulate/EN-Library/Black-Studies/afindep.html>.

Africans in America: America's Journey through Slavery. Dir. Orlando Bagwell and Susan Bellows. WGBH Educ. Foundation. 1998. DVD.

The African Slave Trade and the Middle Passage. PBS Online, n.d. Web. 22 Apr. 2015. <http://www.pbs.org/wgbh/aia/part1/1narr4.html>.

African Tales: Technology and Learning in Every School. Center for Indigenous Knowledge Systems, n.d. Web. 24 Mar. 2015. <http://www.cfiks.org/community/community/central/storytelling.htm>.

Alexander, Elizabeth. "The One Who Went Before." *American Scholar* 75.1 (2006): 122–25. Print.

Amazing Grace. Dir. Michael Apted. Samuel Goldwyn, 2007. Film.

Amistad. Dir. Steven Spielberg. DreamWorks, 1997. Film.

Asante, Molefi K. *The Afrocentric Idea*. Philadelphia: Temple UP, 1987. Print.

———. *Afrocentricity: The Theory of Social Change*. Buffalo: Amulef, 1980. Print.

August Wilson. Films for the Humanities and Sciences, 2003. DVD. Season 14, episode 15, of *The South Bank Show*.

Baker, Houston A., Jr. *Betrayal: How Black Intellectuals Have Abandoned the Ideals of the Civil Rights Era.* New York: Columbia UP, 2008. Print.

———. *Blues, Ideology, and Afro-American Literature: A Vernacular Theory.* Chicago: U of Chicago P, 1984. Print.

Baraka, Amiri. *See* Jones, LeRoi

Barrett, Lindon. "Institutions, Classrooms, Failures: African American Literature and Critical Theory in the Same Small Spaces." *Teaching Contemporary Theory to Undergraduates.* Ed. Dianne F. Sadoff and William E. Cain. New York: MLA, 1994. 218–32. Print.

Bascom, William. "African Dilemma Tales: An Introduction." *African Folklore.* Ed. Richard M. Dorson. Garden City: Doubleday, 1972. 143–55. Print.

Bastide, Roger. *The African Religions of Brazil: Toward a Sociology of the Interpenetration of Civilizations.* Trans. Helen Sebba. Baltimore: Johns Hopkins UP, 1978. Print.

Bearden, Romare. *Mill Hand's Lunch Bucket. Romare Bearden: His Life and Art*. Ed. Myron Schwartzman. New York: Abrams, 1990. 45. Print.

Beavers, Herman. "You Can't Make Life Happen without a Woman: Paternity and the Pitfalls of Structural Design in *King Hedley II* and *Seven Guitars.*" Nadel, *August Wilson* 110–22.

Bell, Catherine. *Ritual: Perspectives and Dimensions.* New York: Oxford UP, 1997. Print.

Bennett, Lerone, Jr. *Before the Mayflower: A History of Black America*. New York: Johnson, 2007. Print.

Bercovitch, Sacvan. *The American Jeremiad.* Madison: U of Wisconsin P, 1978. Print.

Berlin, Ira. *Many Thousands Gone: The First Two Centuries of Slavery in North America.* Cambridge: Harvard UP, 1998. Print.

Beyond the Wilson-Brustein Debate. Spec. issue of *Theater* 27.2–3 (1997): 9–41. Print.

Bigsby, Christopher, ed. *Cambridge Companion to August Wilson.* New York: Cambridge UP, 2007. Print.

———. "The Ground on Which He Stood." Bigsby, *Cambridge Companion* 1–27.

Bissiri, Amadou. "Aspects of Africanness in August Wilson's Drama: Reading *The Piano Lesson* through Wole Soyinka's Drama." *African American Review* 30 (1996): 99–113. Print.

Black Theatre: The Making of a Movement. Dir. Woodie King, Jr. California Newsreel, 1978. Videocassette.

Blind Willie Johnson. *Wikipedia*. Wikimedia Foundation, 13 Apr. 2015. Web. 22 Apr. 2015.

Bloom, Harold, ed. *August Wilson.* New York: Infobase, 2009. Print. Bloom's Modern Critical Views.

———. *Shakespeare: The Invention of the Human.* New York: Riverhead, 1998. Print.

Boccella, Demeatria Gibson. "Veteran Screen, Stage Actor Bill Nunn to Help Students Prepare for August Wilson Monologue Competition." *August Wilson Center for African American Culture*. August Wilson Center for African Amer. Culture, 3 Feb. 2011. Web. 9 Dec. 2014. <http://www.augustwilsoncenter.org/aacc_pdfs/August WilsonMonologue_2.11.pdf>.

Bogumil, Mary. "'Tomorrow Never Comes': Songs of Cultural Identity in August Wilson's *Joe Turner's Come and Gone.*" *Theatre Journal* 46.4 (1994): 463–77. Print.

———. *Understanding August Wilson.* Columbia: U of South Carolina P, 2011. Print.

Bottoms, Stephen. "Introduction: The Man Who Had Three Lives." *The Cambridge Companion to Edward Albee.* Ed. Bottoms. Cambridge: Cambridge UP, 2005. 1–15. Print.

Brantley, Ben. "Voices Warped by the Business Blues." *New York Times*. New York Times, 30 Apr. 2005. Web. 16 Dec. 2015.

Brondum, Lene. "'The Persistence of Tradition': The Retelling of Sea Islands Culture in Works by Julie Dash, Gloria Naylor, and Paule Marshall." Diedrich, Gates, and Pedersen 153–63.

Brown, Alison, and Annali Kristiansen. *Urban Policies and the Right to the City: Rights, Responsibilities, and Citizenship.* UNESCO, Mar. 2009. Web. 24 Mar. 2015.

Brown, Elsa Barkley. "African-American Women's Quilting." *Signs* 14.4 (1989): 921–29. Print.

———. "The Labor of Politics." *From Freedom to "Freedom Now," 1865–1990s.* Ed. Thomas C. Holt and Brown. Boston: Houghton, 2000. 75–86. Print. Vol. 2 of *Major Problems in African American History.*

———. "To Catch the Vision of Freedom: Reconstructing Southern Black Women's Political History, 1865–1880." *African American Women and the Vote, 1837–1965.* Ed. Ann D. Gordon, Bettye Collier-Thomas, John H. Bracey, Arlene Voski Avakian, and Joyce Avrech Berkman. Amherst: U of Massachusetts P, 1997. 68–87. Print.

Browning, Sandra Lee, R. Robin Miller, and Lisa M. Spruance. "Criminal Incarceration Dividing the Ties that Bind: Black Men and Their Families." *Journal of African American Men* 6.1 (2001): 87–102. Print.

Brustein, Robert. "The Lesson of *The Piano Lesson.*" *New Republic* 21 May 1990: 28–30. Print.

———. *Reimagining American Theatre.* New York: Hill, 1991. Print.

———. "Subsidized Separatism." *American Theatre* 13.8 (1996): 26–27, 100–01. Print.

Bryant, William Cullen. "Thanatopsis." *Bartleby.com.* Bartleby.com, Jan. 1999, Web. 17 Dec. 2015.

Bryer, Jackson R., and Mary C. Hartig, eds. *Conversations with August Wilson.* Jackson: UP of Mississippi, 2006. Print.

Camp, Stephanie M. H. *Closer to Freedom: Enslaved Women and Everyday Resistance in the Plantation South.* Chapel Hill: U of North Carolina P, 2004. Print.

Carby, Hazel. "Policing the Black Woman's Body in an Urban Context." *Cultures in Babylon.* London: Verso, 1999. 22–39. Print.

Carlson, Gustav D. "Numbers Gambling: A Study of a Culture Complex." Diss. U of Michigan, 1940. Print.

Catanese, Brandi Wilkins. *The Problem of the Color(blind): Racial Transgression and the Politics of Black Performance.* Ann Arbor: U of Michigan P, 2001. Print.

Caywood, Cynthia, Marilyn Elkins, and Carlton Floyd, eds. *August Wilson.* Spec. issue of *College Literature* 36.2 (2009): ix–xv, 1–129. Web. 9 Dec. 2014.

Caywood, Cynthia, and Carlton Floyd. "She Make You Right with Yourself: Aunt Ester, Masculine Loss and Cultural Redemption in August Wilson's Cycle Plays." Caywood, Elkins, and Floyd 74–95.

Chaudhuri, Una. *Staging Place: The Geography of Modern Drama.* Ann Arbor: U of Michigan P, 1995. Print.

Chonville, Claude, and Patrick Chamoiseau. *The Middle Passage.* Dir. Guy Deslauriers. Kreol Productions and Raphia Film Productions. HBO, 2003. Film.

Christian, Barbara. "But Who Do You Really Belong To—Black Studies or Women's Studies?" Norment 225–28.

Clark, VeVe. "Developing Diaspora Literacy and Marasa Consciousness." *Comparative American Identities: Race, Sex, and Nationality in the Modern Text.* Ed. Hortense Spillers. New York: Routledge, 1991. 40–61. Print.

Clark-Lewis, Elizabeth. *Living In, Living Out: African American Domestics and the Great Migration*. New York: Kodansha America, 1996. Print.

Clear, Todd R. *Imprisoning Communities: How Mass Incarceration Makes Disadvantaged Neighborhoods Worse*. Oxford: Oxford UP, 2007. Print.

Clifford, James. *Routes: Travel and Translation in the Late Twentieth Century.* Cambridge: Harvard UP, 1997. Print.

Colbert, Soyica Diggs. "If We Must Die: Violence as History Lesson in *Seven Guitars* and *King Hedley II*." Nadel, *August Wilson* 97–109.

Collins, Patricia Hill. "It's All in the Family: Intersections of Gender, Race, and Nation." *Hypatia* 13.3 (1998): 62–82. Print.

Coltrane, John. *Central Park West*. *YouTube*. Uploaded by Dale Mcilwain. YouTube, 2 July 2010. Web. 23 July 2015.

Columbia, the Gem of the Ocean. *Wikipedia*. Wikimedia Foundation, 18 Feb. 2015. Web. 22 Apr. 2015.

Comaroff, Jean, and John Comaroff. Introduction. *Modernity and Its Malcontents.* Ed. Comaroff and Comaroff. Chicago: U of Chicago P, 1993. xi–xxxvi. Print.

Condé, Susan. "The Fractal Artist." *Leonardo* 34.1 (2001): 3–10. MIT P, 13 Mar. 2006. Web. 24 Mar. 2015.

Cook, William. "Members and Lames: Language in the Plays of August Wilson." Bloom, *August Wilson* 77–86.

Creel, Margaret Washington. "Gullah Attitudes toward Life and Death." *Africanisms in American Culture*. 2nd ed. Ed. Joseph E. Holloway. Bloomington: Indiana UP, 1990. 69–97. Print.

Crenshaw, Kimberlé. "Demarginalizing the Intersections of Race and Sex: A Black Feminist Critique of Antidiscrimination Doctrine, Feminist Theory, and Antiracist Politics." *University of Chicago Legal Forum* 140 (1989): 139–67. Print.

———. "Mapping the Margins: Intersectionality, Identity Politics, and Violence against Women of Color." *Stanford Law Review* 43.6 (1991): 1241–79. Print.

Crew, Spencer R. *Field to Factory: Afro-American Migration, 1915–1940*. Washington: Smithsonian Inst., 1987. Print.

Crowley, Gregory J. *The Politics of Place: Contentious Urban Redevelopment in Pittsburgh*. Pittsburgh: U of Pittsburgh P, 2005. Print.

Curriculum 21: Essential Education for a Changing World. Ed. Heidi Hayes Jacobs. Alexandria: ASCD, 2010. Print.

Davis, Doris. "'Mouths on Fire': August Wilson's Blueswomen." *MELUS* 35.4 (2010): 165–85. Print.

Day, Randal D. "The G.I. Bill of the Twenty-First Century: Mass Incarceration and How Crime Is Paying." *Applied Developmental Science* 11.4 (2007): 249–53. Print.

deGravelles, Karin H. "You Be Othello: Interrogating Identification in the Classroom." *Pedagogy* 11.1 (2011): 153–75. Print.

Diedrich, Maria, Henry Louis Gates, Jr., and Carl Pedersen, eds. *Black Imagination and the Middle Passage*. New York: Oxford UP, 1999. Print.

The Drama of Creation: Writers on Writing. *Films on Demand*. Films for the Humanities and Sciences, 2006. Web. 27 Mar. 2015. < http://digital.films.com/play/QPMYJ7>.

Du Bois, W. E. B. "Of Our Spiritual Strivings." *The Souls of Black Folk*. 1903. Introd. Brent Hayes Edwards. London: Oxford UP, 2007. 7–14. Print.

Edwards, Gus, Paul Carter Harrison, and Victor Walker, eds. *Black Drama: Ritual in the African Diaspora*. Philadelphia: Temple UP, 2002. Print.

Eglash, Ron. *African Fractals: Modern Computing and Indigenous Design*. New Brunswick: Rutgers UP, 2005. Print.

Elam, Harry J., Jr. "The Dialectics of August Wilson's *The Piano Lesson*." *Theatre Journal* 52.3 (2000): 361–79. Print.

———. *The Past as Present in the Drama of August Wilson*. Ann Arbor: U of Michigan P, 2004. Print.

———. *Taking It to the Streets: The Social Protest Drama of Luis Valdez and Amiri Baraka*. Ann Arbor: U of Michigan P, 1996. Print.

———. "Teaching *Joe Turner's Come and Gone*." *Modern Drama* 50.4 (2007): 582–600. Print.

Elkins, Marilyn, ed. *August Wilson: A Casebook*. New York: Garland, 1994. Print.

Elliot, Robert C. *The Power of Satire: Magic, Ritual, Art*. Princeton: Princeton UP, 1962. Print.

Ellison, Ralph. "King of the Bingo Game." *"Flying Home" and Other Stories*. Ed. John F. Callahan. New York: Knopf, 1998. 123–36. Print.

———. "Richard Wright's Blues." Ellison, *Shadow* 78–79.

———. *Shadow and Act*. New York: Random, 1964. Print.

Emery, Lynne Fauley. *Black Dance in the United States from 1619 to 1970*. New York: Natl., 1972. Print.

Engber, Daniel. "Can Criminals Hide in Church? On the Tradition of Religious Sanctuary." *Slate*. Slate Group, 16 Aug. 2006. Web. 27 Mar. 2015.

Equiano, Olaudah. *The Interesting Life of Olaudah Equiano; or, Gustavus Vassa the African Written by Himself*. Project Gutenberg, 17 Mar. 2005. E-book.

Erickson, Peter. "Afterword: The Blind Side in Colorblind Casting." A. Thompson, *Colorblind Shakespeare* 241–49.

———. "From Lear's Button to Harmond's Paintbrush: A Conversation with Harry Lennix." *Transition* 102 (2009): 68–90. Print.

Euba, Femi. *Archetypes, Imprecators, and Victims of Fate: Origins and Developments of Satire in Black Drama*. New York: Greenwood, 1989. Print.

———. *Poetics of the Creative Process: Organic Practicum to Playwriting*. Lanham: UP of Amer., 2005. Print.

Euell, Kim. "Wilson's Worlds through African Eyes." *American Theatre* 20.5 (2003): 22–23. Print.

Fabian, Ann. *Card Sharps, Dream Books, and Bucket Shops: Gambling in Nineteenth-Century America*. Ithaca: Cornell UP, 1990. Print.

Fabre, Genevieve. "The Slave Ship Dance." Diedrich, Gates, and Pedersen 33–46.

Fabre, Genevieve, and Robert O'Meally. *History and Memory in African American Culture*. Oxford: Oxford UP, 1994. Print.

Finegan, Edward, and John R. Rickford. *Language in the U.S.A.: Themes for the Twenty-First Century*. Cambridge: Cambridge UP, 2004. Print.

Finley, Cheryl, Laurence Glasco, and Joe W. Trotter. *Teenie Harris, Photographer: Image, Memory, History*. Pittsburgh: U of Pittsburgh P, 2011. Print.

Fisher, Philip. Rev. of *King Hedley II*. *British Theatre Guide* (2002). David Chadderton, n.d. Web. 27 Mar. 2015. <http://www.britishtheatreguide.info/reviews/kinghedley-rev.htm>.

Fishman, Joan. "Romare Bearden, August Wilson, and the Traditions of African Performance." Nadel, *May All* 133–49.

Fitzpatrick, Dan. "The Story of Urban Renewal: In East Liberty and Elsewhere, Pittsburgh's Dominant Public Policy Tool Didn't Work Out As Planned." *Pittsburgh Post-Gazette*. Pittsburgh Post-Gazette, 21 May 2000. Web. 27 Mar. 2015. <http://www.post-azette.com/businessnews/20000521eaastliberty1.asp>.

Florida, Richard. *Cities and the Creative Class*. New York: Routledge. 2005. Print.

———. *The Rise of the Creative Class*. New York: Basic, 2002. Print.

Floyd, Samuel A., Jr. "Ring Shout! Literary Studies, Historical Studies, and Black Music Inquiry." *Black Music Research Journal* 11.2 (1991): 265–87. Print.

Franklin, John Hope. *From Slavery to Freedom: A History of African Americans*. New York: McGraw, 2010. Print.

Freedman, Samuel. "A Voice from the Streets." *New York Times*. New York Times, 15 Mar. 1987. Web. 20 Apr. 2015.

Friedman, Mary Lusky. *The Emperor's Kites: A Morphology of Borges' Tales*. Durham: Duke UP, 1987. Print.

Gallaher, Carolyn. "Neoliberalism." *Key Concepts in Political Geography*. London: Sage, 2009. 152–63. Print.

Gantt, Patricia M. "Putting Black Culture on Stage: August Wilson's Pittsburgh Cycle." Caywood, Elkins, and Floyd 1–25.

Gates, Henry Louis, Jr. *Figures in Black: Words, Signs, and the Racial Self*. New York: Oxford, 1987. Print.

———. *The Signifying Monkey: A Theory of African-American Literary Criticism.* New York: Oxford UP, 1988. Print.

Giroux, Henry. *On Critical Pedagogy*. New York: Continuum, 2011. Print.

Glasco, Laurence A. "The Hill and the African American Experience." Glasco and Rawson 29–52.

Glasco, Laurence A., and Christopher Rawson. *August Wilson: Pittsburgh Places in His Life and Plays.* Pittsburgh: Pittsburgh Hist. and Landmarks Foundation, 2011. Print.

Green, Tara T. "Speaking of Voice and August Wilson's Women." Shannon and Williams, *August Wilson* 145–57.

Greene, Robert. *Greenes Groats-worth of Witte*. 1592. *The Norton Shakespeare: Based on the Oxford Edition.* Ed. Stephen Greenblatt et al. New York: Norton, 1997. 3321–22. Print.

Guy-Sheftall, Beverly. "Black Women's Studies: The Interface of Women's Studies and Black Studies." Norment 137–43.

Hackworth, Jason. *The Neoliberal City: Governance, Ideology, and Development in American Urbanism.* Ithaca: Cornell UP, 2006. Print.

Hale, Allean. "Early Williams: The Making of a Playwright." *The Cambridge Companion to Tennessee Williams.* Ed. Matthew C. Roudane. Cambridge: Cambridge UP, 1997. 11–28. Print.

Hale, Thomas A. *Griots and Griottes: Masters of Words and Music.* Bloomington: Indiana UP, 1998. Print.

Haller, Mark M. "Policy Gambling, Entertainment, and the Emergence of Black Politics: Chicago from 1900 to 1940." *Journal of Social History* 24.4 (1991): 719–39. Print.

"Hamlet on the Street: Monologue by Craig Bazan in Camden NJ." *YouTube*. Uploaded by chrisbarrett. YouTube, 19 July 2007. Web. 9 Dec. 2015. <http://www.youtube.com/watch?v=Oa-cfEncd6Y>.

Harris, Trudier. "August Wilson's Folk Traditions." Elkins 49–67.

Harrison, Paul Carter. "August Wilson's Blues Poetics." Wilson, *Three Plays* 291–317.

———. *Kuntu Drama: Plays of the African Continuum.* New York: Grove, 1974. Print.

Harvey, David. *A Brief History of Neoliberalism.* New York: Oxford UP, 2005. Print.

———. "The Right to the City." *New Left Review* 53 (2008): 23–40. Print.

Herrington, Joan. *"I Ain't Sorry for Nothin' I Done": August Wilson's Process of Playwriting.* New York: Limelight, 1998. Print.

Howard-Pitney, David. *The African American Jeremiad: Appeals for Justice in America.* Rev. ed. Philadelphia: Temple UP, 2005. Print.

Howe, Neil, and William Strauss. *Millennials Go to College.* Great Falls: LifeCourse Assocs., 2007. Print.

Hunter, Tera A. *To 'Joy My Freedom: Southern Black Women's Lives and Labors after the Civil War*. Cambridge: Harvard UP, 1998. Print.

Hurston, Zora Neale. *Jonah's Gourd Vine.* New York: Harper, 1934. Print.

Ijimere, Obotunde. *The Imprisonment of Obatala.* The Imprisonment *and Other Plays.* Ed. Ulli Beier. London: Heinemann, 1966. Print.

Isherwood, Charles. "August Wilson, Theater's Poet of Black America, Is Dead at 60." *New York Times.* New York Times, 3 Oct. 2005. Web. 10 May 2014.

Jacobs, Brian. *Strategy and Partnerships in Cities and Regions: Economic Development and Urban Regeneration in Pittsburgh, Birmingham, and Rotterdam.* New York: St. Martin's, 2000. Print.

Jacobs, Heidi. "How Might Interdisciplinary Learning Affect You, Your Colleagues, and Your Students?" *Thirteen Ed Online*. Educ. Broadcasting, n.d. Web. 17 Apr. 2015. <http://www.thirteen.org/edonline/concept2class/interdisciplinary/index_sub2.html>.

———. "A New Essential Curriculum for a New Time." *Curriculum 21: Essential Education for a Changing World*. Ed. Jacobs. ASCD, n.d. Web. 16 Dec. 2015.

———. "What Is Interdisciplinary Learning?" *Thirteen Ed Online*. Educ. Broadcasting, n.d. Web. 17 Apr. 2015. <http://www.thirteen.org/edonline/concet2class/interdisciplinary/index.html>.

Jennings, Caleen Sinnette. "Magic, Royalty, and Inheritance: Teaching Wilson's King Hedley II and Shakespeare's Prince Hamlet Together." *Theatre Topics* 19.1 (2009): 87–93. Print.

Jones, Joni L. "Performance Ethnography: The Role of Embodiment in Cultural Authenticity." *Theatre Topics* 12.1 (2002): 1–15. Print.

Jones, LeRoi. *The Blues People: Negro Music in White America.* Westfield: Greenwood, 1980. Print.

———. "The Changing Same: R&B and New Black Music." *The Black Aesthetic*. Ed. Addison Gayle, Jr. New York: Doubleday, 1972. 118–31. Print.

———. *Dutchman*. Dutchman *and* The Slave, *Two Plays*. New York: Morrow, 1964. 1–38. Print.

Kahn, Si, and Elizabeth Minnich. "Keep the Paying Guests Coming: Filling Up the Prisons." *The Fox in the Henhouse: How Privatization Threatens Democracy.* San Francisco: Berrett-Koehler, 2005. 95–101. Print.

Kapp, Stephen A. "Pathways to Prison: Life Histories of Former Clients of the Child Welfare and Juvenile Justice Systems." *Journal of Sociology and Social Welfare* 27.3 (2000): 63–74. Print.

Karenga, Maulana. "Black Studies and the Problematic of a Paradigm: The Philosophical Dimension." *Journal of Black Studies* 18.4 (1988): 395–414. Print.

Kolin, Philip C. "'Black Up Again': Combating *Macbeth* in Contemporary African-American Plays." *Weyward Macbeth: Intersections of Race and Performance.* Ed. Scott L. Newstok and Ayanna Thompson. New York: Palgrave Macmillan, 2010. 211–21. Print.

Kubitschek, Missy Dehn. "August Wilson's Gender Lesson." Nadel, *May All* 183–99.

Lawal, Babatunde. "The African Heritage of African American Art and Performance." *Black Drama: Ritual in the African Diaspora.* Ed. Gus Edwards, Paul Carter Harrison, and Victor Walker. Temple UP, 2002. 39–64. Print.

Lears, T. Jackson. *Something for Nothing: Luck in America.* New York: Viking, 2003. Print.

Lefebvre, Henri. *The Production of Space.* Trans. Donald Nicholson-Smith. Oxford: Blackwell, 1991. Print.

Lennix, Harry J., and Laurence Fishburne. "Two Actors on Shakespeare, Race, and Performance: A Conversation between Harry J. Lennix and Laurence Fishburne." *Shakespeare Bulletin* 27.3 (2009): 399–414. Print.

Lipman, Pauline. "Whose City Is It Anyways?" *Trashing the Neoliberal City: Autonomous Cultural Practices in Chicago, 2000–2005.* Ed. Emily Forman and Daniel Tucker. Chicago: AREA Chicago, 2007. 5. Print.

Macdonald, Amie A., and Susan Sánchez-Casal. "Introduction: Feminist Reflections on the Pedagogical Relevance of Identity." *Twenty-First-Century Feminist Classrooms:*

Pedagogies of Identity and Difference. Ed. Macdonald and Sánchez-Casal. New York: Palgrave Macmillan, 2002. 1–28. Print.

Magnet, Myron. Introduction. Magnet, *Millennial City* 3–8.

———. *The Millennial City: A New Urban Paradigm for Twenty-First-Century America*. Ed. Magnet. Lanham: Dee, 2001. Print.

Marra, Kim. "Ma Rainey and The Boyz: Gender Ideology in August Wilson's Broadway Canon." Elkins 123–60.

Mauer, Marc. *Race to Incarcerate*. New York: New, 1999. Print.

McKittrick, Katherine. *Demonic Grounds: Black Women and the Cartographies of Struggle*. Minneapolis: U of Minnesota P, 2006. Print.

Mercer, Kobena. "Diaspora Culture and the Dialogic Imagination: The Aesthetics of Black Independent Film in Britain." *Theorizing Diaspora: A Reader*. Ed. Jana Evans Braziel and Anita Mannur. Malden: Blackwell, 2003. 247–60. Print.

Mikkelsen, Nina. "Diamonds within Diamonds within Diamonds: Ethnic Literature and the Fractal Aesthetic." *MELUS* 27.2 (2002): 95–116. Print.

"Millennials (Millenial Generation)." *WhatIs.com*. TechTarget, n.d. Web. 28 Mar. 2015. <http://whatis.techtarget.com/definition/millennials-millennial-generation>.

Milloy, Courtland. "In America, Racial Oppression Is Not Ancient History." *Washington Post*. Washington Post, 7 Feb. 2012. Web. 16 Apr. 2015.

Mohanty, Chandra. "On Race and Voice: Challenges for Liberal Education in the 1990s." *Beyond a Dream Deferred: Multicultural Education and the Politics of Excellence*. Ed. Becky W. Thompson and Sangeeta Tyagi. Minneapolis: U of Minnesota P, 1993. 41–65. Print.

Molana-Allen, Leila. "High School Talent Competition Will Honor August Wilson." *DNAinfo*. DNAinfo, 21 Mar. 2011. Web. 28 Mar. 2015. <http://www.dnainfo.com/new-york/20110321/midtown/high-school-talent-competition-honor-august-wilson>.

Morrison, Toni. *Playing in the Dark: Whiteness and the Literary Imagination*. Cambridge: Harvard UP, 1992. Print.

Moyers, Bill. "August Wilson—A *World of Ideas*—1988." *Bill Moyers Journal*. Public Affairs Television, n.d. Web. 24 Apr. 2014. <http://www.pbs.org/moyers/journal/archives/wilsonwoi_flash.html>.

Mudge, Stephanie Lee. "What Is Neo-liberalism?" *Socio-economic Review* 6.4 (2008): 703–31. Print.

Murphy, Brenda. "The Tragedy of *Seven Guitars*." Bigsby, *Cambridge Companion* 124–34.

Murray, Albert. *The Blue Devils of Nada: A Contemporary American Approach to Aesthetic Statement*. New York: Vintage, 1996. Print.

———. *The Hero and the Blues*. New York: Vintage, 1996. Print.

———. *Stomping the Blues*. New York: Da Capo, 1989. Print.

Nadel, Alan, ed. *August Wilson: Completing the Twentieth-Century Cycle*. Iowa City: U of Iowa P, 2010. Print.

———. Introduction. Nadel, *August Wilson* 1–13.

———. Introduction. Nadel, *May All* 1–8.

———. *Invisible Criticism: Ralph Ellison and the American Canon*. Iowa City: U Iowa P, 1988. Print.

———, ed. *May All Your Fences Have Gates: Essays on the Dramas of August Wilson*. Iowa City: U of Iowa P, 1994. Print.

———. "My Country Too: Time, Place, and Afro-American Identity in the Work of John Williams." *Obsidian II* 2.3 (1987): 25–41. Print.

Nandi, M. "Re/Constructing Black Masculinity in Prison." *Journal of Men's Studies* 11.1 (2002): 91–107. Print.

Nathans, Heather, ed. *August Wilson Celebrated.* Spec. issue of *New England Theatre Journal* 19a (2008): 1–93. Assn. for Theatre in Higher Educ., n.d. Web. 29 Mar. 2015.

———. "Infinite Variety: Introduction to the Special Issue on August Wilson." Nathans, *August Wilson* 1–6.

Ngũgĩ wa Thiong'o. *Penpoints, Gunpoints, and Dreams: Toward a Critical Theory of the Arts and the State in Africa.* Oxford: Clarendon, 1988. Print.

Norment, Nathaniel, Jr. *The African American Studies Reader*. 2nd ed. Durham: Carolina Academic, 2007. Print.

Oblinger, Diana. *Boomers, Gen-Xers, Millennials: Understanding the New Students*. EDUCAUSE, n.d. Web. 16 Dec. 2015.

Okpewho, Isidore. *African Oral Literature: Background, Character, and Continuity.* Bloomington: Indiana UP, 1992. Print.

Okur, Nilgun Anadolu. "Afrocentricity as a Generative Idea in the Study of African American Drama." *Journal of Black Studies* 24.1 (1993): 88–108. Print.

Page, Philip. "Circularity in Toni Morrison's *Beloved.*" *African American Review* 26.1 (1992): 31–40. Print.

Pasquaretta, Paul. "Sacred Chance: Gambling and the Contemporary Native American Indian Novel." *MELUS* 21.2 (1996): 21–33. Print.

Pease, Donald E. "August Wilson's Lazarus Complex." Nadel, *August Wilson* 71–96.

Penningroth, Dylan. *Claims of Kinfolk: African American Property and Community in the Nineteenth-Century South*. Chapel Hill: U of North Carolina P, 2002. Print.

Pereira, Kim. *August Wilson and the African-American Odyssey.* Urbana: U of Illinois P, 1995. Print.

———. "*Joe Turner's Come and Gone:* Seek and You Shall Find." Pereira, *August Wilson* 55–84.

The Piano Lesson. By August Wilson. Dir. Lloyd Richards. Hallmark Home Entertainment, 2002. DVD.

Pinneau, Elyse Lamm. "Critical Performative Pedagogy." *Teaching Performance Studies.* Ed. Nathan Stuckey and Cynthia Wimmer. Carbondale: Southern Illinois UP, 2002. 41–54. Print.

Plimpton, George. "August Wilson: The Art of Theater XIV." *Paris Review* 41.153 (1999): 67–94. Print.

Raboteau, Albert J. *Slave Religion: The "Invisible Institution" in the Antebellum South.* Rev. ed. New York: Oxford UP, 2004. Print.

"*Radio Golf* Reflects the '90s: Wilson's Upwardly Mobile Encounter a Parallel Reality." *Milwaukee Journal Sentinel.* Milwaukee Journal, 31 Jan. 2007. Web. 27 July 2015.

Raphael, Jody, and Brenda Myers-Powell. *From Victims to Victimizers: Interviews with Twenty-Five Ex-Pimps in Chicago*. DePaul U Coll. of Law, 2010. Print.

Rawson, Christopher. "August Wilson: The Ground on Which He Stood." Glasco and Rawson 3–22.

Richards, Sandra L. "Spreading Sweetness: Storytelling in Contemporary Black Theatre." *Worlds in Words: Storytelling in Contemporary Theatre.* Ed. Mateusz

Borowski and Malgorzata Sugiera. Newcastle upon Tyne: Cambridge Scholars, 2010. 90–106. Print.

———. "Yoruba Gods on the American Stage: August Wilson's *Joe Turner's Come and Gone.*" *African Drama and Performance.* Ed. John Conteh-Morgan and Tejumola Olaniyan. Bloomington: Indiana UP, 2004. 94–106. Print.

Rickford, John Russell, and Russell John Rickford. *Spoken Soul: The Story of Black English*. New York: Wiley, 2000. Print.

Robeson. Paul. *Here I Stand.* 1958. *Black Thought and Culture* Alexander Street, n.d. Web. Available by subscription.

Robinson, Beverly J. "Africanisms and the Study of Folklore." *Africanisms in American Culture*. Ed. Joseph E. Holloway. 1st ed. Bloomington: Indiana UP, 1990. 211–24. Print.

Rocha, Mark William. "American History as 'Loud Talking' in *Two Trains Running*." Nadel, *May All* 116–32.

———. "August Wilson and the Four B's: Influences." Elkins 3–16.

———. "Black Madness in August Wilson's 'Down the Line' Cycle." *Madness in Drama*. Ed. James Redmond. Cambridge: Cambridge UP, 1993. 191–201. Print.

———. "A Conversation with August Wilson." *Diversity: A Journal of Multicultural Issues* 1 (1992): 24–42. Print.

Romare Bearden (1911–1988): A Centennial Celebration, August 30, 2011–March 4, 2012. Metropolitan Museum of Art, n.d. Web. 20 Apr. 2014. <http://www.metmuseum.org/exhibitions/listings/2011/romare-bearden-centennial>.

Rooney, David. "Review: *Radio Golf*." *Variety*. Variety Media, 11 May 2007. Web. 14 Apr. 2015.

Roudane, Matthew C. Introduction. *The Cambridge Companion to Tennessee Williams.* Cambridge: Cambridge UP, 1997. 1–10. Print.

Savran, David. "August Wilson." *In Their Own Words: Contemporary American Playwrights.* New York: Theatre Communications Group, 1988. 288–305. Print.

Seidler, Philip D. "'King August': August Wilson in His Time." Bloom, *August Wilson* 131–47.

Shakespeare, William. *Hamlet*. Ed. Ann Thompson and Neil Taylor. London: Arden Shakespeare, 2006. Print. The Arden Shakespeare. Ser. 3.

Shannon, Sandra. "'Ain't I a Woman?': Sojourner Truth's Question Revisited in August Wilson's Female Characters." *MAWA Review* 14.1 (1999): 1–8. Print.

———. "Audience and Africanisms in August Wilson's Dramaturgy: A Case Study." *African American Performance and Theatre History.* Ed. Harry J. Elam and David Krasner. Oxford: Oxford UP, 2001. 149–67. Print.

———, ed. *August Wilson.* Spec. issue of *Zora Neale Hurston Forum* 20 (2006–08): 1–117. Print.

———. *August Wilson's* Fences*: A Reference Guide.* Westport: Greenwood, 2003. Print.

———. *The Dramatic Vision of August Wilson.* Washington: Howard UP, 1995. Print.

———. "'The Ground on Which I Stand': August Wilson's Perspective on African American Women." Nadel, *May All* 150–64.

Shannon, Sandra G., and Dana A. Williams, eds. *August Wilson and Black Aesthetics.* New York: Palgrave Macmillan, 2004. Print.

———. "A Conversation with August Wilson." Shannon and Williams, *August Wilson* 187–95.

Shepard, Tim. *Traditional Storytelling in Africa*. Tim Shepard, n.d. Web. 10 Apr. 2015. < http://www.timsheppard.co.uk/story/dir/traditions/index.html>.

Singh, Roopa. "Anti-Gentrification Rebels." *The Nation*. The Nation, 17 Oct. 2007. Web. 1 Apr. 2015.

Smith, Neil. "Gentrification and Then Rent Gap." *Annals of the Association of American Geographers* 77 (1987): 462–75. Print.

———. "New Globalism, New Urbanism: Globalization as Global Urban Strategy." *Antipode* 34.3 (2002): 427–50. Print.

———. *The New Urban Frontier: Gentrification and the Revanchist City*. London: Routledge, 1996. Print.

Smitherman, Geneva. *Talkin and Testifyin: The Language of Black America*. Boston: Houghton, 1977. Print.

———. *Talkin That Talk: African-American Language and Culture*. New York: Routledge, 2000. Print.

Snodgrass, Mary Ellen. *August Wilson: A Literary Companion*. Jefferson: McFarland, 2004. Print.

Sobel, Mechal. *Trabelin' On: The Slave Journey to an Afro-Baptist Faith*. Westport: Greenwood, 1979. Print.

Soyinka, Wole. *Art, Dialogue, and Outrage: Essays on Literature and Culture*. 2nd ed. New York: Pantheon, 1993. Print.

———. "The Fourth Stage: Through the Mysteries of Ogun to the Origin of Yoruba Tragedy." Soyinka, *Art* 27–39.

———. "Morality and Aesthetics in the Ritual Archetype." *Myth, Literature, and the African World View*. Cambridge: Cambridge UP, 1976. 1–36. Print.

"Standing in My Grandfather's Shoes: A Mellon Interdisciplinary Course Inspired by the Plays of August Wilson. Howard U, n.d. Web. 27 July 2015. <http://library.howard.edu/friendly.php?s=augustwilsoninterdisciplinarycourse>.

Streitfeld, David. "For Pittsburgh, There's Life after Steel." *New York Times*. New York Times, 17 Jan. 2009. Web. 1 Apr. 2015. <www.newyorktimes.com/2009/01/08/business/economy/collapse.html>.

Stuckey, Sterling. *Slave Culture: Nationalist Theory and the Foundations of Black America*. Oxford: Oxford UP, 1987. Print.

Tate, Claudia. *Psychoanalysis and Black Novels: Desire and Protocols of Race*. Oxford: Oxford UP, 1998. Print.

Teaford, Jon. *The Rough Road to Renaissance: Urban Revitalization in America, 1940–1985*. Baltimore: Johns Hopkins UP. 1990. Print.

———. "Urban Renewal and Its Aftermath." *Housing Policy Debate* 11.2 (2000): 443–65. Print.

Thompson, Ayanna, ed. *Colorblind Shakespeare: New Perspectives on Race and Performance*. New York: Routledge, 2006. Print.

———. "In the Blood: William Shakespeare, August Wilson, and a Black Director." A. Thompson, *Colorblind Shakespeare* 137–53.

———. *Passing Strange: Shakespeare, Race, and Contemporary America*. London: Oxford UP, 2011. Print.

———. "Practicing a Theory / Theorizing a Practice: An Introduction to Shakespearean Colorblind Casting." A. Thompson, *Colorblind Shakespeare* 1–26.

Thompson, Robert Farris. *Flash of the Spirit: African and Afro-American Art and Philosophy*. New York: Vintage, 1984. Print.

Tobin, Jacqueline L., and Raymond G. Dobard. *Hidden in Plain View: A Secret History of Quilts and the Underground Railroad.* New York: Anchor, 2000. Print.

Tracy, Steven C. "Appendix: Discography for *Seven Guitars.*" Nadel, *August Wilson* 207–09.

———. "The Holyistic Blues of *Seven Guitars.*" Nadel, *August Wilson* 50–70.

Traylor, Eleanor W. "Two Afro-America Contributions to Dramatic Form." *The Theatre of Black Americans.* Ed. Errol Hill. New York: Applause, 1987. 45–60. Print.

Trotter, Joe W., and Jared N. Day. *Race and Renaissance: African Americans in Pittsburgh since World War II.* Pittsburgh: U of Pittsburgh P, 2010. Print.

Tyndall, C. Patrick. "Using Black Rage to Elucidate African and African American Identity in August Wilson's *Joe Turner's Come and Gone.*" Shannon and Williams 159–73.

Üsekes, Çiğdem. "'We's the Leftovers': Whiteness as Economic Power and Exploitation in August Wilson's Twentieth-Century Cycle of Plays." Bloom 87–101.

Vlach, John Michael. *The Afro-American Tradition in Decorative Arts.* Cleveland: Cleveland Museum of Arts, 1978. Print.

Wall, Cheryl A. *Worrying the Line: Black Women Writers, Lineage, and Literary Tradition.* Chapel Hill: U of North Carolina P, 2005. Print.

Washington, M. Bunch. *The Art of Romare Bearden: The Prevalence of Ritual.* New York: Abrams, 1973. Print.

Watkins, Valethia. "New Directions in Black Women's Studies." Norment 229–40.

———. "Womanism and Black Feminism: Issues in the Manipulation of African Historiography." *African World History Project: The Preliminary Challenge.* 1997. Ed. Jacob H. Carruthers and Leon C. Harris. Los Angeles: Assn. for the Study of Classical African Civilizations, 2002. 245–84. Print.

Welch, Michael. *Corrections: A Critical Approach.* 2nd ed. New York: McGraw, 2003. Print.

Wilkerson, Isabel. *The Warmth of Other Suns: The Epic Story of America's Great Migration.* New York: Random, 2010. Print.

Williams, Tennessee. *A Streetcar Named Desire.* New York: Signet, 1947. Print.

Williams-Forson, Pysche. *Building Houses out of Chicken: Black Women, Food, and Power.* Chapel Hill: U of North Carolina P, 2006. Print.

Wilson, August. "August Wilson Explains His Dramatic Vision: An Interview." Interview by Sandra Shannon. Bryer and Hartig 118–54.

———. "August Wilson on Blackness." Interview by Bill Moyers. *Bill Moyers: A World of Ideas.* Public Affairs Television, 20 Oct. 1988. Web. 29 Mar. 2015.

———. "Blues, History, and Dramaturgy: An Interview with August Wilson." Interview by Sandra Shannon. *African American Review* 27.4 (1993): 539–59. Print.

———. *Fences.* New York: New Amer. Lib., 1986. Print.

———. *Fences.* New York: Plume, 1986. Print.

———. *Fences.* Wilson, *Three Plays* 95–192.

———. *Gem of the Ocean.* New York: Theatre Communications Group, 2007. Print. August Wilson Century Cycle.

———. "The Ground on Which I Stand." *Callaloo: A Journal of African American and African Arts and Letters* 20.3 (1997): 493–503. Print.

———. *The Ground on Which I Stand.* New York: Theatre Communications Group, 1996. Print.

———. Interview by Joan Herrington, 12 Feb. 1994.

———. "An Interview with August Wilson." Interview by Kim Powers. Bryer and Hartig 3–11.

———. "I Want a Black Director." Nadel, *May All* 200–04.

———. *Jitney.* New York: Overlook, 2003. Print.

———. *Joe Turner's Come and Gone.* New York: New Amer. Lib., 1988. Print.

———. *Joe Turner's Come and Gone*. Wilson, *Three Plays* 197–290.

———. *King Hedley II.* New York: Theatre Communications Group, 2007. August Wilson Century Cycle.

———. *Ma Rainey's Black Bottom.* New York: Plume, 1981. Print.

———. "A Note from the Playwright." *Seven Guitars.* New York: Dutton, 1996. N. pag. Print.

———. *The Piano Lesson.* New York: Plume, 1990. Print.

———. Preface. *King Hedley II.* New York: Theatre Communications Group, 2005. vii–xi. Print.

———. *Radio Golf.* New York: Theatre Communications Group, 2007. Print.

———. *Three Plays*. Ed. Paul Carter Harrison. Pittsburgh: U of Pittsburgh P, 1991. Print.

———. *Two Trains Running.* New York: Plume, 1993. Print.

Wolcott, Victoria W. "The Culture of the Informal Economy: Numbers Runners in Interwar Black Detroit." *Radical History Review* 69 (1997): 46–75. Print.

The World Began at Ile-Ife: Meaning and Function in Yoruba Art. Chicago: Art Inst. of Chicago, 1990. Videocassette.

Yates, Jeff, and Andrew B. Whitford. "Race and the War on Drugs: The Social Consequences of Presidential Rhetoric." *Journal of Empirical Legal Studies* 6.4 (2009): 874–98. Print.

Zamora, Lois Parkinson, and Wendy B. Faris, eds. *Magical Realism: Theory, History, Community.* Durham: Duke UP, 1995. Print.

Zewde, Almaz, and Gregory Carr. *African Systems of Thought: Linking the Ethos and Customs of Africa to America*. Howard U Libs., n.d. Web. 23 Dec. 2015. <http://library.howard.edu/content.php?pid=273384&sid=2259478>.

INDEX